Studies in Development Economics and Policy
Series Editor: Finn Tarp

UNU WORLD INSTITUTE FOR DEVELOPMENT ECONOMICS RESEARCH
(UNU–WIDER) was established by the United Nations University as its first research and
training centre and started work in Helsinki, Finland, in 1985. The purpose of the Institute
is to undertake applied research and policy analysis on structural changes affecting the
developing and transitional economies, to provide a forum for the advocacy of policies
leading to robust, equitable and environmentally sustainable growth, and to promote
capacity strengthening and training in the field of economic and social policy–making.
Its work is carried out by staff researchers and visiting scholars in Helsinki and through
networks of collaborating scholars and institutions around the world.

UNU World Institute for Development Economics Research (UNU–WIDER)
Katajanokanlaituri 6 B, FIN-00160 Helsinki, Finland

Titles include:

Tony Addison and Alan Roe (*editors*)
FISCAL POLICY FOR DEVELOPMENT
Poverty, Reconstruction and Growth

Tony Addison, Henrik Hansen and Finn Tarp (*editors*)
DEBT RELIEF FOR POOR COUNTRIES

Tony Addison and George Mavrotas (*editors*)
DEVELOPMENT FINANCE IN THE GLOBAL ECONOMY
The Road Ahead

Tony Addison and Tilman Brück (*editors*)
MAKING PEACE WORK
The Challenges of Social and Economic Reconstruction

George G. Borjas and Jeff Crisp (*editors*)
POVERTY, INTERNATIONAL MIGRATION AND ASYLUM

Ricardo Ffrench-Davis and Stephany Griffith-Jones (*editors*)
FROM CAPITAL SURGES TO DROUGHT
Seeking Stability for Emerging Economies

David Fielding (*editor*)
MACROECONOMIC POLICY IN THE FRANC ZONE

Basudeb Guha-Khasnobis and George Mavrotas (*editors*)
FINANCIAL DEVELOPMENTS, INSTITUTIONS, GROWTH AND POVERTY REDUCTION

Basudeb Guha-Khasnobis, Shabd S. Acharya and Benjamin Davis (*editors*)
FOOD INSECURITY, VULNERABILITY AND HUMAN RIGHTS FAILURE

Basudeb Guha-Khasnobis and Ravi Kanbur (*editors*)
INFORMAL LABOUR MARKETS AND DEVELOPMENT

Basudeb Guha-Khasnobis (*editor*)
THE WTO, DEVELOPING COUNTRIES AND THE DOHA DEVELOPMENT AGENDA
Prospects and Challenges for Trade-led Growth

Aiguo Lu and Manuel F. Montes (*editors*)
POVERTY, INCOME DISTRIBUTION AND WELL-BEING IN ASIA DURING THE TRANSITION

George Mavrotas and Anthony Shorrocks (*editors*)
ADVANCING DEVELOPMENT
Core Themes in Global Economics

George Mavrotas and Mark McGillivray (*editors*)
DEVELOPMENT AID
A Fresh Look

George Mavrotas (*editor*)
DOMESTIC RESOURCE MOBILIZATION AND FINANCIAL DEVELOPMENT

Mark McGillivray (*editor*)
ACHIEVING THE MILLENNIUM DEVELOPMENT GOALS

Mark McGillivray (*editor*)
HUMAN WELL-BEING
Concept and Measurement

Mark McGillivray, Indranil Dutta and David Lawson (*editors*)
HEALTH INEQUALITY AND DEVELOPMENT

Mark McGillivray (*editor*)
INEQUALITY, POVERTY AND WELL-BEING

Robert J. McIntyre and Bruno Dallago (*editors*)
SMALL AND MEDIUM ENTERPRISES IN TRANSITIONAL ECONOMIES

Vladimir Mikhalev (*editor*)
INEQUALITY AND SOCIAL STRUCTURE DURING THE TRANSITION

E. Wayne Nafziger and Raimo Väyrynen (*editors*)
THE PREVENTION OF HUMANITARIAN EMERGENCIES

Wim Naudé (*editor*)
ENTREPRENEURSHIP AND ECONOMIC DEVELOPMENT

Machiko Nissanke and Erik Thorbecke (*editors*)
THE IMPACT OF GLOBALIZATION ON THE WORLD'S POOR
Transmission Mechanisms

Machiko Nissanke and Erik Thorbecke (*editors*)
GLOBALIZATION AND THE POOR IN ASIA

Matthew Odedokun (*editor*)
EXTERNAL FINANCE FOR PRIVATE SECTOR DEVELOPMENT
Appraisals and Issues

Amelia U. Santos-Paulino and Guanghua Wan (*editors*)
THE RISE OF CHINA AND INDIA
Impacts, Prospects and Implications

Laixiang Sun (*editor*)
OWNERSHIP AND GOVERNANCE OF ENTERPRISES
Recent Innovative Developments

Guanghua Wan (*editor*)
UNDERSTANDING INEQUALITY AND POVERTY IN CHINA
Methods and Applications

Studies in Development Economics and Policy
Series Standing Order ISBN 978–0333–96424–8 hardcover
Series Standing Order ISBN 978–0230–20041–8 paperback

You can receive future titles in this series as they are published by placing a standing order. Please contact your bookseller or, in case of difficulty, write to us at the address below with your name and address, the title of the series and the ISBNs quoted above.

Customer Services Department, Macmillan Distribution Ltd, Houndmills, Basingstoke, Hampshire RG21 6XS, England

---

Health Inequality and Development

Edited by

Mark McGillivray,
Indranil Dutta
and
David Lawson

In association with the United Nations University – World Institute for
Development Economics Research (UNU–WIDER)

© United Nations University 2011

All rights reserved. No reproduction, copy or transmission of this publication may be made without written permission.

No portion of this publication may be reproduced, copied or transmitted save with written permission or in accordance with the provisions of the Copyright, Designs and Patents Act 1988, or under the terms of any licence permitting limited copying issued by the Copyright Licensing Agency, Saffron House, 6–10 Kirby Street, London EC1N 8TS.

Any person who does any unauthorized act in relation to this publication may be liable to criminal prosecution and civil claims for damages.

The authors have asserted their rights to be identified as the authors of this work in accordance with the Copyright, Designs and Patents Act 1988.

First published 2011 by
PALGRAVE MACMILLAN

Palgrave Macmillan in the UK is an imprint of Macmillan Publishers Limited, registered in England, company number 785998, of Houndmills, Basingstoke, Hampshire RG21 6XS.

Palgrave Macmillan in the US is a division of St Martin's Press LLC, 175 Fifth Avenue, New York, NY 10010.

Palgrave Macmillan is the global academic imprint of the above companies and has companies and representatives throughout the world.

Palgrave® and Macmillan® are registered trademarks in the United States, the United Kingdom, Europe and other countries

ISBN 978–0–230–28065–6   hardback

This book is printed on paper suitable for recycling and made from fully managed and sustained forest sources. Logging, pulping and manufacturing processes are expected to conform to the environmental regulations of the country of origin.

A catalogue record for this book is available from the British Library.

A catalog record for this book is available from the Library of Congress.

10   9   8   7   6   5   4   3   2   1
20   19   18   17   16   15   14   13   12   11

Printed and bound in Great Britain by
CPI Antony Rowe, Chippenham and Eastbourne

Contents

Foreword

Global health statistics narrate an interesting story: on average, people today live longer and healthier than 50 years ago; infectious diseases have been dramatically reduced and life expectancy improved globally from 48 years in 1955 to 68 years in 2005.

Despite these outcomes, disparities in health achievements are on the rise and of grave concern to policymakers. One telling statistic is that of the life expectancy for African females which was 49 years in 1978 compared to the world average of 63. By 1998 most of the world's women could expect to live six years longer but the average life expectancy for women in Africa increased only by two years, widening the life expectancy gap between them and the rest of the world.

This gap in health outcomes is not widening just across countries, but has increased within countries too, and this alarming trend is not restricted simply to poor developing countries. There are pockets in the developed world where overall health distribution has worsened. Policymakers recognize that better health is a prerequisite and a major contributor to economic growth and social cohesion. It is also recognized that health – owing to its intrinsic and instrumental properties – is a key dimension of wellbeing. The fact that developing country health levels are low, and in some instances declining, makes the achievement of better health a key issue for developing countries.

Health inequality, both within and between countries, and its relationship with development and the need to achieve better health levels in developing countries therefore remain at the forefront of international development challenges. It is against this background that UNU–WIDER decided to pursue the present volume which seeks to provide a better understanding of what drives health achievements in developing countries and health outcomes in sub-Saharan Africa, North Africa, South America and Asia.

This aim of promoting a better understanding of health achievements is reflected in the choice of contributions which look both at inequality in health and health care *within* countries as well as disparities *among* countries. As such the volume adds value to ongoing policy debates and forms part of UNU–WIDER's continuing concern with the welfare and living conditions of the poorest people in the poorest countries.

Finn Tarp
Director, UNU–WIDER

Figures

Tables

Abbreviations

CBS	Central Bureau of Statistics (Kenya)
DCS	Department of Census and Statistics (Sri Lanka)
DHS	Demographic and Health Survey
DPT	diphtheria–pertussis–tetanus
EDHS	Eritrea Demographic and Health Survey
Equitap	Equity in Asia-Pacific Health Systems
GDP	gross domestic product
GMM	generalized method of moments
ICC	intra-class correlation
IMF	International Monetary Fund
ITUSR	Institute for Trade Union and Social Research (Bulgaria)
KDHS	Kenya Demographic and Health Survey
LSMS	Living Standards Measurement Survey (World Bank)
MDG	Millennium Development Goal
MLE	maximum likelihood estimation
MOH	Ministry of Health (Kenya)
NCHS	National Center for Health Statistics (USA)
NGO	non-governmental organization
OECD	Organisation for Economic Co-operation and Development
OLS	ordinary least squares
OOP	out-of-pocket
RIGLS	restricted iterative generalized least squares
SD	standard deviation
SLIS	Sri Lanka Integrated Survey
SSA	sub-Saharan Africa
UNHS	Ugandan national household survey
UNDP	United Nations Development Programme
WHO	World Health Organization

Contributors

Harsha Aturupane is a Lead Education Specialist in the South Asia Region of the World Bank. He has worked and written extensively in the fields of human development, education economics, labour economics, health economics and the economics of poverty. He is at present the World Bank's Human Development Coordinator for Sri Lanka and the Maldives.

Sarah Bridges is a Lecturer in the School of Economics, University of Nottingham. Her research interests lie in the field of applied micro-ecoconomics, with a specific interest in the economics of labour markets, family economics and household indebtedness. She has published in a wide range of journals including the *Journal of Health Economics*, *Economica* and *Labour Economics*.

Anil Deolalikar is Professor of Economics and Associate Dean of Social Sciences at the University of California, Riverside. His research interests include the economics of human capital in Asia and Africa. He has published four books and more than 60 articles in the areas of child nutrition, health, education, poverty and social protection in developing countries. Previously he has taught at the University of Washington (Seattle) and the University of Pennsylvania.

Indranil Dutta is currently a Brooks World Poverty Institute Lecturer in Economics at the University of Manchester. Before this he was a Research Fellow at the World Institute for Development Economics Research of the United Nations University (UNU–WIDER). His primary research interests are mainly in area deprivation and inequality. His papers have been published in the *Journal of Health Economics*, *Economica* and *Mathematical Social Sciences*.

Patrick Guillaumont is Professeur émérite at CERDI, Université d'Auvergne, President of the FERDI (Fondation pour les Etudes et Recherches sur le Développement International), and director of the Revue d'Economie du Développement, and for many years until the end of 2009 was a Member of the United Nations Committee for Development Policy. He is also a Fellow of the Oxford Centre for Studies on African Economies (CSAE). His main research interests are development economics, foreign aid, human resources, and the least developed countries.

Dileni Gunewardena holds a doctorate in economics from American University, Washington DC and a BA(Hons) in economics from the University of Peradeniya, Sri Lanka, where she is a Senior Lecturer. Her research is mainly in development microeconomics and includes empirical analyses relating to poverty measurement, child nutrition, gender wage inequality and ethnic inequality in Sri Lanka and in Vietnam.

Catherine Korachais is currently a PhD student in development economics in the Centre d'Etudes et Recherches sur le Développement International (CERDI) at Université d'Auvergne. Her research topics focus on the effects of foreign aid in the health sector, macroeconomic instability and poverty issues, equity of health financing and applied econometrics.

David Lawson is a Lecturer at the Institute for Development Policy and Management (IDPM) and Senior Research Fellow/Faculty Associate with the Chronic Poverty Research Centre (CPRC)/Brooks World Poverty Institute (BWPI), University of Manchester. He has extensive developing country experience and his research interests are in development economics, but more specifically applied microeconometric analysis, particularly in relation to issues of poverty dynamics, health and gender. He has published in leading development journals, consulted extensively for the World Bank and DFID, and is on the World Health Organisation (WHO) Scientific Resource Group on Equity Analysis and Research. He is lead editor of *What Works for the Poorest: Poverty Reduction Programmes for the Ultra Poor, Practical Action* (2010).

Marie-Claude Martin is the Program Manager at the Think Tank Initiative, a multi-donor initiative at the International Development Research Centre in Ottawa, Canada, dedicated to strengthening independent policy research institutions in developing countries. An economist by background, she obtained a PhD in Public Health from the University of Montreal. Her areas of research include determinants of population health, health economics, poverty analysis and economic modelling.

Mark McGillivray is Research Chair in International Development at the Alfred Deakin Research Institute, Deakin University, Australia. His previous positions include Chief Economist of the Australian Agency for International Development and Deputy Director of the World Institute for Development Economics Research of the United Nations University. Mark's research interests include aid allocation and effectiveness, measuring multidimensional wellbeing achievement and international inequality in wellbeing.

Clive Mutunga is a Research Associate with Population Action International (PAI) (www.populationaction.org). His current research interests include population and climate change as well as aid financing. Prior to PAI, he worked for several years at the Kenya Institute for Public Policy Research & Analysis (KIPPRA), conducting policy research and analysis on a broad range of socioeconomic issues including the environment and health.

Owen O'Donnell is an Associate Professor of Applied Economics at the University of Macedonia and Erasmus University Rotterdam, and a Visiting Professor at the University of Lausanne. He has co-directed two European Union-funded research projects on equity in the finance and provision of health care in Asia and is a co-author of *Analyzing Health Equity Using Household Survey Data* (World Bank 2008).

Mariano Rojas is Professor of Economics at FLACSO-México and at UPAEP, México. He holds a licenciatura degree in economics from Universidad de Costa Rica, and Masters and PhD degrees in economics from Ohio State University. His areas of research are: subjective well-being, quality of life, economic development, health economics, poverty, progress, and applied microeconomics.

Julie Subervie is a researcher at the French National Institute of Agronomic Research (INRA). She received her PhD in development economics from CERDI, Université d'Auvergne, France. Her areas of interest include development economics, agricultural commodity markets, policy evaluation and applied econometrics.

Eddy van Doorslaer is Professor of Health Economics at the Erasmus School of Economics and the Department of Health Policy and Management, both at Erasmus University, Rotterdam. He has directed several international comparative research projects on European countries as well as Asian countries, and has published widely on the measurement and explanation of inequalities in health and health care.

1
Health Inequality and Development: Achieving Better Health in Developing Countries

Mark McGillivray, Indranil Dutta and David Lawson

1 Introduction

Throughout most of the last century there has been steady improvement in health outcomes. Among them are improvements in life expectancy, which has increased significantly across countries. On average people now live longer and healthier than even 50 years ago. Life expectancy improved globally from a lowly 48 years in 1955 to 68 years by 2005, and for a number of countries it currently exceeds 80 years (WHO 1996; UNDP 2007). This substantial increase in longevity has been coupled by a dramatic control of infectious diseases that has further improved the average quality of life. Despite this massive improvement in health outcomes there is a growing concern that disparities in health achievements are increasing. Consider the life expectancy for African females, which was 49 years in 1978 compared to the world average of 63. By 1998, the average life expectancy for females improved by six years, whereas in African countries it only increased by two years, thus widening the life expectancy gap (WHO 1999).

Disparities have emerged not only from slower rates of improvement in life expectancy. In a number of countries, overall life expectancy has declined in recent years while in many other countries, all in sub-Saharan Africa (SSA), it has fallen to as low as 40–43 years in 2005 (UNDP 2007).[1] Added to this is the stark fact that more than 150 million children in developing areas remain underweight, and 182 million remain stunted. Moreover, progress in reducing prevalence rates has slowed in the past two decades, and increased in Africa. As a result, a reduction in the prevalence of underweight children between 1990 and 2015 – one of the MDG indicators – will not be met (Haddad et al. 2003).

This gap in terms of health outcomes is not widening just across countries, but has increased within countries too. This alarming trend is not restricted just to poor developing countries; in the rich world, there are pockets where overall health distribution has worsened, which implies a growing iniquitous outcome in terms of health. While there has been increasing recognition of the issue of health inequality from policymakers and practitioners,[2] the focus, for the most part, has been on improving the overall health outcomes, particularly in developing countries. It is not surprising, therefore, that three out of the eight MDG targets are focused directly on health.[3] At a macrolevel, better health is considered a prerequisite and a major contributor to economic growth and social cohesion (World Bank 1993; WHO 2003). From the wellbeing perspective, there are also strong arguments for prioritizing health, especially in the developing countries, given their low levels of health and overall wellbeing. This is driven by the recognition that health has both intrinsic and instrumental wellbeing values. The intrinsic value of health reflects the fact that it is directly constitutive of an individual's wellbeing. The instrumental or basic value of health relates to the pursuit of the various goals an individual may value (Anand 2004). From an agency-based perspective of individuals, health is perceived as a basic capability because without good health an individual's ability to do and to be becomes restricted. Escaping morbidity and disease and being able to enjoy a longer life both facilitates and enhances achievements in other dimensions of wellbeing. Thus, for Nussbaum (1988) bodily health constitutes one of the essential capabilities for leading a meaningful life.

From a broader societal perspective, in view of the fact that health is a crucial component of wellbeing, health distributions will matter for the overall level of wellbeing, with lower overall wellbeing indicative of higher inequality in health outcomes. The capability-augmenting aspect of health also implies a stronger focus on the distribution based on the Rawlsian notion of justice where equality in terms of opportunity is important. A highly unequal distribution of health will imply a higher inequality in terms of opportunity as well. Further, there is growing evidence from surveys indicating strong public opinion against health inequality (Abasolo and Tsuchiya 2004). People may be willing to tolerate some inequality in income, but when it comes to health there is strong desire for greater equality. These arguments reinforce the notion that even though health achievements are important, the distribution of health outcomes also matters in the overall welfare or wellbeing of a society.

A growing body of research, however, demonstrates that health inequality itself may be very much affected by socioeconomic inequalities. In a pioneering study on Whitehall employees in the UK, Marmot et al. (1991) find that lower socioeconomic status leads to lower health achievements. Differential access to health services was not an issue in this case because Whitehall employees are civil servants and all have access to the same medical service facilities. Yet the study notes that people in the lower civil service ranks had a greater experience of coronary diseases. There is an ever-growing literature on socioeconomic research issues such as the determinants of ill-health (Strauss and Thomas 1998) and the economic costs of ill-health, including implications of lower labour productivity and the impact of impaired child development (World Bank 1993). Wagstaff (2004), using concentration curves, studies how socioeconomic inequalities affect child mortality in nine developing countries. He finds that Brazil has the highest health inequality while Pakistan and Nepal have the lowest. Thus, the need to further our understanding of these issues – especially in the context of low-income countries where small changes in health or health care programmes can have critical effects on physical wellbeing (Pitt 1993; Deaton 2003) – is immense.

This chapter has three main goals. The first is to provide a contextual background for the chapters in this volume by briefly identifying some of the complexities surrounding health inequalities and discussing existing literature related to the topics covered. These topics relate to child health, gendered health outcomes, the measurement of health satisfaction and the analysis of health inequality. The second objective is to outline the rationale guiding the selection of chapter topics and the overall framework that links each topic together. And finally, this chapter aims to provide an outline of the volume's contents and conclusions. We complement this purpose by also highlighting some of the main conclusions from a policy perspective.

2   Health inequality: complexities

In order to understand health inequality, several major issues arise: some of these are discussed briefly in the next sections.

Health and income

Although we have tried to establish the importance of health – and specifically of health inequality – one can argue that health is highly correlated with income with the implication that health inequality may yield very little additional information to income inequality. As high-lighted by Deaton (2006), a common starting point for understanding the changing relationship between health and income, particularly in relation to inequalities, is the Preston Curve (1975), showing ultimately, but with variation across countries, that income poverty and health poverty are positively correlated. A similar line of argument emphasizing the co-movement of income and health has been propounded by Pritchett and Summers (1996).[4]

We, however, find significant differences in health and income inequality. Figure 1.1 provides a comparison of the inequality with respect to GDP per capita and child mortality across six regions. It is clear from Figure 1.1 that while the coefficient of variation of GDP per capita has, at best, increased slightly, there has been a steady increase in child mortality. Therefore, while all regions have been able to increase their income almost at a similar pace, child mortality in the worse-off regions has not improved as much as in the better-off regions, thus indicating a higher level of inequality in health.

If one looks more closely at the data, it is not surprising to see that in the early 1970s it is the East Asia and Pacific region that was the worst in terms of both income and health, followed by South Asia and then SSA. Over the years, however, the East Asia and Pacific region made

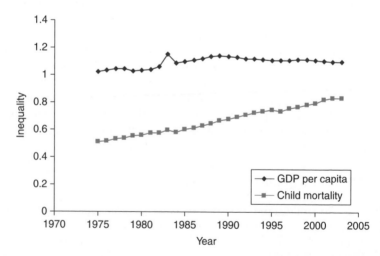

Figure 1.1: Coefficient of variation of GDP per capita and child mortality from 1975 to 2003 across six regions
Source: McGillivray et al. (2009).

substantial progress in both dimensions while SSA has stagnated. South Asia, on the other hand, has had some improvement in GDP per capita but has not kept pace with similar advancements in child mortality. This is a broad description of developments with respect to health inequality at the interregional level, but the story may be starker on the intraregional scene.

Health indicators

Although in most discussions we may have a broad idea of what is meant by health, but when it comes to a precise definition, the term often remains ambiguous. To some extent, this is because health is a multidimensional concept, quite broad and difficult to pin down.

At the macrolevel, the overall health of the country can be indicated through several different measures, such as life expectancy, child mortality and infant mortality, among others. At the individual level popular indicators include anthropometric measures (such as height-to-weight ratios), and subjective assessment of health measures in which individuals evaluate their own state of health. Given this wide variety of indicators, it is not easy to choose any one particular marker as the measure of health. These indicators not only reflect the plurality that is present in the concept of health but also add to the complexities of measuring health inequality (Kawachi et al. 2002).

One approach is to distinguish between the different aspects of health we may wish to consider. We may have to rely on an entirely different set of indicators if we want to measure health inequality with regard to health access rather than outcomes. For instance, a plausible indicator for health access can be the percentage of births attended by medical personnel, whereas if we want to think in terms of health outcomes, we may have to look into maternal deaths due to childbirth. This distinction between health access and health outcomes helps not only to narrow down the choice of health indicators, but also raises further issues about which of these two concepts should be chosen. One may claim that we would want to reduce inequality in terms of access to health since reduction of such structural inequalities is the best we can do. In such a case, the individual becomes responsible for their own health outcomes, as should be the case especially if they engage in activity that may be damaging to health. In our efforts to guarantee equal access to health services, however, we may end up with very unequal health outcomes, as people with congenital health issues may be unfairly disadvantaged in the process. On the other hand, an effort to reduce inequality in health outcomes may imply increased inequality of health access.[5]

In a survey of eight developing countries, Makinen et al. (2002) find that the rich have better access to medical services and are able to avail themselves more readily of the services than the poor, although in absolute terms they do outspend the poor on health issues. What it reflects is that unequal access to health in fact may exacerbate the social gradient with respect to health. Therefore, measuring and understanding inequality both in terms of health outcomes and health access is crucial from a policy perspective.

Another option that enables the choice of indicators to be narrowed is to think in terms of ordinal or cardinal measures. While most anthropometric measures have the advantage of being cardinal and allow us to make detailed interpersonal comparisons, ordinal data, such as the subjective health evaluations, constitute a more comprehensive measure which includes both physical and emotional wellbeing instead of relying purely on physical health status, as is done in most of the standard measures. The self-reported health status, however, can be influenced by an individual's socioeconomic status and thus may include more than just the level of health. This has led some researchers to speculate that increased educational levels among respondents might be positively associated with reported sickness because of heightened awareness of the symptoms of disease (see Lawson and Appleton 2007 for further review).[6]

It has to be noted that the standard mean-based measures of inequality will not be adequate with regard to self-reported health status. Hence, a different methodology is needed to measure inequality in order to satisfy basic conditions of consistency (Allison and Foster 2005).[7] Using appropriate methodology, Madden (2008) demonstrates that the level of health inequality varies significantly with the choice of ordinal or cardinal variables.

These different criteria allow us, on one hand, to narrow the choice of variables but also demonstrate, on the other hand, the difficulties that come with measuring health, particularly health inequality. We are concerned about health inequality but it is debatable whether this should be in terms of inequality to access or in terms of health outcomes. Similarly, our concern about health inequality does not provide us with an easy answer to the question of choice between cardinal indicators of health or self-reported health. These measurement issues reflect the inherent complexities of health inequality, and our objective here is to highlight these factors, instead of providing a decisive answer.

Analysing health deprivation and equity

From a theoretical perspective, the issue of health inequalities and wellbeing outcomes can be studied at many levels. Bloom and Canning (2000) outline parts of the interaction that can be understood through several key mechanisms. Notably, in the context of this volume, this concerns the consideration of issues such as the demographic dividend (lowering of mortality),[8] education (healthier people live longer, have stronger incentives to invest in developing their skills, and influence intrahousehold allocation), and through productivity (healthier populations tend to have higher labour productivity).

Using a variety of techniques, the chapters of this volume deal with some of these complexities and draw our attention to health deprivation and inequity, including intrahousehold discrimination. Given the adverse social and economic consequences of child ill-health, both in the short and long term, perhaps no starting point for analysing health issues in developing countries is more fundamental or important than child health. Malnutrition during infancy and childhood substantially raises vulnerability to infection and disease, and increases the risk of premature death. It is also believed to impair cognitive achievement, labour productivity during adulthood, and lifetime earnings. Hence, child health has a fundamental long-term impact on economy-wide issues.

A common approach to analysing child health is through the use of anthropometric-based measures, regarded as health indicators partly because past ill-health impairs a child's physical development. For example, bouts of illness reduce a child's ability to absorb food. Furthermore, poor anthropometric status is associated with adverse future health outcomes, including mortality. However, in the consideration of child health, environmental, behavioural and socioeconomic factors associated with mortality are also important, particularly from the perspective of SSA (see Mutunga, Chapter 5 in this volume). Prior research based on both anthropometry and mortality is sometimes a little restricted in the methods of analysis utilized. For example, econometric approaches to analyse malnutrition (see Chapter 4 of this volume for a literature review) have commonly not studied the entire extent of malnutrition, and in the case of mortality, survival analysis has been used less frequently. Both the aforementioned chapters advance the technical approaches that could be used to analyse child health by slightly varying the more traditional research methods, and thus have, by extension, potentially major policy implications.

Similarly, there is a large amount of earlier empirical work that has focused on the intrahousehold allocation of resources and how this may, for example, impact on gendered health inequalities. Evidence, such as that presented in Behrman (1988a, 1988b); Sen and Sengupta (1983) and Dasgupta (1987) for India, suggests that intrahousehold distribution may not be equal across a family. Behrman (1988a, 1988b) and Chen et al. (1981) both find that compared to boys, poorer health status tends to persist for girls, although this may simply reflect a cultural bias. However, intrahousehold issues extend beyond the probability of a person becoming ill, and can impact on facts such as the effect of illness on an individual's satisfaction, happiness and level of perceived health. This area is covered to a lesser extent in the health literature.

This, of course, brings up the question of how to measure health. Adult-based analysis commonly relies on self-reported health measures, and this may raise concerns or produce alternative approaches (see Rojas, Chapter 7 in this volume). For example, self-reported durations of illness may be inaccurate (Schultz and Tansel 1997). In addition, self-reported morbidity can be a particular problem in considering health and labour issues, for example, because there is a concern about the potential endogeneity of health, and notably self-reported health in this setting (Stern 1989; Bound 1991; Bridges and Lawson, Chapter 9 in this volume). Measurement issues also raise concern about other dimensions such as the impact of health on poverty and whether typical measures of impoverishment can take full account of health care needs because of the variability and unpredictability of related costs (van Doorslaer and O'Donnell, Chapter 2 in this volume).

3   Contents of this volume

This collection aims to provide a better understanding of the various health outcomes in developing countries in SSA, North Africa, South America and Asia. *Health Inequality and Development* contains eight chapters, in addition to this introductory chapter. Details of each chapter are provided below, but let us first outline the rationale for the selection and ordering of these studies. This, in essence, turns to what we hope to achieve with the book, extending beyond the coverage of various health-related issues in developing countries. The book is based on two arguments, which stem from the material above. First, health – owing to its intrinsic and instrumental properties – is a key dimension of wellbeing, as was also noted above. The recognition that developing-country health levels are low, and in some instances declining, makes the achievement of better health a key issue for developing countries. The second argument is that there is no case whatsoever for tolerating inequalities in health, especially in developing countries. The main aim of the volume, therefore, is to promote a better understanding of what drives health achievement in developing countries.

This aim of promoting a better understanding of health achievements is reflected in the choice and ordering of the chapters. Chapter 2 looks at income-related inequality in health and health care, mainly in low-income settings, focusing on inequality *within* countries, while Chapter 3 looks at inequality in health, with a particular emphasis on disparities *among* countries. The remaining chapters concentrate mainly on the drivers of health achievement in developing countries. Chapters 4 to 6 look at the various determinants of child health through a unique micro-based approach, and conclude with a macro mortality perspective. Chapter 7 examines health from a subjective wellbeing approach and Chapters 8 and 9 review the health of females. Recognizing that health inequality is, by definition, disparity in health, these chapters implicitly look at what drives such inequality. They do not strive to provide a formal decomposition of the inequality observed in Chapters 2 and 3, but they do offer insights as to the context in which disparities in health achievement in developing countries arise. Let us now provide more detail on these chapters.

In Chapter 2, 'Measurement and Explanation of Inequality in Health and Health Care in Low-income Settings', Eddy van Doorslaer and Owen O'Donnell provide a comparative study of 14 Asian countries. The structure of health finance in low-income countries, in particular the heavy reliance on out-of-pocket payments, means that equity issues in finance are quite different from those that concern high-income countries. The primary concern is not with the distribution of contributions to pre-payment mechanisms but with the deterrent effect of payments on utilization and the distribution of uninsured payment risks.

Chapter 2 reviews the standard measurement approach, the required adaptation or qualification for the analysis of equity in low-income settings, and the findings derived to date in Asian comparisons for each of three distributions relevant to health equity analysis: health payments, health care utilization and health status. The concern over these three factors stems mostly from the widely perceived social aversion to inequality in the distribution of both health and income. Chapter 2 recognizes that the distribution of income alone is not always instrumental to health sector equity; sometimes it is the distribution of fundamental interest, and the equity concern is related to how the health sector impacts on it. Chapter 2 makes this clear with some examples taken from the Asian comparative study. Starting with a discussion of the distributional consequences of health care payments, the chapter goes on to discuss equity analyses of the distribution of health care utilization and addresses the measurement and explanation of health inequality.

Chapter 3, 'Global Inequality in Health: Disparities in Human Longevity among Countries', by Mark McGillivray, seeks to contribute to the literature on global inequality in health by empirically examining inter-country disparities in human longevity. It applies a number of inequality measures, including the Gini coefficient and two measures from the Theil entropy class, both population and non-population weighted, to life expectancy data for a sample of 169 countries for the years 1992–2004. The chapter also examines, for comparative purposes, disparities in education and income per capita for the same sample of countries and time period. It reports increased inequality in health since 1992, and either declining or largely stable inequality in education and income variables. It finds that the increase in inequality is primarily driven by the widely reported and discussed declines in life expectancy among countries in the lower ranges of this variable. The results reported in Chapter 3 add weight to the case for a better understanding of health achievement in developing countries.

Earlier literature on child malnutrition – and in particular research which investigates the economic, social and policy determinants of malnutrition – focuses overwhelmingly on direct interventions and estimations of the mean effect on child nutrition of such variables as the child's gender, the schooling of its mother, and household income. These estimates miss a point that is crucial for policymakers: socioeconomic background variables and policy interventions may affect child nutrition differently at different points of the conditional nutritional distribution. Indirect policy interventions, such as improved infrastructure, could have as large an effect on child nutrition as direct nutritional interventions but are relatively rarely examined.

This imbalance is addressed in Chapter 4, 'The Determinants of Child Weight and Height in Sri Lanka: A Quantile Regression Approach', by Harsha Aturupane, Anil Deolalikar and Dileni Gunewardena. It provides estimates of quantile regressions to analyse the socioeconomic and policy determinants of child nutrition at different points of the conditional distribution of child nutrition. The findings of Chapter 4 suggest that income and maternal education may improve health, but not that of the least healthy cohorts. The implication for policy, therefore, is suggestive that general interventions (parental schooling, infrastructure and income growth) are ineffective in raising the nutritional status of children at the lower tail of the conditional weight and height distribution range. Hence, it may be important to target direct nutritional interventions, such as food supplementation programmes, to 'at-risk children'. A policy message that ultimately reinforces the general – and growing – developing-country perspective is that integrated packages of maternal and child health services are needed in order to address child malnutrition and promote child growth.

In Chapter 5, entitled 'Environmental Determinants of Child Mortality in Kenya', Clive J. Mutunga extends the focus on child health and development through an SSA-based country case study, by considering the literature on mortality, and the increasingly important issue of environmental determinants of child mortality. Focusing on the determinants of infant and child mortality, it specifically examines how infant and child mortality is related to the household's environmental and socioeconomic characteristics, such as the mother's education, source of drinking water, sanitation facility, type of cooking fuels and access to electricity. A hazard rate framework is used to analyse the determinants of child mortality. Duration models are directly applicable to the problem of child mortality, as this type of model is able to account for problems of right-censoring, which traditional econometric techniques cannot handle adequately.

Reducing child mortality is a universally accepted goal. There is, however, considerable debate over the means to be used to achieve substantial and sustained reductions, especially in the least developed countries (LDC). The evidence shows that a household's socioeconomic and environmental characteristics have a significant impact on child mortality, reinforcing the wealth-effect finding of the earlier chapter that better survival prospects are found to exist for children born in wealthier families. Environmental characteristics are noted to be significantly related to child mortality with lower mortality rates experienced in households that have, for example, access to safe drinking water, access to sanitation facilities, and those using low-polluting fuels as their main source of cooking. From a policy perspective, these are, once again, potentially interesting conclusions, suggesting that sectoral programmes that focus on mother and child illness should be emphasized – particularly given the wealthier household dimension to the above findings. Greater efforts should also be geared towards promoting the use of low-polluting fuels and, in particular, discouraging the use of firewood and charcoal, which cause deforestation and other environmental problems.

However, without underestimating the importance of these interventions, it seems increasingly obvious that the rate of reduction of child mortality is heavily influenced by the macroeconomic environment. Chapter 6 provides a broader perspective by investigating child mortality through a macro lens, thus providing a useful complement to the prior two micro-based child development chapters. The chapter, 'How Growth Related Instabilities Lower Child Survival', by Patrick Guillaumont, Catherine Korachais and Julie Subervie, shows how macroeconomic instability influences the level of child mortality. The effect of exogenous shocks is first examined through a variable measuring income instability. The study is then extended by examining primary instabilities, defined in terms of the instability of world agricultural commodity prices, the export of goods and services and agricultural production. The findings suggest that addressing issues of macroeconomic instability is a significant way to improve health levels in developing countries. Public health policy, which aims at developing insurance mechanisms/tools for instance, should take into account the deterioration of the macroeconomic environment induced by income shocks. The real argument is not that inequality threatens public health policy outcomes, but rather that public health policy should target the most vulnerable populations, many points of which highlight the concerns and direction of policy highlighted in the early part of the volume.

Following on from the child health discussion, Chapter 7, 'Intrahousehold Arrangements and Adult Health Satisfaction: Evidence From Mexico', by Mariano Rojas, analyses the key issue of household 'arrangements' in relation to an individual's health satisfaction, through a subjective wellbeing approach. The chapter also considers the impact of household arrangements on health satisfaction across different income groups in Mexico, and complements the volume with an interesting methodological variation away from the rather more typical microeconometric quantitative data. One of the main foci is on the intrahousehold distribution of health satisfaction in economically poor families, as the unequal distribution of relevant health-satisfaction resources is expected to be more harmful for this particular income group.

The chapter contrasts two main theories of the family. First is the altruistic/communitarian theory, which emphasizes altruism within the family and implies that the within-household allocation of relevant health-satisfaction resources leads to an egalitarian distribution of health satisfaction. Second is the cooperative-bargaining theory, which holds that the family emerges as a cooperative-equilibrium outcome from the unilateral interests of each household member. Thus, each household member takes advantage of his or her bargaining power to attain an equilibrium that favours their personal interests. The cooperative-bargaining approach implies a within-household allocation of the relevant health-satisfaction resources that leads to a distribution of health satisfaction that closely follows the distribution of bargaining power. The main finding from the investigation is that household income has a larger explanatory capability in health satisfaction than personal income, and that income-based poverty measures are very limited in serving as a proxy for some relevant wellbeing aspects, such as health satisfaction. Gender disparities also exists, and daughters in low-income families, for example, enjoy lower health satisfaction than fathers or sons.

Chapter 8, 'Individual and Collective Resources and Women's Health in Morocco', by Marie-Claude Martin, looks at the interaction between available individual and collective resources in the determination of health in developing countries. The chapter analyses the role public resources play in the perception that rural women in Morocco have of their health. These resources are taken to contribute directly and indirectly to the improvement of individual health by providing, on the one hand, a health-promoting environment and by improving the individual's ability to produce health on the other. In exploring the question of the contribution of public resources to women's capacity to produce better health and of the potential interactions between collective and individual resources and vulnerability factors, the chapter utilizes theoretical proposals and analytic tools favoured by the capability approach. This approach provides a unique perspective since it recognizes the importance of considering the freedom of individuals to convert public and private resources and instrumental capabilities (such as education) into health and other benefits. It makes the distinction between access to resources and the freedom and the capacity to use them to achieve a set of functions. A consistent production function for health is derived and then estimated, using empirical techniques. The findings suggest that any intervention that jointly tackles individual, family, communal or regional mediators of women's socioeconomic status is likely to help improve their health. The results validate the proposition that individual resources contribute to improved health status and that individuals' freedoms to convert these resources into health depend on their vulnerability factors.

Chapter 9, 'Health and Female Labour Market Participation: The Case of Uganda', by Sarah Bridges and David Lawson, is based on the recognition of the key instrumental importance of health, and the associated growing literature that accepts female labour market participation to be a vital ingredient in the economic development process. Specifically, the chapter focuses on labour force participation of women, and to what extent health determines this. Uganda, having experienced rapid economic growth in the 1990s, provides a particular and interesting case study from a development perspective. The study empirically models the abovementioned link between health and labour force participation employment outcomes for a representative sample of working-age adults. A specific interest of the chapter is whether the key gender disparities commonly observed in Uganda (and most other SSA countries) between males and females in terms of health and household responsibilities also affect labour market outcomes.

4   Achieving better health: looking ahead with a policy lens

A number of conclusions that contribute to advancing health knowl-edge emerge from the volume. Many of these have been clearly articu-lated in the chapters, but it is useful to briefly mention some of the findings here.

Understanding child health, and offering variations to the approaches of how we analyse these issues, is extremely important for advancing our understanding and for establishing a solid base from which an economy can grow in the future. Income-generating interventions, while very important for a number of other social outcomes, are found unlikely to be effective in raising the nutritional levels of the children at greatest risk of malnutrition. In fact, it is integrated packages of maternal and child health services that are perhaps of greater importance in address-ing child malnutrition and promoting child growth. For example, these can be packages that promote, from inception, antenatal care to ensure foetal growth and wellbeing as well as breastfeeding, appropriate wean-ing and growth monitoring, and other issues such as immunization programmes and prevention of infections such as water-borne diseases. Such policies and schemes need to be complemented by health and nutrition education. However, it is perhaps equally important to ensure the synergy – and evaluation – of nutrition policies and programmes across different sectors and ministries within a country to ensure a coherent and efficient approach to reducing child malnutrition.

If we consider the impacts of household environmental issues on child mortality, we find that policies aimed at achieving the goal of reduced child mortality should be directed towards improving the household's environmental and/or socioeconomic status. Macroeconomic instabili-ties are also likely to affect under-five survival in addition to their impact through lower economic growth. These instabilities have an irreversible influence on child mortality due to the asymmetry in the reaction of child health to fluctuations in economic variables. Developing-country primary instabilities, the main exogenous sources of income instability, appear to have a direct effect on child survival but income instability also has a long-run effect.

It is also shown in this volume that income-based poverty measures are a very limited proxy for some relevant wellbeing aspects, such as health satisfaction. The limitations of income-based poverty measures with respect to health satisfaction are threefold. First, these measures usually rely on household *per capita* income, while it has been shown that household income *per se* is the relevant variable for health satisfaction. Second, health satisfaction is not distributed uniformly within a household; thus, there are important intrahousehold disparities within a given *household* income. Third, these intrahousehold disparities in health satisfaction can be explained by cultural patterns that discriminate against women, and by cooperative-bargaining elements that are present in family arrangements. Variation in the state of health is also associated with the presence of collective resources. However, the higher the level of the women's individual wealth, the less the characteristics of the community in which they live seem to be associated with their health, and the less potential vulnerability factors seem to constrain their ability to maintain or improve health.

The results suggest that collective investments derived from various areas of activity will be more favourable to improving health, insofar as they are adapted to the initial capacity of women to benefit from them. Health has a strong effect on labour market outcomes. Not only are those in the poorest health less likely to participate but, conditional on participation, they are also less likely to be in the formal labour market. In addition and perhaps more worryingly, these negative effects are stronger for women than men. Ill-health represents a gender disadvantage to women.

Financing health care systems affects both income and health. The method of financing can largely alter equity issues in the sector and reforms aimed at improving financial equity should focus on a reduction of out-of-pocket-based financing. Health care systems that largely rely on out-of-pocket payments affect both income inequalities and utilization. Out-of-pocket-based health care financing can substantially increase poverty and social exclusion. In low-income countries, the better-off tend to pay more for health care, both absolutely and in relative terms, but they also consume more health care. Health care is financed largely according to the benefit principle. Assessing the distributional performance of health systems in low-income settings therefore requires examination of finance and utilization simultaneously. Future changes in the health care system have to take into account these deepening problems and adopt targeted programmes for the excluded groups. Only then can the system prevent negative long-term consequences

Several of the findings of this book highlight the importance of appropriate health policy. In general the real argument is not that inequality threatens public health policy outcomes, but rather that public health policy should target the most vulnerable populations – issues that are all accentuated, through varying dimensions, in this volume. Hence, income-generating interventions, although very important for a number of other social outcomes, are in isolation unlikely to be effective in raising the nutritional levels of those at the greatest risk of malnutrition. A policy message that ultimately reinforces a general and growing perspective is that focused integrated health packages are required – for example, maternal and child health services to address child malnutrition and promote child growth, or female empowerment to ensure the full economic benefits of female labour market participation.

The topics covered in this volume provide a useful illustration of the range of current research on various aspects of health. It is hoped that each of its chapters will stimulate further research along similar lines, and provide the basis for expansion of different type of research that can further enhance our understanding of the key health and development issues. Above all, however, it is hoped that the book will contribute to the design and implementation of more effective health policy interventions and, of course, better health outcomes worldwide.

Acknowledgements

The authors gratefully acknowledge the research assistance provided for the preparation of this chapter by Nora Markova. The usual disclaimer applies.

Notes

1. The overall life expectancy in SSA has dramatically fallen over the past 10 years, mostly because of the HIV/AIDS epidemic. Life expectancy dropped for females from 51.1 years to 46.3 years and from 47.3 years to 44.8 years for males (WHO 2008).
2. Under the UK's presidency of the EU in 2005, health inequalities were a major focus. The World Health Organization through its annual *World Health Reports* has consistently highlighted the growing health inequalities.

3. The three MDG health targets are: reducing child mortality, improving maternal health and combatting communicable diseases such as HIV/AIDS and malaria.

4. Cross-country research has tended to find a positive correlation between average incomes and life expectancy, pithily expressed in 'Wealthier Is Healthier', the title of a paper by Pritchett and Summers (1996). Studies of individual and household survey data have also found such correlations. For example, in a recent study of 12 developing countries, multivariate models revealed strong relations between income and one health indicator, preschoolers' weight-for-age (Haddad et al. 2003). See Deaton (2006) and Haddad et al. (2003) for a good summary of additional health inequality indicators cross-referenced with income-related variables.

5. See Sen (1992) for a discussion of interlinkages between the inequalities along the different dimensions of wellbeing.

6. However, some studies of self-reported health status have found it to be a reliable indicator of future mortality (Idler and Kasl 1991; Idler and Benyamini 1997; Ferraro and Farmer 1999). It should be noted, nonetheless, that these studies have used data from industrialized countries, where higher levels of health awareness and understanding of disease may reduce the kind of systematic reporting biases that have concerned researchers looking at developing-country data.

7. Naga and Yalcin (2007) generalize the Allison-Foster approach and provide characterization of parametric indices that can be used for measuring inequality under ordinal data.

8. Mortality then declines, concentrated among infants and children, typically initiating the transition and triggering subsequent declines in fertility.

References

Abasolo, I. and A. Tsuchiya (2004) 'Exploring Social Welfare Functions and Violation of Monotonicity: An Example from Inequalities in Health', *Journal of Health Economics*, 23 (2): 313–29.

Allison, R. A. and J. E. Foster (2004) 'Measuring Health Inequality Using Qualitative Data', *Journal of Health Economics*, 23 (3): 505–25.

Anand, S. (2004) 'The Concern for Equity in Health', in S. Anand, F. Peter and A. Sen (eds), *Public Health, Ethics and Equity* (Oxford: Oxford University Press).

Behrman, J. R. (1988a) 'Intrahousehold Allocation of Nutrients in Rural India: Are Boys Favoured? Do Households Exhibit Inequality Aversion?', *Oxford Economic Papers*, 40 (1): 55–73.

Behrman, J. R. (1988b) 'Nutrition, Health, Birth Order and Seasonality: Intrahousehold Allocation among Children in Rural India', *Journal of Development Economics*, 28 (1): 43–62.

Bloom, D. and D. Canning (2000) 'The Health and Wealth of Nations', *Science*, 287 (5456): 1207–09.

Bound, J. (1991) 'Self-Reported versus Objective Measures of Health in Retirement Models', *Journal of Human Resources*, 25 (1): 106–38.

Chen, L., E. Huq and S. DeSouza (1981) 'Sex Bias in the Family Allocation of Food and Health Care in Bangladesh', *Population and Development Review*, 7 (1): 55–70.

Dasgupta, M. (1987) 'Selective Discrimination against Female Children in Rural Punjab, India', *Population and Development Review*, 13 (1): 77–100.

Deaton, A. (2003), 'Health, Inequality and Economic Development', *Journal of Economic Literature*, 41 (1): 113–58.

Deaton, A. (2006) 'Global Patterns of Income and Health: Facts, Interpretations, and Policies', NBER Working Paper 12735 (Cambridge, MA: National Bureau of Economic Research).

Ferraro, K. and M. Farmer (1999) 'Utility of Health Data from Social surveys: Is There a Gold Standard for Measuring Morbidity?', *American Sociological Review*, 64 (2): 303–15.

Haddad, L., H. Alderman, S. Appleton, L. Song and J. Yisehac (2003) 'Reducing Child Malnutrition: How Far Does Income Growth Take Us?, *World Bank Economic Review*, 17 (1): 107–31.

Idler, E. and Y. Benyamini (1997) 'Self-Rated Health and Mortality: A Review of Twenty Seven Community Studies', *Journal of Health and Social Behaviour*, 38 (1): 21–37.

Idler, E. and S. Kasl (1991) 'Health Perceptions and Survival: Do Global Evaluations of Health Status Really Predict Mortality?', *Journal of Gerontology: Social Sciences*, 46 (2): S55–65.

Kawachi, I., S. V. Subramanian and N. Almeida-Filho (2002) 'A Glossary for Health Inequalities', *Journal of Epidemiology and Community Health*, 56: 647–52.

Lawson, D. and S. Appleton (2007) 'Child Health in Uganda – Policy Determinants and Measurement', *European Journal of Development Research*, 19 (2): 210–33.

Madden, D. (2008) 'Ordinal and Cardinal Measures of Health Inequality: An Empirical Comparison', Discussion paper, University of York.

Makinen, M., H. Waters, M. Rauch, N. Almagambetova, R. Bitran, L. Gilson, M. McIntyre, A. L. Prieto, G. Ubilla and S. Ram (2002) 'Inequalities in Health Care Use and Expenditures: Empirical Data for Eight Developing Countries and Countries in Transition', *Bulletin of World Health Organizations*, 78 (1): 55–65.

Marmot, M., D. Smith, G. Davey Smith and S. Stansfeld (1991) 'Health Inequalities among British Civil Servants: The Whitehall II Study', *Lancet*, 337: 1387–93.

Naga, R. H. A. and T. Yalcin (2007) 'Inequality Measurement for Ordered Response Health Data', *Journal of Health Economics*, 27 (6): 1614–25.

Nussbaum, M. (1988), 'Nature, Function and Capability: Aristotle on Political Distribution', *Oxford Studies in Ancient Philosophy*, Supplementary 1: 145–84.

Pitt, M. (1993) 'Analysing Human Resource Effects: Health', in L. Demery, M. Ferroni and C. Grootaert (eds), *Understanding the Social Effects of Policy Reform*. World Bank Study (Washington, DC: World Bank).

Pritchett, L. and L. H. Summers (1996) 'Wealthier Is Healthier', *Journal of Human Resources*, 31 (4): 841–68.

Sen, A. (1992). *Inequality Re-examined* (London: Russell Sage Publishers).

Sen, A. and S. Sengupta (1983) 'Malnutrition of Rural Children and the Sex Bias', *Economic and Political Weekly*, May: 855–63.

Schultz, P. and A. Tansel (1997) 'Wage and Labour Supply Effects of Illness in Côte d'Ivoire and Ghana', *Journal of Development Economics*, 53 (2): 251–86.

Stern, S. (1989) 'Measuring the Effect of Disability on Labour Force Participation', *Journal of Human Resources*, 24: 361–95.

Strauss, J. and D. Thomas (1998) 'Health, Nutrition, and Economic Development', *Journal of Economic Literature*, 36: 766–817.

UNDP (United Nations Development Programme) (2007) *Human Development Report 2007/2008* (Basingstoke: Palgrave Macmillan).

Wagstaff, A. (2004) 'Health and Poverty, What's the Problem? What to Do?', available at: http://web.worldbank.org/WBSITE/EXTERNAL/COUNTRIES/ AFRICAEXT/EXTAFRHEANUTPOP/0,,contentMDK:20183097~pagePK: 34004173~piPK:34003707~theSitePK:717020~isCURL:Y,00.html (accessed 21 July 2010).

World Bank (1993) *World Development Report* (Oxford: Oxford University Press).

WHO (World Health Organization) (1996–2008) *World Health Reports* (Geneva: WHO).

2
Measurement and Explanation of Inequality in Health and Health Care in Low-Income Settings

Eddy van Doorslaer and Owen O'Donnell

Equity in relation to health and health care are extremely important and the public attaches greater importance to the achievement of equity than to efficiency (MacLachlan and Maynard 1982). Whether this is justified or not can be debated but, even if health equity is not given primary importance, it is certainly a goal that attracts strong support in many countries. This is beginning to be reflected in academic research. Recent decades have witnessed a dramatic expansion of the literature on health equity. Not only has the number of articles with the word 'equity' in the abstract grown rapidly, but their share of all articles published in Medline, for instance, has grown by 260 per cent in the past 25 years (O'Donnell et al. 2007b). Various factors have contributed to this development. An increased interest and awareness among international organizations, governments and non-governmental organizations worldwide is certainly one factor. But the increased availability of micro data sets and the development of new analytic methods also must have played an important role.

In the health economics literature, the work on the measurement and explanation of inequalities in health and health care has drawn a lot on analogies with the literature on the measurement of inequalities in – and the redistribution of – income. Wagstaff and van Doorslaer (2000a) reviewed this literature up to 2000 with respect to three key topics: equity in health care finance, equity in health care delivery, and inequalities in health. With the focus exclusively income-related, all inequity analyses proposed and used draw heavily on rank-based measures of inequality, such as concentration curves and indices. These methods were widely used for comparisons both within and across countries of the extent to which health care systems were achieving their egalitarian goals with respect to health finance (for example, Wagstaff et al. 1999), health care delivery (for example, Van Doorslaer et al. 2000) and population health (for example, Van Doorslaer et al. 1997).

In recent years, attempts have been made to apply similar methods to the analysis of health equity in low-income countries, which typically lack breadth of coverage with respect to both population and services. Some of the methods that have proved fruitful for the examination of equity in the finance and delivery of health systems in countries of the Organisation for Economic Co-operation and Development (OECD) appear to be almost directly transferable to low-income contexts. In other cases, however, conceptual and/or practical considerations make the methods less suited to the analysis of the primary health equity issues of low-income countries. In this chapter we aim to review what we have learned from a recently completed large-scale cross-country comparative research project about health equity and the challenges of analysing it in low-income countries. The Equitap project on equity in the finance and delivery of health care in the Asia-Pacific region has the explicit aim of examining to what extent the methods developed for the analysis of equity in European health care systems could provide similarly useful information for the equity comparison of Asia-Pacific health systems.[1]

For each of the three distributions relevant to equity analysis – health payments, health care utilization and health status – we will review briefly: (a) the standard measurement approach; (b) the required adaptation or qualification for the analysis of equity in low-income settings; and (c) the findings derived to date in the Asian comparisons. The concern about these three distributions derives mostly from the widely perceived social aversion to inequality in the distributions of both health and income. In the following discussion we recognize that the distribution of income is not always only of instrumental interest to health sector equity; sometimes it is the distribution of fundamental interest and the equity concern consists of how the health sector impacts on it. In what follows, we aim to make this clearer using some examples taken from the Asian comparative study. We start with a discussion of the distributional consequences of health care payments. We then discuss equity analyses of the distribution of health care utilization and address the measurement and explanation of health inequality. The final section provides conclusions and a discussion, all of which should also be cross-related to the policy issues raised in the conclusion of Chapter 1 of this volume.

1   The distribution of health care payments

The analysis of equity in the finance of health care has traditionally focused on the measurement of progressivity (Wagstaff et al. 1992; Wagstaff et al. 1999) and on the income redistributive effect (Van Doorslaer et al. 1999) of health sources in high-income countries. The main motivation was to determine the extent to which alternative financing mechanisms complied with the *ability-to-pay principle*. Progressivity analysis was used to measure *vertical equity*, that is, the extent to which those with unequal incomes make unequal contributions to the financing of health care, by assessing the deviation of the health payment concentration curve from the Lorenz curve describing the income distribution. The degree to which payments departed from proportionality to incomes was summarized using the progressivity index proposed by Kakwani (1977). *Horizontal inequity*, that is, the degree to which equals contribute unequally, was measured as the additional redistributive effect, over and above that due to departures from proportionality, resulting from the differential payments of those on equal incomes, using an approach introduced by Aronson et al. (1994).

To a large extent, the distribution of the economic burden of health care is determined by the structure of financing and the split between direct payments, which are charged in relation to actual costs, and private insurance premiums, which are related to (pooled) expected costs. Taxation and social insurance break the link between use of health care (realized or expected) and financial liability. Instead, liability can be made a function of ability to pay. Taxation directs the bill for health care to the taxpayer and, indirectly, it is mostly workers and consumers who pick up this bill. Social insurance places the main burden on workers. Private insurance accumulates funds from those who choose to insure against the cost of future illness. Analyses of the distribution of health payments in OECD countries were instructive in showing how alternative mixes of health care financing sources (taxes, social insurance, private insurance and direct payments) may lead to very different consequences for progressivity and redistribution.

Distribution of health financing in Asia

O'Donnell et al. (2008) have analysed the structure and distribution of health care financing in 13 territories accounting for 55 per cent of the Asian population. Private insurance plays a relatively minor role in most of the health systems considered. The main distinguishing factor

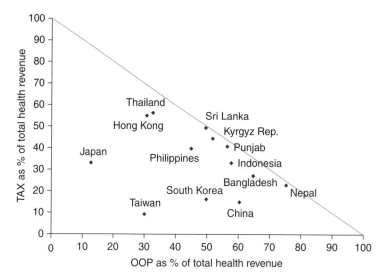

Figure 2.1: Out-of-pocket (OOP) and general government taxes (TAX) as share of total expenditure on health
Source: O'Donnell et al. (2008).

in these health financing systems is the balance between public pre-payment and private out-of-pocket (OOP) payment. The latter accounts for at least 30 per cent of total expenditure on health in all territories except Japan.

As is clear from the health financing triangle in Figure 2.1, these Asian countries and territories conform to the stylized fact that reliance on OOP payments declines with the level of development. Nepal, Bangladesh, Kyrgyz, Punjab and Sri Lanka are all very close to the 45° line, indicating that health care is financed almost exclusively from OOP and general government revenues. Nepal and Bangladesh rely more heavily on OOP, while the burden is close to being evenly split in Kyrgyz, Punjab and Sri Lanka. The distance from any point to the 45° line gives the share contributed by insurance – social and/or private. The high and middle-income territories lying furthest below the 45° line – Japan, Taiwan and South Korea – have significant social insurance systems.

Using survey data on household payments, incidence assumptions and Health Accounts data on aggregate expenditures by source, O'Donnell et al. (2008) have estimated the distributions of each financing source and of total health financing by ability to pay. In summary, they found that direct taxation is the most progressive source of finance and is most progressive in poorer economies with a narrow tax base. The distribution of OOP payments also depends on the level of development. In high-income economies with widespread insurance coverage, OOP payments absorb a larger fraction of the resources of low-income households. In poor economies, it is apparently the better-off who spend relatively more on OOP payments. At first sight, this appears to contradict much of the evidence on the regressiveness of direct payments in high-income economies (Wagstaff et al. 1999), but it may merely illustrate that the poor simply cannot afford to pay for health care in low-income economies.

So the short answer to the question 'Who pays for health care in Asia?' is that the better-off pay more. Does this mean that health care financing in these countries is very redistributive? No, the picture is somewhat misleading because, with the exception of Hong Kong, South Korea, Taiwan and Japan, and, more recently, Thailand, none of these countries has ensured close to universal coverage of a fairly comprehensive package of health services. Only these higher-income countries have divorced the link between payment for care (on the basis of the *ability-to-pay principle*) and receipt of health care (largely on the basis of the *need principle*, see below), and a redistribution interpretation can be placed on the progressivity of health payments, as in other OECD countries. For all others, the lack of coverage for a substantial share, if not the majority, of the population and the reliance on out-of-pocket direct payments for funding at least 50 per cent – and often much more – of their health care, means that it is the *benefit principle* that predominantly governs the distribution of payments for health care.

The distribution of OOP payments largely reflects the distribution of benefits (in the absence of fee waivers) and must be interpreted as such. Whereas in high-income economies the distribution of health financing is of interest largely because of its implications for the distribution of income, in low-income economies it is the consequences of health care financing for the distribution of health care, and subsequently of health, that are primarily of interest. Although health payments can have a substantial effect on the economic welfare of households, it is the income risk arising from these payments that is of greatest interest. With restricted health insurance cover, large, unforeseen expenditures on health care can have catastrophic consequences for living standards and, in the extreme, may push households into, or further into, poverty (Wagstaff and van Doorslaer 2003; Xu et al. 2003). In the next two sections we discuss how the threat that out-of-pocket health payments pose to living standards can be analysed and illustrate the methods with findings for Asian countries.

Catastrophic health payments in Asia

In the absence of insurance cover, households with severe and immediate medical needs can be forced to spend a large fraction of the household budget on health, which can result in a financing strategy that may be labelled 'catastrophic'. The concept of catastrophic payments has been put into operation by defining them as occurring once OOP payments cross some threshold share of household total expenditure (Berki 1986; Wyszewianski 1986; Pradhan and Prescott 2002; Wagstaff and van Doorslaer 2003; Xu et al. 2003). Although it is acknowledged that the choice of threshold is arbitrary, 10 per cent of total expenditure has been a common choice (Pradhan and Prescott 2002; Ranson 2002; Wagstaff and van Doorslaer 2003).

The prevalence of catastrophic payments can be measured by a headcount – the percentage of households spending more on health care than some threshold fraction of resources. The threshold may be defined as a fraction of total expenditure or, given that food spending is close to subsistence level and is less discretionary in very poor households, of non-food expenditure. Wagstaff and van Doorslaer (2003) and Van Doorslaer et al. (2007) have estimated the prevalence of catastrophic health payments in 14 countries and territories in Asia, together accounting for 81 per cent of the Asian population.

In summary, first they found that heavy reliance on OOP financing has important consequences for household living standards. For example, OOP payments for health care absorb more than 10 per cent of household resources in at least one-tenth of all households in Bangladesh, China, India, South Korea and Vietnam. Since the majority of the population do not incur catastrophic payments, the prevalence tends to dominate such statistics and the general pattern across countries is similar to that for the headcount (Van Doorslaer et al. 2007).

Second, the lower-income countries, with usually higher OOP finance shares, have a higher prevalence of catastrophic payments (Figure 2.2), although there is still substantial variation in similar OOP financing contributions. China, for instance, relies on OOP financing only slightly more than Indonesia, but the prevalence of catastrophic payments is much higher in China than in Indonesia.

Third, they found important differences across countries in the distribution of catastrophic payments. In high-income territories, catastrophic payments tend to be evenly distributed, or even slightly concentrated among the less well-off. In most low-income countries, however, it is households with higher total expenditure that are more likely to spend a large fraction of those resources on health care. This reflects the inability

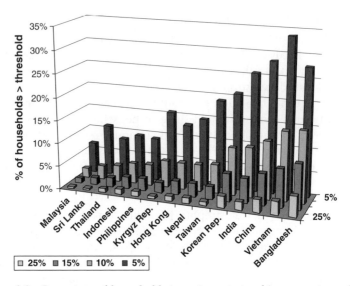

Figure 2.2:   Percentage of households incurring catastrophic payments: various thresholds for OOP as % of total expenditure
Source: Van Doorslaer et al. (2007).

of the poorest of the poor to divert resources from basic needs. But in some countries, it also seems to reflect the protection of the poor from user charges. In China, Kyrgyz and Vietnam, where there are no exemptions of the poor from charges, the poor are as likely, or even more likely, to incur catastrophic payments.

In sum, Van Doorslaer et al. (2007) found cross-country variation in the prevalence and distribution of catastrophic payments that seems to be attributable to differences in national income, financing structure and user-charging policy. Economic development is certainly an important determinant of the degree to which household welfare is put at risk by health payments, but there is no iron law that condemns the households of low-income countries to suffer financial hardship because of these payments. Some countries, in particular Malaysia, the Philippines, Sri Lanka and Thailand, have managed to contain the OOP health financing share below the average level. In contrast, Bangladesh, China, India and Vietnam stand out in relying heavily on OOP financing and having a high incidence of catastrophic payments. Although the second group of countries is, in general, poorer, there is little difference between the average incomes, for instance, of China and Sri Lanka.[2]

Impoverishment

Paying for health care may push households into, or further into, poverty. Such impoverishment is not captured by the standard, house-hold-resource-based, measures of poverty; the poverty line cannot take full account of health care needs because of the variability and unpredictability of health care costs. If expenditures on health care were completely non-discretionary, constituting resources that are not available to meet other basic needs, then it would be appropriate to assess poverty on the basis of household resources net of payments for health care.[3] Of course, not all expenditures on health care are made without discretion. There is ample evidence that such expenditures are responsive to incomes and prices. Nonetheless, it is likely that households make great sacrifices in order to meet needs for vital health care. It seems inaccurate to categorize a household as non-poor simply because high medical expenses raise its total spending above the poverty line, while its spending on food, clothing and shelter is below subsistence levels.

The difference between poverty estimates derived from household expenditures gross and net of OOP payments for health care provides a rough approximation of the poverty impact of such payments (Wagstaff and van Doorslaer 2003; Gustaffson and Li 2004). Van Doorslaer et al. (2006b) have estimated the change in the poverty headcount ratios for 11 low-to-middle-income countries in Asia by comparing household consumption/expenditure both gross and net of OOP health payments relative to two poverty lines. In summary, the results, shown in Table 2.1, are quite consistent with those of the World Bank (Chen and Ravallion 2004). At the US$1.08 poverty line, subtracting OOP payments from total resources results in a 3.8 percentage point increase in the headcount in Bangladesh, equivalent to almost 5 million people, a 3.7 percentage point increase in India (over 37 million people) and a 2.6 percentage point increase in China (32.4 million people). The total estimated increase in the poverty headcount is 78.16 million people, or 2.7 per cent of the population of these 11 low-/middle-income Asian countries. Ultimately, the figure tells us how many individuals are not counted as poor despite the fact that the value of their consumption of all goods and services other than health care is less than the extreme poverty line of US$1.08 per day.

In absolute percentage point terms, the largest increases in poverty at the lower poverty line are in Bangladesh, India, China and Nepal. Of course, the number of individuals pushed into poverty by OOP payments is greatest in India and China. The relative increase in poverty is greatest, by far, in Vietnam, where the poverty rate rises by one-third.

Table 2.1: Poverty headcounts: effect of taking account of OOP payments for health care

Poverty line	US$1.08 per day					US$2.15 per day				
	(1) Pre-payment headcount (%)	(2) Post-payment headcount (%)	Change in poverty headcount			(6) Pre-payment headcount (%)	(7) Post-payment headcount (%)	Change in poverty headcount		
			(3) Percentage point change	(4) Number of individuals	(5) Percentage change			(8) Percentage point change	(9) Number of individuals	(10) Percentage change
Bangladesh	22.5	26.3	**3.8**	4,940,585	16.8	73.0	76.5	**3.6**	4,653,875	4.9
China	13.7	16.2	**2.6**	32,431,209	18.8	44.6	46.4	**1.8**	23,198,460	4.1
India	31.1	34.8	**3.7**	37,358,760	11.9	80.3	82.4	**2.1**	20,638,361	2.6
Indonesia	7.9	8.6	0.7	1,440,395	8.7	58.2	59.9	**1.7**	3,493,767	2.9
Kyrgyz Rep.	2.2	2.7	0.1	5,989	4.7	32.2	34.1	**1.9**	94,793	6.0
Malaysia	1.0	1.1	0.1	10,562	4.4	11.8	12.1	0.3	58,626	2.1
Nepal	39.3	41.6	**2.2**	515,933	5.7	80.4	81.7	**1.3**	290,280	1.6
Philippines	15.8	16.4	0.6	445,680	3.7	50.2	51.2	**1.1**	790,333	2.1
Sri Lanka	3.8	4.1	0.3	60,116	8.3	39.1	40.8	**1.7**	325,783	4.3
Thailand	2.1	2.3	0.2	100,201	7.9	24.2	24.9	0.7	417,626	2.8
Vietnam	3.6	4.7	**1.1**	848,870	30.1	36.9	41.4	**4.5**	3,492,321	12.1
TOTAL	19.3	22.0	2.7	78,158,299	14.0	58.8	60.8	2.0	57,454,225	3.4

Source: Van Doorslaer et al. (2006b).

Notes: Column (3) = (2)−(1). Column (4) = (3)*population. Column (5) = (3)/(1). Bold figures in columns (3) and (8) denote statistically significantly different from 0 at the 5% significance level.

It rises by 18.9 per cent in China, 16.8 per cent in Bangladesh, and 11.9 per cent in India. As we saw in previous sections, these are the countries with the highest OOP budget shares and prevalence of catastrophic payments. It would appear to be both the high levels of OOP payments and their even distribution throughout the income distribution that are responsible for the very high poverty impacts in Vietnam and China. But there are still large poverty impacts in Bangladesh and India, where OOP payments are more heavily concentrated among the better-off.

Regression analysis confirms that the percentage point change in the poverty headcount is positively correlated with the OOP financing share and, as would be expected, with the initial headcount (Van Doorslaer et al. 2006b). Deviations from the positive correlation between the initial poverty headcount and the absolute poverty impact are more interesting than the relationship itself. For example, the initial headcount is higher in the Philippines than it is in China, but the poverty impact is more than four times greater in China. And initial headcounts are similar in Sri Lanka and Vietnam but the poverty impact in Vietnam is four times that in Sri Lanka. These differences point to the consequences of a high reliance on OOP financing in China and Vietnam. However, substantial cross-country variation was found in the extent to which vulnerable individuals are protected from the impoverishing effects of health payments. For example, roughly one-half of the population live on US\$1–2 per day in Bangladesh, India and Indonesia (see Figure 2.3).

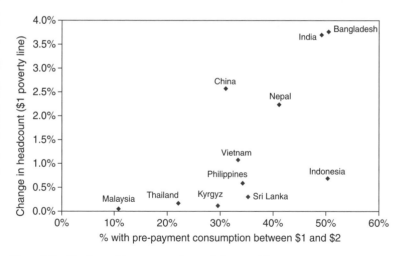

Figure 2.3: Headcount increase and population at risk
Source: Van Doorslaer et al. (2006b).

However, whereas 3.7 per cent of the population slip below the US$1 threshold in both Bangladesh and India after subtracting payments for health care, only 0.7 per cent of Indonesians are impoverished. In the five countries in which 30–40 per cent of the population lie between the two poverty thresholds, there are substantial differences in the poverty impacts. Over 2 per cent are impoverished in China and Nepal, 1.2 per cent in Vietnam and much less than 1 per cent in the Philippines and Sri Lanka. Again, these differences reflect different degrees of reliance on OOP financing. But this does not explain all the differences. Vietnam is more heavily reliant on OOP payments than China but is apparently more successful in limiting their impoverishing effect.

2   Inequality and inequity in health care utilization

The distribution of health care in relation to income is of interest for many reasons. Foremost are the consequences for health inequality: if the poor are relatively deprived of effective health care interventions, income-related inequalities in health will be exacerbated and economic growth retarded (Sala-i-Martin 2005). Health care distribution may also be examined to assess whether there is equity in the allocation of health care resources. This is the motivation that has been predominant in research focused on the distribution of health care in OECD countries (Van Doorslaer et al. 1992; Van Doorslaer et al. 2000; Van Doorslaer 2006a). The aim has been to establish whether the distribution of health care obeys the principle of horizontal equity, defined as equal treatment for equal need. The evidence suggests that many OECD countries are close to achieving their horizontal equity objectives, although the results often differ markedly by type of utilization. This approach has also proved feasible in three of the higher-income countries in the Asian study with near universal coverage (Lu et al. 2006).

Application in low-coverage settings runs into two problems. The first is conceptual. The horizontal equity approach uses the observed average relationship between use and need characteristics (while appropriately controlling for other factors) as the implicit norm to identify needed or need-expected use. In other words, it assumes that, 'on average, the system gets it right' (Van Doorslaer et al. 2000). This assumption is clearly more likely to be violated in systems with very partial coverage of population and services. The second problem concerns data requirements, which for this analysis include measures of income, health care use and need for the same individuals. In the OECD-focused research, need has been proxied by demographics and self-reported measures of health.

Its application to low-income countries is currently constrained by the availability and reliability of self-reported health measures, which often fail to show the income gradients that are observable in more objective, but less general, measures of health, such as infant mortality (Murray 1996; Wagstaff 2002).

Considering these problems in low-income settings, this is not a major concern if there is little or no variation in need. Then, inequality in utilization represents inequity. Variation in need will often be limited provided that the population group and treatment of interest are defined to be sufficiently homogeneous. For example, all children within a certain age band are in need of immunization against measles, tuberculosis and so on. Although it could legitimately be argued that the benefit from immunization varies with the prevalence of the disease in the child's locality, such variation in need is limited in comparison with that for adults' visits to a doctor. Demographic and Health Survey data show clear pro-rich disparities in child immunization rates, use of antenatal care, and medically attended births (Gwatkin et al. 2003).

Conclusions about equity can sometimes be inferred from the distribution of utilization if there is prior knowledge of the distribution of need. For example, it is well established that rates of mortality and malnutrition are higher among poorer children in many low-income countries (Gwatkin et al. 2003). Poor children, and quite probably poor adults, are in greater need of medical interventions. If the distribution of health care is not skewed toward the poor, then this is sufficient to reject the proposition of equity. Pro-rich inequality in utilization then provides a lower bound to the degree of pro-rich inequity. In high-income countries, this approach is not helpful since the poor tend to use health care more than the rich. There the question is whether the greater utilization by the poor matches their greater need such that equity is achieved. In low-income countries, however, inequality in utilization often does not favour the poor and it is possible to make a statement about inequity without simultaneously measuring need. It is evidently not possible, however, to make precise estimates of the degree of inequity, which limits the ability to make cross-country or other comparisons.

The Equitap study has examined whether public spending on health care was: (a) pro-poor; and (b) inequality-reducing in eight Asian countries and three Chinese provinces or regions (O'Donnell et al. 2007a). These questions were addressed by testing the dominance of the concentration curve of the public health subsidy against the 45° line, representing an equal distribution, and the Lorenz curve of household consumption, respectively. Formal statistical tests of dominance were used for inference (Bishop et al. 1992). By way of example, subsidy concentration curves and Lorenz curves for Malaysia and India are presented in Figure 2.4. The concentration curve in Malaysia lies (significantly) above the diagonal – it is pro-poor. In India, by contrast, the curve lies below the diagonal – the poor get less than a proportionate share of public health care. The subsidy concentration curve in India appears to be slightly inside the Lorenz curve, but the difference is not statistically significant. The hypothesis that public spending on health care in India has no impact on inequality in living standards cannot be rejected.

Dominance results for all countries included in the study are summarized in Table 2.2. Public spending on health care is pro-poor only in the three highest-income countries. Sri Lanka is the only low-income country that distributes public health care equally. Spending on health care is pro-rich in all the other low-income countries, although in most cases it is also inequality reducing. The two exceptions are India and Nepal, where the share of public spending received by the poor does not even surpass their share of total consumption. The concentration indices presented in Figure 2.5 measure the degree of income-related inequality in the distribution of public health spending. The pro-poor inequality in Hong Kong, indicated by a negative concentration index,

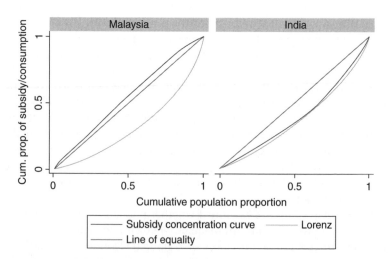

Figure 2.4: Concentration curve of public health subsidy and Lorenz curve of household consumption per equivalent adult
Source: Derived from data and analysis reported in O'Donnell et al. (2007a).

Table 2.2   Distribution of public health subsidy in Asia

	Inequality-reducing	Inequality-neutral
Pro-poor	Hong Kong SAR Malaysia Thailand	
Equal	Sri Lanka	
Pro-rich	Vietnam Bangladesh Indonesia Gansu (China) Heilongjiang (China)	India Nepal

Source: Derived from results reported in O'Donnell et al. (2007a), Table 9.1.
Notes:
Pro-poor – concentration curve statistically dominates (lies above) the 45° line of equality.
Pro-rich – concentration curve is statistically dominated by the 45° line.
Equality – concentration curve is statistically indistinguishable from the 45° line.
Inequality-reducing – concentration curve statistically dominates the Lorenz curve.
Inequality-neutral – concentration curve is statistically indistinguishable from (India) or crosses (Nepal) the Lorenz curve.

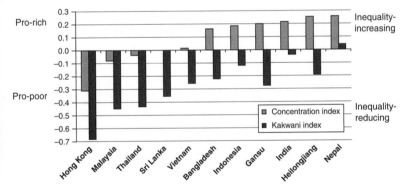

Figure 2.5:   Concentration and Kakwani indices for public health subsidy
Source: O'Donnell et al. (2007a), Table S.3.

is much greater than that in Malaysia and Thailand. As anticipated from the result of the dominance test, the index is zero in Sri Lanka, indicating equality. It is only very slightly positive in Vietnam, suggesting that the pro-rich inequality detected by the dominance test is marginal.

The pro-rich bias is more substantial in the other low-income countries and is greatest in the poorest country – Nepal. The Kakwani index – equal to the concentration index less the Gini coefficient – is negative in all countries but Nepal, indicating inequality reduction, as could be anticipated from the dominance tests.

O'Donnell et al. (2007a) also looked at the cross-country differences in the distribution of public health care, assessed by tests of dominance between concentration curves. In summary, they found the distribution in Hong Kong is more pro-poor than that in all other countries. The distributions in Malaysia, Thailand and Sri Lanka are indistinguishable. Malaysia and Thailand dominate all other distributions and Sri Lanka dominates all others except Vietnam and Bangladesh. Vietnam dominates the remainder of countries. So, countries/provinces can be broadly grouped as follows in relation to the distribution of public health care: (a) Hong Kong (very pro-poor); (b) Malaysia, Thailand and Sri Lanka (mildly pro-poor to neutral); (c) Vietnam (mildly pro-rich); (d) Bangladesh, Indonesia, India, Gansu, Heilongjiang and Nepal (very pro-rich).

The interpretation of these results requires consideration of two questions. First, in the many low-income countries in which the poor do not get their share of public health care, does this necessarily represent a failure of public policy? Second, why is it that public health care is more pro-poor in Malaysia, Thailand, Sri Lanka and, to a lesser extent, Vietnam than in other developing countries of Asia?

The answer to the first of these questions largely depends on the objectives of the public health spending. If the aim is to ensure that the poor get more public health services than the better-off, then the objective is clearly not being achieved in most cases. Alternatively, subsidizing health care may be part of a wider policy to reduce relative differences in living standards between rich and poor. With the exceptions of India and Nepal, the subsidy achieves this objective – it is inequality-reducing. But those concerned about inequalities within the health sector may not be content with a reduction in general economic inequality. From this perspective, is the fact that the poor get less of the subsidy necessarily a failure? Despite its name, benefit incidence analysis provides information about the incidence of public health expenditures rather than the benefits from these expenditures. Even though the poor get a lower than proportionate share of the subsidy, the impact on their health can be greater if the marginal product is declining with the initial level of health (given a positive relationship between income and health) (Filmer et al. 2002).

The evidence shows that, on average, the better-off typically receive most of the subsidy. But this is informative about the distributional implications of a policy change only if marginal changes in the subsidy were delivered in strict proportion to current utilization (Younger 2003). Of course, many policy reforms will deliver marginal gains that differ from average gains (Lanjouw and Ravallion 1999).

Although relatively high levels of public spending can ensure adequate technical quality in the public sector, universality of access leads to long waiting times and minimal amenities, creating incentives for the better-off to opt out of the public sector. These incentives become stronger as the economy grows, as it has done most impressively in Malaysia and Thailand, and there is an expansion of middle- and higher-income groups with not only the desire but also the means to purchase higher-quality care in the private sector (Hammer et al. 1995). Figure 2.6 shows clear discrepancies between the distributions of public and private inpatient care in Hong Kong, Malaysia, Sri Lanka and Thailand. In Bangladesh, India and Indonesia, in contrast, the distribution of private sector care is only slightly more pro-rich than is care in the public sector. In these countries there does not yet exist a large middle class with the effective demand for the greater convenience of private sector care. In addition, quality differentials between the sectors can be limited. In Bangladesh and India, the poor make extensive use of unqualified private sector providers, who may be cheaper and more accessible than public sector alternatives. In Hong Kong, Malaysia,

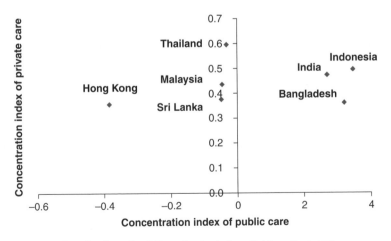

Figure 2.6: Distribution of public and private hospital inpatient care
Source: Somanathan et al. (2005).

Sri Lanka and Thailand, private sector care is pro-rich whereas the public sector is pro-poor or neutral.

In summary, the analysis shows that the pervasive outcome of a pro-rich distribution of public health care in most Asian and other low-income countries is not unavoidable but that effective targeting is easier to realize at higher national incomes. Hong Kong, Malaysia, Sri Lanka and Thailand have demonstrated that the allocation of sufficient public resources coupled with a policy of universal access can ensure far greater benefits to the poor than may have hitherto been assumed. Higher incomes not only make such policies more feasible, they also make them more effective with respect to the target efficiency of spending, by allowing the private sector opt-out.

Descriptive analysis such as that presented above is useful in identifying a problem. It shows that public spending on health care does not predominantly reach the poor in most low-income countries. Hypotheses can be offered to explain this and solutions can be proposed. But from a descriptive analysis it is not possible to identify the likely effectiveness of any policy reforms in shifting the distribution of health care towards the poor. For this, an evaluative approach is required.

3   Health inequality

Two issues of importance to the study of health inequality in low-income countries are considered in this section: (a) reporting heterogeneity in measures of health; and (b) decomposition of health inequality and of changes in inequality.

Reporting heterogeneity in health measures

The difficulty confronted in obtaining an accurate measure of health for a study of health inequality varies with the type of inequality one is seeking to examine. If the purpose is to measure the total variation in health across the population, then detailed measures of health available from administrative records or health surveys can be used. The task is more difficult if the aim is to measure socioeconomic-related inequality in health. Data that provide measures of health and of socioeconomic status for the same individuals are then required. There is usually a trade-off between the use of health surveys that provide more detailed measures of health but less detailed measures of economic status, such as income and consumption, and the use of general household and expenditure surveys that measure income and/or consumption more accurately but have cruder instruments for the measurement of health. In recent years, the Demographic and Health Surveys (DHS) have weakened this trade-off by being able to construct an index of household wealth.

However, the DHS do not provide a measure of general health in the adult population and, as already noted in the previous section, self-reported measures of health have proved to be less useful in low-income countries. Case vignettes have been proposed as an instrument to correct for systematic heterogeneity in the reporting of health (Tandon et al. 2003; King et al. 2004). The idea is to identify variation in reporting behaviour from individuals' ratings of defined cases. For example, sample respondents may be asked to rate, on a five-point scale, the health of someone who cannot walk 100 metres without stopping to catch breath. Variation in the ratings depending on respondents' characteristics, such as gender, age, income, education and nationality, allows estimation of the effects of these characteristics on reporting behaviour. Assuming that respondents report on the vignettes in the same way that they report their own health, the identified reporting effect can be purged from the rating of own health. Inequality in this cleansed measure of health should then reflect variation only in true health conditions and not in the reporting of these conditions.

Bago d'Uva et al. (2008) used vignette data collected for Indonesia, Andrah Pradesh (India) and three Chinese provinces (Gansu, Henan, and Shan-dong) as part of the World Health Organization's Multi-Country Survey Study of Health and Responsiveness (Sadana et al. 2002) to examine the effect of removing systematic reporting heterogeneity from measured disparities in health by income, education, demographics and urban/rural location.

This study found that the way in which individuals report their health varies significantly with their socioeconomic and demographic characteristics, and this biases measures of income-related inequality in health downward. In most cases, however, the magnitude of the effect is rather small. This may reflect the difficulty poorly educated individuals have in completing the vignette exercise, which requires a considerable degree of abstract thought. Although it is certainly an approach that deserves further experimentation, the jury remains out on whether it does offer a sufficiently more accurate way of measuring health for the purpose of examining socioeconomic inequality in health in low-income countries.

Decomposition of health inequality

Measurement of health inequality is a first step toward understanding the socioeconomic determinants of health and of health sector inequities. A natural next step is the explanation of the sources of health inequality and the factors contributing to its change over time. Decomposition techniques can be used to provide such explanations. The method presented in this section decomposes income-related health inequality, as measured by the concentration index, into the contribution of various factors. The approach can also be used to explain change in the concentration index.

Wagstaff et al. (2003) demonstrate that the concentration index of health can be written as the sum of the contribution of factors, such as demographics, education and region, to income-related health inequality, where each contribution is the product of the elasticity of health with respect to the factor and the concentration index of the factor.[4] Wagstaff et al. used these decomposition methods to explain the level and change in income-related inequality in child height-for-age z-scores, a measure of long-term nutritional status, in Vietnam in 1993 and 1998. They found the concentration index was negative in both years, indicating that nutritional status was lower among poorer children. The largest contribution was the direct effect of household consumption, the measure of economic status against which inequality is assessed. There was also a very large contribution to consumption-related nutrition inequality from commune fixed effects. This suggests that nutrition and consumption both varied across communes and this commune-level covariance made an important contribution to the measured inequality in nutrition. There was a smaller contribution from access to sanitation and to safe drinking water in 1998. Age differences in nutrition and consumption shifted the inequality in the other direction, toward lower nutrition among the better-off, but this was outweighed by the other contributions. The concentration index increased in absolute value between 1993 and 1998 from –0.075 to –0.102, indicating an increase in consumption-related inequality in the child height deficit. Most of this increase in inequality is explained by changes in the distribution and effect of household consumption and in the contribution of the commune-level covariance between nutrition and consumption.

Measurement of horizontal inequity in the utilization of health care, as described above, involves measuring income-related inequality in utilization after standardizing for differences in need. The decomposition approach provides a convenient way of doing this. One simply needs to deduct the contributions of the need-standardizing variables from total inequality (Van Doorslaer et al. 2004). An advantage is that the analyst can avoid imposing judgements about which factors should be counted as need and therefore justifiably giving rise to variation in utilization. The full decomposition results can be presented and the user can choose which factors to standardize.

4 Conclusion

This review has served to illustrate that, in moving attention from high-
to low-income countries, some of the standard measurement methodology that has been proposed and used to measure income-related
inequality in health payments, medical care use and health status
cannot straightforwardly be applied in low-income countries with low
health insurance coverage. Some of the reasons for this are conceptual
and relate to different equity priorities concerning the finance and
provision of health care in such countries. Others derive from measurement problems.

With respect to finance, it is obvious that, in systems with small rev-
enue shares deriving from pre-payments, questions of income redistribution or deviations from proportionality are secondary to questions of
income protection. This is why measures of the incidence and intensity
of catastrophic out-of-pocket payments and their impoverishing effect
are required to assess the equity performance of health financing systems.
Measures of progressivity and redistributive effect may even be misleading if used to examine the distribution of payments that are mainly
driven by the benefit principle rather than the ability-to-pay principle.
In low-income countries, the rich clearly pay more, even proportionally
more, but mainly for receipt of their own care. Unlike in universal coverage systems, which tend to require payments according to ability to
pay and receipt according to need, in low-coverage countries, payments
and receipt of care are still very much linked and it can be misleading
to analyse them separately. The measures of catastrophic payments and
impoverishment that have been proposed and used to date are rather ad
hoc and certainly do not have the sort of conceptual underpinnings that
have been developed for progressivity measures. Further consideration
should be given to the development of a conceptual basis for catastrophic
health payments from which a measure can be derived.

With respect to equity in access to and use of medical care, again
a straightforward application of approaches based on the need principle, which requires those in equal need to be treated equally, runs into
two problems. One is, as above, that a lot of care is simply allocated on
the basis of market principles – you get what you pay for – and therefore the standard approach of using the average need–use relationship
as the norm breaks down. Second, self-reported health measures appear
much less reliable in low-income/low-education settings (see Rojas,
Chapter 7 in this volume, for further discussion), and are therefore less
appropriate for need standardization procedures. Given these problems,

analysis is confined to examination of the distribution of health care with no standardization for need. Conclusions about equity can still possibly be drawn if there is prior knowledge of the distribution of need. Examination of the distribution of public health care is of additional interest since it reveals whether public spending dollars predominantly benefit the rich or the poor. This is integral to evaluation of the effectiveness of government anti-poverty policies. The Asian study shows that public spending on health care – despite being inequality-reducing – does not predominantly reach the poor in most low-income countries. It was found to be most pro-poor in Malaysia, Thailand and Sri Lanka, three countries that seem to have achieved better-targeted public care subsidies as a result of a combination of (near) universal public provision with limited user charges on the poor, geographically dispersed health services and facilities, a private sector offering an attractive alternative, and incomes that make demand for this alternative effective.

With respect to inequalities in health itself, most studies hitherto have concentrated on objective measures such as adult or child survival or nutrition (see, for example, Aturupane et al., Chapter 4, and Mutunga, Chapter 5, both in this volume) because of presumed measurement biases in self-reported measures of health. This has generated a large and useful literature, ranging from descriptive to explanatory to evaluative, and such measures are clearly more appropriate the lower the level of development. With rising levels of development, however, other aspects of health than nutrition and survival will gain importance and require measurement. Reports of weak, missing or even the 'wrong' gradients in self-reported measures of health and illness have generated scepticism concerning their usefulness and worries about strong and systematic reporting biases. The use of case vignettes has been suggested, both as a tool to test for reporting tendencies but also as a potential remedy to correct its biases. The evidence to date is still thin on the extent to which vignette-based modelling techniques will be able meet these promises.

Although most of the evidence reviewed in this chapter concerns inequality measurement and explanation, it is obvious that there is an even more urgent need to complement this with evaluative evidence that is capable of demonstrating not only how inequality compares across time and place, or can be decomposed into (partial) associations with other inequalities, but also how it can be impacted upon by policy interventions. This calls for well-controlled, possibly even experimental designs, which may give us harder evidence on the causes and consequences of health inequalities, but may come at the price of lower generalizability. Advancing health equity will require accumulating evidence from a multitude of micro studies on what interventions in which settings are effective in changing the distributions of health payments, health care and health.

Acknowledgements

This chapter is a revised version of a paper prepared for the UNU–WIDER conference on Advancing Health Equity, Helsinki, 29–30 September 2006. We are grateful to the European Commission INCO-DEV programme for funding the Equitap project (ICA4-CT-2001-10015) from which this paper derived and to the Equitap partners for permission to use illustration material from the joint working papers.

Notes

1. 'Equity in Asia-Pacific Health Systems', available at: www.equitap.org.
2. Van Doorslaer et al. (2007) should be consulted for a further discussion of the limitations associated with studies of catastrophic payments.
3. A National Academy of Sciences Panel made this recommendation as the appropriate approach to measuring poverty in the USA (Cirto and Michael 1995). Alternative estimates of US poverty based on the approach are available (Short et al. 1999; Short and Garner 2002).
4. See Wagstaff et al. (2003) for equations.

References

Aronson, J. R., P. Johnson and P. J. Lambert (1994) 'Redistributive Effect and Unequal Tax Treatment', *Economic Journal*, 104: 262–70.
Bago d'Uva, T., E. van Doorslaer, M. Lindeboom, O. O'Donnell et al. (2008) 'Does Reporting Heterogeneity Bias the Measurement of Health Disparities?', *Health Economics*, 17 (3): 351–75.
Berki, S. E. (1986) 'A Look at Catastrophic Medical Expenses and the Poor', *Health Affairs*, 5 (4): 138–45.
Bishop, J. A., J. P. Formby and P. D. Thistle (1992) 'Convergence of the South and Non-South Income Distributions, 1969–1979', *American Economic Review*, 82 (1): 262–72.
Chen, S. and M. Ravallion (2004) 'How Have the World's Poor Fared since the Early 1980s?', *World Bank Research Observer*, 19 (2): 141–69.
Cirto, C. and R. Michael (1995) *Measuring Poverty: A New Approach* (Washington, DC: National Academy Press).
Filmer, D., J. Hammer and L. Pritchett (2002) 'Weak Links in the Chain II: A Prescription for Health Policy in Poor Countries', *World Bank Research Observer*, 17 (1): 47–66.

Gustaffson, B. and S. Li (2004) 'Expenditures on Education and Health Care and Poverty in Rural China', *China Economic Review*, 15: 292–301.

Gwatkin, D. R., S. Rustein, K. Johnson, R. Pande, et al. (2003) *Initial Country-Level Information about Socio-economic Differentials in Health, Nutrition and Population*, Vols I and II (Washington, DC: World Bank, Health, Population and Nutrition).

Hammer, J. S., I. Nabi and J. A. Cercone (1995) 'Distributional Effects of Social Sector Expenditures in Malaysia, 1974–89', in D. van de Walle and K. Nead (eds), *Public Spending and the Poor* (Baltimore: Johns Hopkins University Press).

Kakwani, N. C. (1977) 'Measurement of Tax Progressivity: An International Comparison', *Economic Journal*, 87 (345): 71–80.

King, G., C. J. L. Murray, J. Salomon and A. Tandon (2004) 'Enhancing the Validity and Cross-Cultural Comparability of Measurement in Survey Research', *American Political Science Review*, 98 (1): 184–91.

Lanjouw, P. and M. Ravallion (1999) 'Benefit Incidence, Public Spending Reforms and the Timing of Program Capture', *World Bank Economic Review*, 13 (2), 257–73.

Lu, J.-F. R., G. M. Leung, S. Kwon, K. Y. Tin et al. (2006) 'Horizontal Equity in Health Care Utilization – Evidence from Three High-Income Asian Economies', *Social Science & Medicine*, 64: 199–212.

MacLachlan, G. and A. Maynard (1982) 'The Public/Private Mix in Health Care: The Emerging Lessons', in G. MacLachlan and A. Maynard, *The Public/Private Mix in Health Care: The Relevance and Effects of Change* (London: Nuffield Provincial Hospital Trust),

Murray, C. J. L. (1996) 'Epidemiology and Morbidity Transitions in India', in M. Dasgupta, C. L. Chen and T. N. Krishnan (eds), *Health, Poverty and Development in India* (Delhi: Oxford University Press), 122–47.

O'Donnell, O., E. van Doorslaer, R. Rannan-Eliya A. Somanathan, S. R. Adhikari, D. Harbianto, C. C. Garg, P. Hanvoravongchai, M. N. Huq, A. Karan, G. M. Leung, C. W. Ng, B. R. Pande, K. Tin, K. Tisayaticom, L. Trisnantoro, Y. Zhang and Y. Zhao (2007a) 'The Incidence of Public Spending on Health Care: Comparative Evidence from Asia', *World Bank Economic Review*, 21 (1): 93–123.

O'Donnell, O., E. van Doorslaer, A. Wagstaff and M. Lindelow (2007b) *Analyzing Health Equity Using Household Survey Data: A Guide to Techniques and Their Implementation* (Washington DC: World Bank Institute, World Bank).

O'Donnell, O., E. van Doorslaer, R. Rannan-Eliya, A. Somanathan, S. R. Adhikari, B. Akkazieva, D. Harbianto, C. C. Garg, P. Hanvoravongchai, A. N. Herrin, M. N. Huq, S. Ibragimova, A. Karan, S. M. Kwon, G. M. Leung, J. F. Lu, Y. Ohkusa, B. R. Pande, R. Racelis, K. Tin, K. Tisayaticom, L. Trisnantoro, Q. Wan, B. M. Yang and Y. Zhao (2008) 'Who Pays for Health Care in Asia?', *Journal of Health Economics*, 27 (2): 460–75.

Pradhan, M. and N. Prescott (2002) 'Social Risk Management Options for Medical Care in Indonesia', *Health Economics*, 11: 431–46.

Ranson, M. K. (2002) 'Reduction of Catastrophic Health Care Expenditures by a Community-Based Health Insurance Scheme in Gujarat, India: Current Experiences and Challenges', *Bulletin of the World Health Organization*, 80 (8): 613–21.

Sadana, R., A. Tandon, C. J. L. Murray, I. Serdobova, Y. Cao, W. J. Xie, S. Chatterji and B. L. Ustun (2002) *Describing Population Health in Six Domains: Comparable Results from 66 Household Surveys* (Geneva: World Health Organization).

Sala-i-Martin, X. (2005) 'On the Health-Poverty Trap', in G. Lopez-Casasnovas, B. Rivera and L. Currais (eds), *Health and Economics Growth: Findings and Policy Implications* (Cambridge MA: MIT Press).

Short, K. and T. Garner (2002) 'Experimental Poverty Measures: Accounting for Medical Expenditures', *Monthly Labor Review*, 125: 3–13.

Short, K., T. Garner, D. Johnson and P. Doyle (1999) 'Experimental Poverty Measures: 1990 to 1997', U.S. Census Bureau, *Current Population Reports, Consumer Income, 60-205* (Washington, DC: US Government Printing Office).

Somanathan, A., O. O'Donnell, E. van Doorslaer, R. P. Rannan-Eliya, et al. (2005) 'Who Gets Health Care in Asia?', EQUITAP Working Paper No. 4, Erasmus University, Rotterdam, and IPS, Colombo.

Tandon, A., C. J. L. Murray, J. A. Salomon and G. King (2003) 'Statistical Models for Enhancing Cross-Population Comparability', in C. J. L. Murray and D. B. Evans (eds), *Health Systems Performance Assessment: Debates, Methods and Empiricisms* (Geneva: World Health Organization), 727–46.

Van Doorslaer, E., A. Wagstaff, S. Calonge, T. Christiansen et al. (1992) 'Equity in the Delivery of Health Care: Some International Comparisons', *Journal of Health Economics*, 11 (4): 389–411.

Van Doorslaer, E., A. Wagstaff, H. Bleichrodt, S. Calonge et al. (1997) 'Income-Related Inequalities in Health: Some International Comparisons', *Journal of Health Economics*, 16 (1): 93–112.

Van Doorslaer, E., A. Wagstaff, H. van der Burg, T. Christiansen et al. (1999) 'The Redistributive Effect of Health Care Finance in Twelve OECD Countries', *Journal of Health Economics*, 18 (3): 291–313.

Van Doorslaer, E., A. Wagstaff, H. van der Burg, T. Christiansen et al. (2000). 'Equity in the Delivery of Health Care in Europe and the US', *Journal of Health Economics*, 19 (5): 553–84.

Van Doorslaer, E., X. Koolman and A. M. Jones (2004) 'Explaining Income-Related Inequalities in Doctor Utilization in Europe', *Health Economics*, 13 (7): 629–47.

Van Doorslaer, E., C. Masseria and X. Koolman for the OECD Health Equity Research Group (2006a) 'Inequalities in Access to Medical Care by Income in Developed Countries', *Canadian Medical Association Journal*, 174: 177–83.

Van Doorslaer, E., O. O'Donnell, R. P. Rannan-Eliya, A. Somanathan, et al. (2006b) 'Effects of Payments for Health Care on Poverty Estimates in 11 Countries in Asia: An Analysis of Household Survey Data', *The Lancet*, 368: 1357–64.

Van Doorslaer, E, O. O'Donnell, R. Rannan-Eliya, A. Somanathan, S. R. Adhikari, C. C. Garg, D. Harbianto, A. N. Herrin, M. N. Huq, S. Ibragimova, A. Karan, T. J. Lee, G. M. Leung, J. F. Lu, C. W. Ng, B. R. Pande, R. Racelis, S. Tao, K. Tin, K. Tisayaticom, L. Trisnantoro, C. Vasavid and Y. Zhao (2007) 'Catastrophic Payments for Health Care in Asia', *Health Economics*, 16 (11): 1159–84.

Wagstaff, A. (2002). 'Poverty and Health Sector Inequalities', *Bulletin of the World Health Organization*, 80 (2): 97–105.

Wagstaff, A. and E. van Doorslaer (2000a). 'Equity in Health Care Finance and Delivery', in A. J. Culyer and J. P. Newhouse (eds), *Handbook of Health Economics* (Amsterdam: Elsevier North-Holland), 1B, 1803–62.

Wagstaff, A. and E. van Doorslaer (2000b) 'Measuring and Testing for Inequity in the Delivery of Health Care', *Journal of Human Resources*, 35 (4): 716–33.

Wagstaff, A., and E. van Doorslaer (2003) 'Catastrophe and Impoverishment in Paying for Health Care: With Applications to Vietnam 1993–98', *Health Economics*, 12: 921–34.

Wagstaff, A., E. van Doorslaer, S. Calonge, T. Christiansen et al. (1992) 'Equity in the Finance of Health Care: Some International Comparisons', *Journal of Health Economics*, 11 (4): 361–88.

Wagstaff, A., E. van Doorslaer, H. van der Burg, S. Calonge et al. (1999) 'Equity in the Finance of Health Care: Some Further International Comparisons', *Journal of Health Economics*, 18 (3): 263–90.

Wagstaff, A., E. van Doorslaer and N. Watanabe (2003) 'On Decomposing the Causes of Health Sector Inequalities, with an Application to Malnutrition Inequalities in Vietnam', *Journal of Econometrics*, 112 (1): 219–27.

Wyszewianski, L. (1986) 'Financially Catastrophic and High Cost Cases: Definitions, Distinctions and Their Implications for Policy Formulation', *Inquiry*, 23 (4): 382–94.

Xu, K., D. E. Evans, K. Kawabate, R. Zeramdini, et al. (2003) 'Household Catastrophic Health Expenditure: A Multicountry Analysis', *The Lancet*, 362: 111–17.

Younger, S. D. (2003) 'Benefits on the Margin: Observations on Marginal Benefit Incidence Analysis', *World Bank Economic Review*, 17 (1): 89–106.

3
Global Inequality in Health: Disparities in Human Longevity among Countries

Mark McGillivray

1 Introduction

Increasing disparity in life expectancy among countries has been widely documented and discussed. The depressing and disturbing story is well-known but worth reiterating briefly. Global life expectancy, as was noted in Chapter 1, has improved continually from 48 years in the early 1950s to 68 years in the early 2000s (WHO 1996; UNDP 2007). The star regional performer has been Asia, which has achieved an increase in life expectancy from 41.1 to 67 years over the same period (Dorling et al. 2006). Life expectancy in many countries now exceeds 80 years. The highest achievers are Japan and Hong Kong, in which life expectancy was 82.3 and 81.9 years, respectively (UNDP 2007). The experience for many other countries has been radically different. Life expectancy in sub-Saharan Africa increased steadily from 38.2 years in the early 1950s to 50.1 years in the early 2000s. It fell to 48.8 years by the early 2000s, some 33 years less than in OECD countries, owing mainly to the HIV/ AIDS pandemic experienced in the region (Dorling et al. 2006). Four sub-Saharan African countries in the early 2000s recorded life expectancies that were less than 42.4 years, which was the regional achievement some 40 years earlier (UNDP 2007). Life expectancy had fallen by the mid-2000s to 39.2 years in Lesotho, more than 43 years less than in Japan during the same period (UNDP 2007). Sub-Saharan Africa is not alone in experiencing declines. Life expectancy in a number of former Soviet, Eastern European countries fell during the 1990s. Between the early 1970s and early 2000s it fell from 71.5 to 68.4, 69 to 64.8 and 70.1 to 67.6 years in Belarus, Russia and Ukraine, respectively.

These divergent trends and the global disparities they imply have not been ignored by the researchers. There is, in fact, a huge literature on them. Recent studies of global disparity in life expectancy include, but are by no means limited to, Goesling and Firebaugh (2004), Dorling et al. (2006), Ram (2006) and McGillivray et al. (2009). All report increases in life expectancy disparity among countries. Goesling and Firebaugh and Ram, based on the application of various population-weighted inequality measures to samples of 169 and 163 countries, respectively, report increased inequality from the early to mid-1990s. McGillivray et al. report non-population-weighted Gini coefficients for a sample of 93 countries for five-year intervals covering 1962 to 2002. A selection of the McGillivray et al. results are shown in Table 3.1. These results show declines in inequality to 1987, and increases from 1992. The increase in inequality was attributed in the latter to declining life expectancy among countries with the lowest achievement in this variable.[1] Sub-Saharan African (SSA) countries dominate this country group. Dorling et al. also report an increase in inequality in life expectancy, but provide estimates of the extent to which AIDS has contributed to this outcome. Noting that six years of difference in life expectancy between the United States and SSA during the 2000s is due to AIDS in the former, Dorling et al. point out that in the absence of this disease inequality in life expectancy would have continued in the 2000s the slight downward trend of earlier periods.

This chapter also looks at global disparities in life expectancy. It looks specifically at the period from the early 1990s, during which life expectancy inequality is considered to have increased, employing a time invariant sample of 169 countries. It continues the focus of Chapter 2 by looking at inequality, thus providing a broad contextual

Table 3.1:   Inequality in life expectancy among countries

Year	Gini coefficient	Mean life expectancy	
		Bottom quintile	Second bottom quintile
1962	0.126	38	42
1967	0.117	40	44
1972	0.108	42	46
1977	0.101	43	48
1982	0.096	46	51
1987	0.094	46	52
1992	0.101	42	51
1997	0.109	42	49
2002	0.117	40	47

Source: McGillivray et al. (2009).

background for the chapters that follow in this volume. The main difference between this and the preceding chapter is that it looks at inter-country as opposed to within-country inequality. Aside from providing further background for subsequent chapters, the chapter makes two contributions to the literature on disparities among countries in human longevity. The first relates to robustness of measurement and the second to comparative perspectives.

It is well-known that inequality measures are subjective and have different properties, as Atkinson (1970), Sen (1973) and others observe. Bourguignon and Morrisson (2002) actually show that different measures can yield different results. Some are more sensitive to changes in the variable in question at the upper end of its range, while others are more sensitive to changes either at the middle or bottom of this range (Champemowne 1974; Fields 2001). Each of the studies just cited is concerned with income inequality, but it is clear that the same fundamental point applies to inequality in other spaces, including life expectancy. The literature on life expectancy inequality appears not to be sufficiently cognizant of it. This chapter reports, therefore, values of six inequality measures. Applying a range of inequality measures is interesting in its own right, but also provides information on whether the results obtained are robust with respect to the choice of any one measure over another. In particular, the chapter in a single study will be able to assess whether the widely reported abovementioned increases in inequality are robust with respect to the choice of inequality measure. It also applies population-weighted and non-population-weighted (for convenience, hereinafter referred to as 'unweighted') inequality measures. Whether one should rely on the former or the latter is a vexed question in the various inequality literatures. Studies of life expectancy disparities tend to report values of one but not the other class of measures. Referring to the above-cited studies, Goesling and Firebaugh (2004) and Ram (2006) report only population-weighted measures while McGillivray et al. (2009) and, it seems, Dorling et al. (2006) report only unweighted measures. This chapter reports both classes of measures, thus ascertaining in the context of life expectancy disparity whether the choice of one is robust with respect to the other.

Life expectancy is a key indicator of health, and health is a key well-being dimension. It has already been noted in Chapter 1 above that many perceive health as the most important dimension due to its intrinsic and in particular instrumental value. Yet it is not the only dimension, and as such one should also pay attention to inequalities in other wellbeing dimensions. This is not at all to say that an increase in health inequality is in some way compensated for by decreased inequality in another dimension. It is difficult to envisage any situation in which increased inequality in health can be tolerated. Comparing inequalities among wellbeing dimensions might reveal information that guides further investigation and policy interventions. This would be the case particularly if there is steady or declining inequality in some dimensions and increasing inequality in others. If, say, inequality in health is increasing and inequality in other dimensions is decreasing, then this would appear to provide a strong case for better understanding why the former is occurring and for allocating resources to address it. This need not necessarily mean allocating resources directly to health, of course. For these reasons this chapter also looks at inequality in indicators of health and the material standard of living.

The chapter consists of five more sections. Section 2 discusses inequality concepts, seeking to provide conceptual clarity for the empirical analysis that follows. Section 3 presents and defines both the population-weighted and unweighted representations of the six inequality measures used to examine life expectancy inequality, alongside that in education and the material standard of living. Section 4 describes the data used. Section 5 reports the results obtained from the application of the inequality measures to these data. Section 6 concludes.

2   Basic inequality concepts

It is important to be very clear regarding the inequality type or concept addressed in any study of this topic. Health research has differentiated between two types of health inequality. The first is disparity in mean health status across population subgroups. These subgroups can be defined in terms of age, sex, race or social class (Goesling and Firebaugh 2004). Stewart (2002) describes this as horizontal inequality. The second type of inequality examined in health research is the uneven distribution of health across all units in a population, independent of the population subgroup (Goesling and Firebaugh 2004). This can be in the context of within countries, as in the previous chapter, or among or between countries. This is also known as a vertical inequality (Stewart 2002). Wolfson and Rowe (2001) label this as a univariate approach to inequality as it does not condition health on other variables such as income, as is the case in a number of studies.

Further clarity is necessary, however, as there are different types of vertical inequality. Milanovic (2005) distinguishes between three global income inequality concepts: (i) inequality between countries in terms of GDP per capita; (ii) inequality between countries in terms of GDP per capita weighted by population size; and (iii) inequality among world citizens, irrespective of the country in which they live. Milanovic's concepts can also be applied to indicators other than GDP per capita, including those relating to health.

Following the comments provided at its outset, this chapter looks at vertical inequality in life expectancy. It also follows from these comments that it is not concerned with concept (iii) vertical inequality. This leaves concepts (i) and (ii) inequality. Firebaugh (1999) and others argue that a nation's contribution to global inequality should be relative to its population size. That is, large countries like China and India, with populations of more than one billion, should have a greater impact on an inequality measure than tiny countries such as St Lucia and Samoa, with populations of fewer than 200,000. While this argument might seem compelling, there is still no consensus in the literature that might guide whether one bases inequality comparisons on either concept (i) or (ii) inequalities. This chapter, consequently, reports levels of both of these inequality types.

3 Inequality measures

As mentioned at the outset of this chapter, it has become commonplace in studies of inequality to report results from the application of a range of inequality measures given that all of these measures are subjective and have different properties and can, therefore, yield different results. The measures used in this chapter are the Gini coefficient (G), two from the Theil Entropy class of measures (T and I), the Wolfson exponential measure (W), the squared coefficient of variation (CV) and the variance of logarithms measure (VL). Each of these measures has been widely used in inequality research and satisfies various desirable properties (Bourguignon 1979).[2] Both population-weighted and non-population (unweighted) versions of these measures are used, which measure concept (ii) and (i) inequality, respectively.

The population-weighted versions of the G, T, I, W, CV and VL measures may be respectively written as follows, for the chosen health measure h:

$$G_h^w = \sum_{i=1}^{n} p_i \left(\frac{h_i}{\mu_h} \right) (q_{h,i} - Q_{h,i}),$$

$$T_h^w = \sum_{i=1}^{n} p_i \left(\frac{h_i}{\mu_h} \right) \ln \left(\frac{h_i}{\mu_h} \right),$$

$$I_h^w = \sum_{i=1}^{n} p_i \ln\left(\frac{\mu_h}{h_i}\right),$$

$$W_h^w = \sum_{i=1}^{n} p_i e^{\left(\frac{-h_i}{\mu_h}\right)}$$

$$CV_h^w = \sum_{i=1}^{n} p_i \left(\frac{h_i}{\mu_h} - 1\right)^2 \qquad \text{and}$$

$$VL_h^w = \sum_{i=1}^{n} p_i \left(\ln\frac{h_i}{\mu_h} - E\left[\ln\frac{h_i}{\mu_h}\right]\right)^2$$

where

$$\mu_h = \sum_{i=1}^{n} p_i s_{h,i}$$

and the superscript w denotes population weighted, p_i is the ratio of the population of country i to total population among n countries, h_i is the chosen health indicator for country i, $s_{h,i}$ is country i's share of the world value of h, $q_{h,i}$ is the proportion of population in countries that has lower health achievement in h than country i, $Q_{h,i}$ is the proportion of population in countries that has higher health achievement in h than country i (so that $p_i + q_i + Q_i = 1$) and E is the mean value operator.

The non-population-weighted (unweighted) versions of the above measures are respectively written as follows:

$$G_h = \frac{2}{n^2} \sum_{i=1}^{n} \frac{h_i}{\nu_h}\left(i - \frac{n+1}{2}\right),$$

$$T_h = \frac{1}{n} \sum_{i=1}^{n} \left(\frac{h_i}{\nu_h}\right) \ln\left(\frac{h_i}{\nu_h}\right),$$

$$I_h = \frac{1}{n} \sum_{i=1}^{n} \ln\left(\frac{\nu_h}{h_i}\right),$$

$$W_h = \frac{1}{n} \sum_{i=1}^{n} e^{\left(\frac{-h_i}{\nu_h}\right)},$$

$$CV_h = \frac{1}{n} \sum_{i=1}^{n} \left(\frac{h_i}{\nu_h} - 1 \right)^2 \quad \text{and}$$

$$VL_r = \frac{1}{n} \sum_{i=1}^{n} \left(\ln \frac{h_i}{\nu_h} - E\left[\ln \frac{h_i}{\nu_h} \right] \right)^2$$

where $\nu_{h,r}$ is the arithmetic mean of $h_{r,i}$ among n countries and all other variables are as above. The formulae for the above measures are taken from or derived from Ram (1980, 1992); Wolfson (1986, 1994); Firebaugh (1999); Fields (2001) and Lambert (2001).

Two comments on the weighted mean, μ_r, of the ordering principle, in this case h_i, are warranted. McGillivray and Markova (2010) have already pointed to the issues that follow, but they are worthy of reiteration in the context of health disparities. First, a number of wide studies of concept (ii) global income and health inequality (Firebaugh 1999; Goesling and Firebaugh 2004; Dowrick and Akmal 2005) have also used the Gini coefficient, along with a number of other inequality measures. The formula for the weighted Gini was the same as that written above, with one important apparent difference in addition to the ordering principle being income per capita. That difference was that the variable used in those studies to normalize the equivalent of h_i above in those studies (national income per capita or life expectancy) was a simple arithmetic mean, rather than a weighted mean as outlined above. Using the former makes little sense. Second, in previous studies of inequality in human development (Ram 1992; Pillarisetti 1997; McGillivray and Pillarisetti 2004) the ordering principle is not the equivalent of h_i but h_i multiplied by i's population size. These studies follow the approach typically used in studies of the distribution of incomes by household within countries, which use total family income rather than average family income. This approach seems questionable, both in the contexts of inter-country human development and health disparities, and is not followed in this chapter.

4 Data

All data used in this chapter are obtained from the UNDP *Human Development Report*. Life expectancy data for a sample of 169 countries for each of the years 1992 to 1995 and 1997 to 2004 were taken from the 1995 to 2006 *Reports* (UNDP, 1995–2006). Countries were selected on the basis of life expectancy data for them being available for each of these years. It follows that the sample of 169 countries was the largest that could be constructed. These countries are listed in Appendix A to this chapter. Data for 1996 could not be used as they were not published in any *Report*.

As mentioned, this chapter also looks at disparities in other wellbeing indicators. Data on three such indicators for the same sample of countries and years were also obtained from UNDP (1995–2006). The three indicators are the adult literacy rate, the combined gross enrolment ratio for primary, secondary and tertiary schools and purchasing power parity (PPP) GDP per capita. The logarithm of PPP GDP per capita was taken, on the widely accepted grounds that there are diminishing returns to the conversion of income into wellbeing. Inequality in (non-logarithmic) PPP GDP per capita is also reported (Anand and Sen 2000; McGillivray 2005). The labelling below refers to these four variables as the rth indicators, where $r = 1, 2, 3$ or 4 and thus to G^w_r, T^w_r and so on.

5   Results

Results obtained from applying the six population-weighted inequality measures to life expectancy are shown in Table 3.2. In all cases increases in inequality are shown over the 13-year period in question. While the Gini coefficient and variance of logarithms measure decline in 1995, in all cases continual increases in inequality are shown for all years until towards the end of this period. The Gini, Wolfson and coefficient of variation measures all peak in 2003 and stabilize thereafter. The variance of logarithms and Theil I measures reach their maximum values in 2002 and stabilize thereafter, whereas the Theil T does likewise from 2001.

Table 3.3 shows results from the application of the unweighted measures to life expectancy data. An overall pattern of increasing inequality is shown, although there is a key difference to the results obtained from the population-weighted measures. All unweighted measures reach their maximum values in either 2001 or 2002, but unlike their weighted versions do not stabilize thereafter. In all cases except the Wolfson measure they actually fall. It will be particularly important to monitor non-population-weighted, or Milanovic concept (i), inequality over the coming years to confirm or otherwise whether this trend continues.

Global inequality over the period 1992 to 2004 for the four non-health variables is shown in Tables 3.4 to 3.7. These results from the application of all inequality measures, both weighted and un-weighted, are striking in comparison to those for life expectancy. Milanovic concepts (i) and (ii) inequality decreases for adult literacy and school

Table 3.2: Population-weighted inequality in life expectancy, 1992–2004

Year	G^w_h	T^w_h	I^w_h	W^w_h	CV^w_h	VL^w_h
1992	0.064	0.007	0.007	0.370	0.013	0.015
1993	0.064	0.007	0.007	0.370	0.013	0.015
1994	0.065	0.007	0.008	0.371	0.014	0.017
1995	0.064	0.007	0.007	0.370	0.014	0.016
1997	0.065	0.008	0.008	0.371	0.014	0.018
1998	0.065	0.008	0.008	0.371	0.014	0.018
1999	0.068	0.008	0.009	0.371	0.015	0.019
2000	0.068	0.008	0.009	0.371	0.015	0.019
2001	0.072	0.010	0.010	0.371	0.018	0.024
2002	0.072	0.010	0.011	0.371	0.018	0.025
2003	0.074	0.010	0.011	0.372	0.019	0.025
2004	0.074	0.010	0.011	0.372	0.019	0.026

Source: Author's calculations.

Table 3.3: Unweighted inequality in life expectancy, 1992–2004

Year	G_h	T_h	I_h	W_h	CV_h	VL_h
1992	0.086	0.013	0.013	0.372	0.024	0.028
1993	0.086	0.012	0.007	0.372	0.024	0.028
1994	0.093	0.015	0.008	0.373	0.029	0.037
1995	0.091	0.014	0.007	0.373	0.027	0.033
1997	0.092	0.015	0.016	0.373	0.028	0.034
1998	0.092	0.015	0.016	0.373	0.028	0.034
1999	0.097	0.016	0.018	0.374	0.031	0.038
2000	0.098	0.008	0.018	0.374	0.031	0.038
2001	0.104	0.020	0.022	0.375	0.036	0.047
2002	0.105	0.020	0.023	0.375	0.038	0.050
2003	0.103	0.019	0.021	0.375	0.035	0.046
2004	0.104	0.019	0.021	0.375	0.036	0.047

Source: Author's calculations.

enrolment remains stable for the logarithm of PPP GDP per capita. This is the case for all six inequality measures. For adult literacy the population-weighted Gini, for example, falls from 0.153 in 1992 to 0.112 in 2004, while its population unweighted counterpart falls from 0.168 to 0.127 over the same period. The population weighted Gini for school enrolment falls from 0.137 in 1992 to 0.118 in 2004, while over the same period its population unweighted counterpart falls from 0.169 to 0.147. The weighted Gini for the logarithm of PPP GDP per capita falls from 0.065 in 1992 to 0.063 in 2004, while unweighted Gini (*to p.58*)

Table 3.4: Population-weighted inequality in education indicators

Year	Adult literacy						Gross school enrolment					
	G^w_r	T^w_r	I^w_r	W^w_r	CV^w_r	VL^w_r	G^w_r	T^w_r	I^w_r	W^w_r	CV^w_r	VL^w_r
1992	0.153	0.044	0.050	0.384	0.080	0.113	0.137	0.037	0.043	0.381	0.071	0.099
1993	0.156	0.045	0.051	0.384	0.082	0.117	0.131	0.033	0.037	0.380	0.064	0.084
1994	0.149	0.041	0.047	0.383	0.076	0.106	0.133	0.034	0.037	0.380	0.064	0.084
1995	0.146	0.040	0.045	0.382	0.073	0.102	0.133	0.032	0.036	0.379	0.061	0.082
1997	0.139	0.036	0.041	0.381	0.067	0.092	0.138	0.034	0.038	0.380	0.063	0.087
1998	0.134	0.033	0.037	0.380	0.061	0.083	0.146	0.036	0.041	0.381	0.069	0.092
1999	0.131	0.032	0.036	0.379	0.059	0.080	0.145	0.036	0.041	0.381	0.068	0.093
2000	0.129	0.031	0.035	0.379	0.058	0.078	0.146	0.037	0.041	0.381	0.069	0.093
2001	0.128	0.031	0.035	0.379	0.057	0.078	0.138	0.034	0.037	0.380	0.067	0.079
2002	0.125	0.030	0.035	0.379	0.054	0.082	0.138	0.034	0.036	0.380	0.065	0.079
2003	0.124	0.030	0.035	0.379	0.054	0.081	0.128	0.030	0.033	0.379	0.058	0.071
2004	0.112	0.025	0.028	0.377	0.046	0.065	0.118	0.026	0.028	0.377	0.048	0.063

Source: Author's calculations.

Table 3.5: Population-weighted inequality in income per capita

Year	PPP GDP per capita (log)						PPP GDP per capita					
	G^w_r	T^w_r	I^w_r	W^w_r	CV^w_r	VL^w_r	G^w_r	T^w_r	I^w_r	W^w_r	CV^w_r	VL^w_r
1992	0.065	0.008	0.008	0.371	0.016	0.016	0.520	0.566	0.576	0.545	1.511	1.074
1993	0.065	0.008	0.008	0.371	0.016	0.015	0.519	0.561	0.563	0.543	1.520	1.037
1994	0.064	0.007	0.007	0.371	0.015	0.015	0.518	0.557	0.556	0.542	1.513	1.022
1995	0.064	0.007	0.007	0.371	0.015	0.015	0.514	0.545	0.546	0.538	1.481	1.010
1997	0.064	0.007	0.007	0.371	0.015	0.014	0.519	0.557	0.555	0.542	1.517	1.007
1998	0.062	0.007	0.007	0.370	0.014	0.014	0.511	0.542	0.535	0.537	1.484	0.965
1999	0.063	0.007	0.007	0.370	0.014	0.014	0.511	0.535	0.535	0.535	1.459	0.982
2000	0.063	0.007	0.007	0.370	0.014	0.014	0.512	0.535	0.535	0.535	1.458	0.986
2001	0.061	0.006	0.006	0.370	0.013	0.013	0.502	0.518	0.511	0.530	1.423	0.938
2002	0.063	0.007	0.007	0.370	0.014	0.013	0.509	0.525	0.527	0.532	1.436	0.980
2003	0.063	0.007	0.007	0.370	0.013	0.013	0.505	0.515	0.517	0.528	1.403	0.969
2004	0.063	0.007	0.007	0.370	0.013	0.013	0.501	0.497	0.508	0.524	1.337	0.974

Source: Author's calculations.

Table 3.6: Unweighted inequality in education indicators

Year	Adult literacy						Gross school enrolment					
	G_r	T_r	I_r	W_r	CV_r	VL_r	G_r	T_r	I_r	W_r	CV_r	VL_r
1992	0.168	0.054	0.067	0.387	0.094	0.162	0.169	0.052	0.063	0.386	0.092	0.153
1993	0.166	0.053	0.051	0.387	0.092	0.155	0.168	0.050	0.037	0.386	0.090	0.144
1994	0.160	0.049	0.047	0.385	0.086	0.144	0.167	0.050	0.037	0.386	0.089	0.142
1995	0.151	0.044	0.045	0.384	0.077	0.130	0.165	0.049	0.036	0.385	0.088	0.142
1997	0.146	0.042	0.050	0.383	0.073	0.122	0.170	0.052	0.063	0.386	0.093	0.153
1998	0.143	0.040	0.048	0.382	0.070	0.116	0.172	0.052	0.062	0.386	0.095	0.144
1999	0.140	0.039	0.046	0.382	0.068	0.111	0.172	0.052	0.061	0.386	0.094	0.143
2000	0.137	0.031	0.045	0.381	0.065	0.108	0.173	0.037	0.061	0.386	0.095	0.143
2001	0.134	0.037	0.044	0.381	0.064	0.107	0.164	0.046	0.053	0.384	0.084	0.121
2002	0.134	0.038	0.048	0.381	0.064	0.121	0.160	0.044	0.050	0.384	0.081	0.114
2003	0.133	0.038	0.049	0.381	0.064	0.125	0.156	0.041	0.047	0.383	0.077	0.105
2004	0.127	0.034	0.042	0.380	0.058	0.102	0.147	0.037	0.043	0.381	0.068	0.098

Source: Author's calculations.

Table 3.7: Unweighted inequality in income per capita

Year	PPP GDP per capita (log)						PPP GDP per capita					
	G_r	T_r	I_r	W_r	CV_r	VL_r	G_r	T_r	I_r	W_r	CV_r	VL_r
1992	0.074	0.008	0.008	0.371	0.017	0.017	0.518	0.442	0.516	0.511	1.023	1.119
1993	0.075	0.008	0.008	0.371	0.017	0.017	0.528	0.463	0.563	0.517	1.087	1.132
1994	0.076	0.009	0.007	0.371	0.017	0.018	0.531	0.467	0.556	0.518	1.102	1.172
1995	0.075	0.009	0.007	0.371	0.017	0.017	0.532	0.469	0.546	0.518	1.103	1.171
1997	0.075	0.009	0.009	0.371	0.017	0.017	0.538	0.479	0.557	0.522	1.121	1.181
1998	0.077	0.009	0.009	0.371	0.018	0.018	0.535	0.472	0.563	0.520	1.089	1.232
1999	0.077	0.009	0.009	0.371	0.018	0.018	0.534	0.470	0.565	0.518	1.096	1.251
2000	0.077	0.007	0.009	0.371	0.018	0.018	0.536	0.535	0.573	0.520	1.116	1.268
2001	0.075	0.009	0.009	0.371	0.017	0.018	0.532	0.468	0.557	0.517	1.106	1.228
2002	0.078	0.009	0.009	0.371	0.018	0.019	0.546	0.497	0.597	0.525	1.194	1.318
2003	0.077	0.009	0.009	0.371	0.018	0.018	0.540	0.486	0.584	0.522	1.166	1.295
2004	0.077	0.009	0.009	0.371	0.018	0.018	0.541	0.488	0.593	0.522	1.165	1.328

Source: Author's calculations.

(*from p.53*) rises from 0.074 to 0.077 over the same period. The most appropriate conclusion to draw, given the tiny magnitude of these changes, is that inequality in this variable remained relatively stable over the period under consideration. Concept (ii) inequality for (non-logarithmic) PPP GDP per capita decreases, while concept (i) inequality in it increases. Recalling that for our current purposes, this variable, unlike the others examined in this chapter, is not interpreted as a measure of wellbeing, the only point that needs to be made regarding this finding is that population weighting does actually matter.

So, to briefly recap, this chapter's finding is that while life expectancy inequality has increased over the period in question, inequality in measures of achievement in other wellbeing dimensions has either decreased or remained the same. This finding is further highlighted in Figures 3.1 and 3.2, which show, respectively, the weighted and unweighted Gini coefficients for life expectancy, adult literacy and the logarithm of PPP GDP per capita. There is no need to chart the other inequality measures, as it follows from the results shown in Tables 3.2 to 3.7 they are robust with respect to the chosen measure, albeit among those used in this chapter.

Two main observations are emphasized by Figures 3.1 and 3.2, both for concept (i) (population-weighted) and concept (ii) (unweighted) inequality. The first is that while life expectancy inequality is slightly higher than that of an indicator of material wellbeing, the logarithm of PPP GDP per capita, it is lower than that in literacy and schooling. The second is that if trends over the period 1992 to 2004 continue, life expectancy inequality will in the not-so-distant future surpass that in literacy or schooling. This adds to the case for addressing inequality in life expectancy.

As mentioned at the outset of this chapter, the literature has linked increasing life expectancy to declines in the level of this variable among countries in its lower ranges. It is instructive to consider this issue in the context of the time period and sample of countries used in this chapter. Accordingly, Figure 3.3 shows the mean life expectancy for various countries groups drawn from this sample. Specifically, it shows means for all countries in the sample of 169 countries, the bottom two quintiles (nine and ten), all countries in quintiles one to nine and all countries in quintiles one to eight. The decline in the mean life expectancy of the bottom quintiles relative to that of all countries and those in higher quintiles is clear from Figure 3.3. In all years under consideration, all countries in the bottom quintile and no fewer than 13 in second bottom quintile (and only one from 2001 onward, Haiti) are in sub-Saharan Africa.

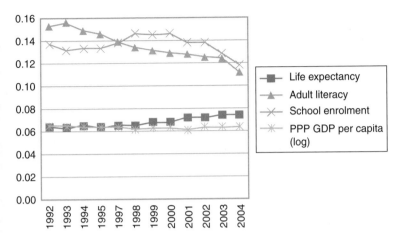

Figure 3.1: Population-weighted Gini coefficient, 1992–2004
Source: Computed by the author.

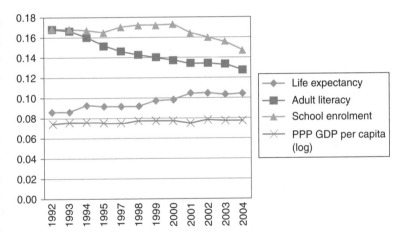

Figure 3.2: Unweighted Gini coefficient, 1992–2004
Source: Computed by the author.

6   Conclusion

This chapter has contributed to the literature on global inequality in health by empirically examining inter-country disparities in human longevity. It applied a number of inequality measures, including the Gini coefficient, two from Theil entropy class, both population- and non-population weighted, to life expectancy data for a sample of 169 countries for the years 1992 to 2004. The chapter also examines, for

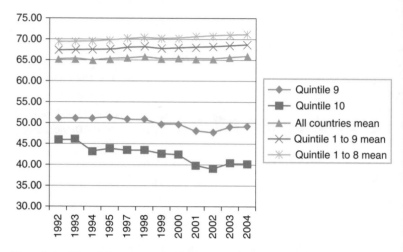

Figure 3.3:   Mean life expectancy by country groups, 1992–2004
Source: Computed by the author.

comparative purposes, disparities in education and income per capita for the same sample of countries and time period. It reports increased inequality in health since 1992, and either declining or largely stable inequality in education and income variables. While inequality in the education variables in question, adult literacy and gross school enrolment, is higher than that in life expectancy, if recent trends are maintained into the future, this will no longer be the case.

The chapter also finds that the increase in life expectancy inequality is primarily driven by the widely reported and discussed declines in life expectancy among countries in the lower ranges of this variable. This, of course, is not a new finding, but it does reinforce the view that if the decrease in life expectancy is to be combated it requires interventions that countries with low life expectancies. In large part this involved continuing to tackle HIV/AIDS, but also other conditions that cause people to have not only shorter life expectancies but poor health in general. To these extents the contents of the chapters that follow in this volume should be read with great interest.

Appendix A: sample of countries

Albania	Georgia	Oman
Algeria	Germany	Pakistan
Angola	Ghana	Panama
Antigua and Barbuda	Greece	Papua New Guinea

Argentina	Grenada	Paraguay
Armenia	Guatemala	Peru
Australia	Guinea	Philippines
Austria	Guinea-Bissau	Poland
Azerbaijan	Guyana	Portugal
Bahamas	Haiti	Qatar
Bahrain	Honduras	Romania
Bangladesh	Hong Kong, China (SAR)	Russian Federation
Barbados	Hungary	Rwanda
Belarus	Iceland	Saint Kitts and Nevis
Belgium	India	St Lucia
Belize	Indonesia	Saint Vincent and the Grenadines
Benin	Iran, Islamic Rep. of	Samoa (Western)
Bhutan	Ireland	Sao Tome and Principe
Bolivia	Israel	Saudi Arabia
Botswana	Italy	Senegal
Brazil	Jamaica	Seychelles
Brunei Darussalam	Japan	Sierra Leone
Bulgaria	Jordan	Singapore
Burkina Faso	Kazakhstan	Slovakia
Burundi	Kenya	Solomon Islands
Cambodia	Korea, Rep. of	South Africa
Cameroon	Kuwait	Spain
Canada	Kyrgyzstan	Sri Lanka
Cape Verde	Lao People's Dem. Rep.	Sudan
Central African Republic	Latvia	Suriname
Chad	Lebanon	Swaziland
Chile	Lesotho	Sweden
China	Libyan Arab Jamahiriya	Switzerland
Colombia	Lithuania	Syrian Arab Republic
Comoros	Luxembourg	Tajikistan
Congo	Madagascar	Tanzania, U. Rep. of
Congo, Dem. Rep. of	Malawi	Thailand
Costa Rica	Malaysia	Togo
Côte d'Ivoire	Maldives	Trinidad and Tobago
Cuba	Mali	Tunisia
Cyprus	Malta	Turkey
Czech Republic	Mauritania	Turkmenistan
Denmark	Mauritius	Uganda
Djibouti	Mexico	Ukraine
Dominica	Moldova, Rep. of	United Arab Emirates
Dominican Republic	Mongolia	United Kingdom
Ecuador	Morocco	United States
Egypt	Mozambique	Uruguay
El Salvador	Myanmar	Uzbekistan
Equatorial Guinea	Namibia	Vanuatu
Estonia	Nepal	Venezuela
Ethiopia	Netherlands	Viet Nam

Fiji	New Zealand	Yemen
Finland	Nicaragua	Zambia
France	Niger	Zimbabwe
Gabon	Nigeria	
Gambia	Norway	

Notes

1. Table 3.1 shows the declines from 1992 in life expectancy of the bottom on second bottom quintiles of the sample of countries used by McGillivray et al. (2009). The mean life expectancies of all other quintiles recorded increases in life expectancy from 1992.
2. Note, however, that as Foster and Ok (1999) point out, the variance of logarithms measure under certain circumstances violates the transfer principle. At the upper end of the distribution of the variable in question, a transfer from a relatively rich person to a relatively poor one may increase the numerical value of this measure. One should express, therefore, some caution over results obtained from this measure.

References

Anand, S. and A. Sen (2000) 'The Income Component of the Human Development Index', *Journal of Human Development*, 1 (1): 83–106.

Atkinson, A. (1970) 'On the Measurement of Inequality', *Journal of Economic Theory*, 2: 244–63.

Bourguignon, F. (1979) 'Decomposable Income Inequality Measures', *Econometrica*, 47 (4): 901–20.

Bourguignon, F. and C. Morrisson (2002) 'Inequality among World Citizens: 1820–1992', *American Economic Review*, 92 (4): 727–44.

Champernowne, D. (1974) 'A Comparison of Measures of Inequality of Income Distribution', *Economic Journal*, 84: 787–816.

Dorling, D., M. Shaw and G. D. Smith (2006), 'Global Inequality of Life Expectancy Due to AIDS', *British Medical Journal*, 332: 662–4.

Dowrick, S. and M. Akmal (2005) 'Contradictory Trends in Global Income Inequality: A Tale of Two Biases', *Review of Income and Wealth*, 51 (2): 201–30.

Fields, G. (2001) *Distribution and Development: A New Look at the Developing World* (New York: Russell Sage Foundation).

Firebaugh, G. (1999) 'Empirics of World Income Inequality', *The American Journal of Sociology*, 104: 1597–630.

Foster, J. and E. Ok (1999) 'Lorenz Dominance and the Variance of Logarithms', *Econometrica*, 67 (4): 901–8.

Goesling, B. and G. Firebaugh (2004) 'The Trend in International Health Inequality', *Population and Development Review*, 30 (1): 131–46.

Lambert, P. (2001) *The Distribution and Redistribution of Income* (Manchester: Manchester University Press).

McGillivray, M. (2005) 'Measuring Non-economic Well-being Achievement', *Review of Income and Wealth*, 51 (2): 337–64.

McGillivray, M. and N. Markova (2010) 'Global Inequality in Well-being Dimensions', *Journal of Development Studies*, 46 (2): 371–8.

McGillivray, M., N. Markova and I. Dutta (2009) 'Health Inequality and Deprivation', *Health Economics*, 18 (S1): 1–12.

McGillivray, M. and J. R. Pillarisetti (2004) 'International Inequality in Human Well-being', *Journal of International Development*, 16: 563–74.

Milanovic, B. (2002) 'True World Income Distribution, 1988 and 1993: First Calculation Based on Household Surveys Alone', *Economic Journal*, 112: 51–92.

Milanovic, B. (2005) *Worlds Apart: Measuring International and Global Inequality* (Princeton and Oxford: Princeton University Press).

Pillarisetti, J. R. (1997) 'An Empirical Note on Inequality in the World Development Indicators', *Applied Economics Letters*, 4: 145–7.

Ram, R. (1980) 'Physical Quality of Life Index and Inter-country Inequality', *Economics Letters*, 5: 195–9.

Ram, R. (1992) 'International Inequalities in Human Development and Real Income', *Economics Letters*, 38: 351–4.

Ram, R. (2006) 'State of the "Life Span Revolution" between 1980 and 2000', *Journal of Development Economics*, 80: 518–26.

Sen, A. (1973) *On Economic Inequality* (New York: Oxford University Press).

Sala-i-Martin, X. (2006) 'The World Distribution of Income: Falling Poverty and Convergence, Period', *Quarterly Journal of Economics*, 121 (2): 351–97.

Stewart, F. (2002) 'Horizontal Inequalities: A Neglected Dimension of Development'. WIDER Annual Lecture No. 5 (Helsinki: UNU–WIDER).

WHO (World Health Organization) (1996) *World Health Report* (Geneva: WHO).

Wolfson, M. (1986) 'Stasis Among Change – Income Inequality in Canada 1965–1983', *Review of Income and Wealth*, 32: 337–70.

Wolfson, M. (1994) 'When Inequalities Diverge', *American Economic Review, Papers and Proceedings*, 84: 353–8.

Wolfson, M. and G. Rowe (2001) 'On Measuring Inequalities in Health', *Bulletin of the World Health Organisation*, 79 (6): 553–60.

(UNDP) United Nations Development Programme (1995–2006) *Human Development Report* (New York: Oxford University Press).

(UNDP) United Nations Development Programme (2007) *Human Development Report 2007/2008* (New York: Palgrave Macmillan).

4
Determinants of Child Weight and Height in Sri Lanka: A Quantile Regression Approach

Harsha Aturupane, Anil B. Deolalikar and Dileni Gunewardena

1 Introduction

As highlighted in the introductory chapter of the volume, reducing child malnutrition is a key goal of most developing countries. A number of studies have documented the wide range of adverse economic and social consequences of child malnutrition. For instance, malnutrition during infancy and childhood substantially raises vulnerability to infection and disease, and increases the risk of premature death. It is also believed to impair cognitive achievement, labour productivity during adulthood, and lifetime earnings.[1] Thus, combatting child malnutrition is of central importance to the economic development and the overall economic and social welfare of countries.

To combat child malnutrition with the right set of interventions, policymakers need to have a better understanding of its economic, social, and policy determinants. While there have been several studies that have analysed the socioeconomic correlates of child nutrition,[2] they suffer from two major shortcomings. First, they do not focus enough on indirect policy interventions, such as improved infrastructure, that could have as large effects on child nutrition as direct nutritional interventions (such as food supplementation schemes). Second, and more importantly, previous studies have almost exclusively concerned themselves with estimating the mean effect on child nutrition of variables such as a child's sex, the schooling of its mother and household income. Such estimates miss a point that is crucial for policymakers, namely, that socioeconomic background variables and policy interventions may affect child nutrition differently at different points of the conditional nutritional distribution. For example, whereas some interventions may not matter for child nutrition 'on average', they may matter a great deal for children at the bottom of the conditional nutritional distribution (that is, children at the highest risk of malnutrition).[3]

This chapter attempts to address these shortcomings of the existing literature. Using data from Sri Lanka, we estimate quantile regressions to analyse the socioeconomic and policy determinants of child nutrition at different points of the conditional distribution of child nutrition. This allows us to address not only the question 'can policy influence child nutrition?' but, more importantly, the question 'for whom do policy interventions matter the most?'. To our knowledge, no previous study has addressed the latter question.

2 Child malnutrition in Sri Lanka

Child malnutrition in Sri Lanka is very high. Nearly one in three children aged 3–59 months is underweight, and about one in seven children in this age group suffers chronic or acute malnutrition. An international comparison of child malnutrition rates relative to per capita income, based on cross-sectional data for 2002 on 113 low- and middle-income countries (UNDP 2002) shows that Sri Lanka has a significantly higher child underweight rate than would be expected on the basis of its per capita GDP (Figure 4.1). This is in sharp contrast to Sri Lanka's celebrated performance on other social indicators, such as primary education enrolment, adult literacy, infant mortality and

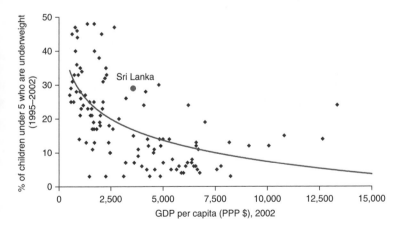

Figure 4.1: Relationship between child underweight rates (1995–2002) and GDP per capita (2002) across a cross-section of low- and medium-human development countries
Source: Computed by authors using data from UNDP (2002).

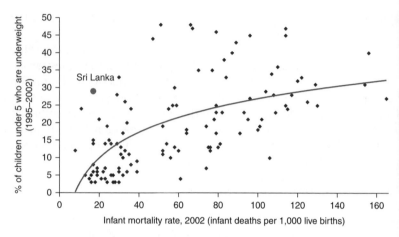

Figure 4.2: Relationship between the percentage of children under five who were underweight in 1995–2002 and the infant mortality rate in 2002 across a cross-section of low- and medium-human development countries
Source: Computed by authors using data from UNDP (2002).

life expectancy, where the country performs well above the levels that would normally be expected at its level of per capita income. Indeed, Figure 4.2 indicates that Sri Lanka has a child underweight rate that may be three times as high as what would be expected of a country with its level of infant mortality. There is thus a big disconnect between Sri Lanka's performance on child health and its performance on child malnutrition. This incongruence is difficult to understand as most factors that are associated with low rates of infant and child mortality (for example, delivery and utilization of high-quality health services, high female literacy, and good hygiene and health practices) typically also influence child malnutrition rates.[4]

3   Data

The data for this chapter are drawn from the 2000 round of the Demographic and Health Survey (DHS). The DHS 2000 is the sixth in a series of surveys conducted by Sri Lanka's Department of Census and Statistics since 1975 to collect data on fertility, family planning and other reproductive health information (DCS 2000). The survey is based on a multi-stage stratified sample of nearly 8,000 households (and 6,385 women in childbearing years), and provides anthropometric data for 2,576 children under 5 years of age, as well as information on the health of children and mothers, schooling and work (occupation) of both parents, and hygiene, feeding and contraception practices. In addition, the survey includes questions on housing conditions, access to safe drinking water, and sanitation. One shortcoming of all DHS surveys is that they do not contain information on household income or expenditure; however, detailed data are available on asset ownership and characteristics of dwellings, which are used to construct a measure of living standards in this chapter.[5]

4 Child malnutrition patterns

The DHS data indicate that about 29 per cent of children 3–59 months are moderately or severely underweight (Table 4.1).[6] A smaller, but still unacceptably high, proportion (14 per cent) of children in this age group suffer from stunting and wasting. These findings imply that children suffer from short-term acute food deficits, reflected in low weight for age, as well as longer-term chronic undernutrition, manifested in high rates of stunting.[7]

Malnutrition for a large proportion (about a fifth) of children begins after the sixth month of life (Table 4.2). Reasons for this include low birth weights, inadequate breastfeeding, poor weaning practices and insufficient consumption of nutritious food. The risk of malnutrition increases sharply in the second year of life (beginning at age 12 months), when most children stop breastfeeding and begin relying almost exclusively on solid foods. The insufficiency and inadequacy of weaning diets in Sri Lanka increases the risk of malnutrition among infants.

Rates of moderate child malnutrition are fairly similar across boys and girls (Table 4.2). However, severe malnutrition shows significant gender differences, with girls having a 40 per cent and 70 per cent greater likelihood of being severely stunted and underweight, respectively, than boys (Table 4.2). Of course, rates of severe malnutrition are

Table 4.1: Malnutrition rates of children aged 3–59 months, 2000 (%)

Indicator	Underweight (weight-for-age)	Stunting (height-for-age)
Moderate or severe	29 (1.03)	14 (0.76)
Severe	5 (0.46)	3 (0.37)

Notes: The malnutrition rates reported here cover seven of the eight provinces, excluding the conflict-affected North-Eastern Province, where the DHS could not be conducted in 2000. Standard errors in parentheses.
Source: Calculations from DCS (2000).

68

Table 4.2: Child malnutrition rates by age and sex, 2000

Age in months	Moderate or severe malnutrition				Severe malnutrition			
	Weight-for-age		Height-for-age		Weight-for-age		Height-for-age	
	Male	Female	Male	Female	Male	Female	Male	Female
3–5	0.90 (0.90)	0.00 (0.00)	6.12 (2.98)	1.83 (1.81)	0.90 (0.90)	0.00 (0.00)	3.23 (2.27)	1.83 (1.81)
6–11	23.50 (3.59)	14.54 (3.93)	6.17 (2.04)	5.02 (2.39)	1.71 (0.99)	4.30 (2.49)	1.64 (1.10)	1.76 (1.74)
12–23	30.57 (3.21)	26.87 (3.09)	11.74 (2.19)	21.53 (2.85)	5.04 (1.58)	4.27 (1.30)	2.89 (1.14)	3.76 (1.28)
24–35	31.95 (3.23)	36.26 (3.75)	10.54 (2.02)	14.47 (2.41)	4.5 (1.34)	7.09 (1.71)	1.74 (0.90)	4.41 (1.41)
36–47	26.69 (3.08)	35.23 (3.49)	12.02 (2.18)	14.76 (2.48)	1.72 (0.80)	7.59 (1.89)	1.03 (0.58)	2.84 (1.01)
48–59	38.20 (3.51)	37.47 (3.64)	18.95 (2.81)	19.28 (2.98)	3.99 (1.31)	6.93 (1.93)	4.43 (1.37)	3.49 (1.46)
All	29.04 (1.43)	29.81 (1.51)	11.90 (0.99)	15.34 (1.17)	3.37 (0.54)	5.80 (0.75)	2.41 (0.46)	3.35 (0.58)

Note: Standard errors in parentheses.
Source: Calculations from DCS (2000).

significantly lower than those of moderate malnutrition among both boys and girls.

There is a very clear pattern of child malnutrition rates increasing with the birth order of children (Table 4.3). For sixth- and higher-order children, the risk of malnutrition is nearly two times as large as that for first-born children. In the case of stunting, gender appears to interact with birth order, such that higher-order girls have a significantly greater likelihood of being stunted than higher-order boys.

5 Model

The focus of this chapter is on the reduced-form demand relations for child weight and height as dependent on income and other child, household and community characteristics. Such relations are consistent with constrained maximization of a unified preference function or with the bargaining framework emphasized by Folbre (1984a, 1984b, 1986), Manser and Brown (1980), and McElroy and Horney (1981). In either case, household preferences are defined over levels of and changes in various child anthropometric indicators, and the constraints typically include a budget or income constraint and biological child growth production functions that characterize the 'production' of weight or height in anthropometric indicators from food consumption, unobserved endowments of a child, the state of health technology (embodied in, say, the education of the health care provider at home – typically, the mother), and various environmental influences (such as the availability of clean drinking water).

The household maximization process results in a system of reduced-form demand equations for weight and height as well as derived demand equations for food consumption. These reduced-form equations have as arguments food and other prices, household income, child characteristics, and relevant family- and location-specific environmental variables.

The previous literature has typically estimated these reduced-form equations for the average child (that is, at the conditional mean levels of child weight or height). However, since the objective of policy is to improve the nutritional status of malnourished children, it may be more meaningful to investigate the effect of income and other interventions on child anthropometry at the lowest quantiles of the child weight or height distribution. In this chapter, we estimate the reduced-form child anthropometry equations at different points of the dependent variable's conditional distribution, using the quantile regression technique.

Table 4.3: Child malnutrition rates by birth order and sex, 2000

Child's birth order	Moderate or severe malnutrition				Severe malnutrition			
	Weight-for-age		Height-for-age		Weight-for-age		Height-for-age	
	Male	Female	Male	Female	Male	Female	Male	Female
First-born	23.50 (2.00)	25.46 (2.16)	8.55 (1.27)	10.42 (1.46)	3.27 (0.84)	4.96 (1.62)	1.32 (0.51)	2.25 (0.70)
Second	31.97 (2.62)	30.87 (2.73)	11.41 (1.71)	16.03 (2.20)	2.14 (1.01)	5.30 (0.71)	2.10 (0.75)	3.56 (1.09)
Third–fifth	35.21 (3.22)	36.28 (3.38)	18.85 (2.67)	23.53 (2.90)	4.37 (1.26)	8.02 (1.27)	4.12 (1.28)	4.81 (1.45)
Sixth and over	48.16 (11.74)	47.79 (13.07)	25.07 (10.03)	33.88 (12.76)	15.88 (8.61)	10.00 (9.32)	15.88 (8.62)	11.77 (9.34)
All	29.04 (1.43)	29.81 (1.51)	11.90 (0.99)	15.34 (1.17)	3.37 (0.54)	5.80 (0.75)	2.41 (0.46)	3.35 (0.58)

Note: Standard errors in parentheses.
Source: Calculations from DCS (2002).

The quantile regression technique was initially developed as a 'robust' regression technique that would allow for estimation where the typical assumption of normality of the error term might not be strictly satisfied (Koenker and Bassett 1978). More recently, it has been used to understand the relationship between the dependent and independent variables over the entire distribution of the dependent variable, not just at the conditional mean (Buchinsky 1994, 1995; Eide and Showalter 1998).

Our dependent variables are the z-scores of height and weight – that is, the number of standard deviations that a child is below (or above) the NCHS/WHO reference weight for his/her age and sex. A child is typically considered moderately malnourished (underweight or stunted) when his/her weight or height is more than two standard deviations below the NCHS/WHO reference. Severe malnutrition is said to occur when the relevant nutritional indicator is more than three standard deviations below the NCHS/WHO reference.

The independent variables include a number of child-level characteristics, such as a child's birth order, age (represented by dummy variables for six discrete age categories: 0–5, 6–11, 12–23, 24–35, 36–47 and 48–59 months), and sex.[8] In addition, the model includes several household-level variables, including log household expenditure per capita,[9] mother's and father's schooling (represented by four discrete schooling categories), ethnicity (whether Sinhalese; Sri Lankan Tamil; Indian Tamil; or Moor, Malay, Burgher and other), access to piped water, and availability of a flush toilet. Another infrastructure variable – access to electricity – is captured at the provincial level by the number of electricity connections per capita in a province.

The model is estimated using the least-absolute value minimization technique described by Koenker and Bassett (1978). Because of the potential non-independence of the error term, the errors in the deciles may be heteroscedastic, and the quantile regression variances may be biased. Therefore, bootstrap estimates of the asymptotic variances of the quantile coefficients are calculated with 100 repetitions (see, for example, Efron 1979; Chamberlain 1994) and are used in the reported asymptotic t-ratios.

6   Results

The quantile regression estimates of child weight are reported in Table 4.4, while those for child height are reported in Table 4.5. For comparison purposes, we also report ordinary least squares (OLS) estimates in both tables.[10]

Table 4.4: OLS and quantile regressions for child weight (z-score), 2000

Independent variable	OLS		Quantile									
			0.10		0.25		0.50		0.75		0.90	
	Coeff.	t-ratio	Coeff.	t-ratio	Coeff.	t-ratio	Coeff.	t-ratio	Coeff.	t-ratio	Coeff.	t-ratio
Whether child is aged:[a]												
6–11 months[b]	−0.535	−4.81	−0.793	−6.54	−0.638	−4.50	−0.622	−4.44	−0.490	−3.34	−0.264	−0.92
12–23 months[b]	−1.032	−10.18	−0.968	−8.09	−1.003	−6.71	−1.040	−8.35	−1.036	−7.29	−1.127	−6.05
24–35 months[b]	−1.085	−10.83	−1.265	−10.01	−1.046	−6.84	−1.089	−8.76	−0.977	−6.46	−1.049	−5.64
35–47 months[b]	−1.035	−10.29	−0.935	−8.57	−0.887	−6.10	−1.038	−8.77	−0.994	−6.93	−1.192	−6.80
48–59 months[b]	−1.085	−10.67	−1.053	−9.27	−0.999	−6.86	−1.115	−9.34	−0.954	−5.81	−1.097	−5.60
Whether child is female[b]	−0.054	−1.24	−0.124	−2.02	−0.118	−2.15	−0.087	−1.69	−0.054	−1.03	0.079	0.97
Birth order of child	−0.044	−2.27	−0.034	−1.00	−0.056	−2.79	−0.049	−2.20	−0.082	−2.68	−0.040	−0.94
Predicted log household expenditure per capita[c]	0.093	2.21	0.007	0.15	0.073	1.44	0.092	1.43	0.066	1.08	0.190	2.17
Whether child's father has:[d]												
Primary schooling[b]	0.032	0.28	0.187	1.10	0.196	1.44	−0.056	−0.35	−0.023	−0.11	−0.190	−0.82
Secondary schooling[b]	0.028	0.24	0.207	1.08	0.257	1.69	−0.015	−0.10	−0.056	−0.28	−0.359	−1.53
O level or equivalent[b]	0.015	0.11	0.270	1.37	0.253	1.64	−0.035	−0.22	0.003	0.02	−0.558	−2.55
A level or equivalent[b]	0.245	1.77	0.433	1.90	0.448	2.65	0.193	1.10	0.184	0.81	−0.189	−0.68
Whether child's mother has:[d]												
Primary schooling[b]	−0.045	−0.41	−0.146	−1.46	0.055	0.37	−0.008	−0.07	−0.146	−0.88	0.105	0.54
Secondary schooling[b]	0.161	1.49	−0.052	−0.51	0.169	1.26	0.156	1.39	0.059	0.38	0.375	1.97
O level or equivalent[b]	0.238	1.94	−0.018	−0.14	0.221	1.41	0.311	2.40	0.119	0.64	0.516	2.22
A level or equivalent[b]	0.400	3.00	0.084	0.62	0.274	1.66	0.349	2.46	0.389	2.12	1.124	4.57

No. of electrical connections per capita in province of residence	**1.309**	3.17	**0.843**	1.91	0.713	1.39	**1.123**	2.30	**1.816**	3.16	**2.393**	3.06
Whether household has flush toilet in home	0.083	1.49	0.083	1.20	0.038	0.60	**0.121**	2.01	0.070	1.02	0.061	0.59
Whether household has piped water	**0.208**	3.53	**0.202**	2.78	**0.249**	3.73	**0.149**	2.09	**0.215**	2.21	**0.322**	2.68
Whether household belongs to following ethnic group:[e]												
Sri Lankan Tamil	−0.073	−0.73	−0.167	−1.12	−0.051	−0.35	−0.019	−0.16	−0.069	−0.49	−0.355	−1.45
Indian Tamil	**−0.228**	−2.73	**−0.318**	−2.74	**−0.272**	−2.26	**−0.262**	−2.60	−0.175	−1.54	**−0.351**	−2.93
Moor, Malay, Burgher and other	0.059	0.71	**0.176**	1.96	0.139	1.35	0.023	0.25	0.113	0.84	−0.047	−0.30
Intercept	**−2.076**	−5.19	**−2.350**	−4.84	**−2.459**	−4.73	**−1.965**	−3.34	**−1.402**	−2.28	**−1.998**	−2.40
No. of observations	2,423		2,423									
R^2	0.15		0.08		0.08		0.09		0.09		0.12	

Note: Table shows asymptotic *t*-ratios (heteroscedasticity robust for OLS; bootstrapped for quantiles). Figures in bold indicate statistical significance of the estimated coefficient at the 10% or lower level. R-squared range is in line with the cross section data work of this type for other countries.

[a] Excluded category is 3–5 months.

[b] Dichotomous variables.

[c] See Appendix for a discussion of how the predicted per capita expenditure variable was generated.

[d] Excluded category is no schooling.

[e] Excluded category is Sinhalese.

Source: Calculations from DCS–DHS (2000).

Table 4.5: OLS and quantile regressions for child height (z-score), 2000

Independent variable	OLS		Quantile									
			0.10		0.25		0.50		0.75		0.90	
	Coeff.	t-ratio	Coeff.	t-ratio	Coeff.	t-ratio	Coeff.	t-ratio	Coeff.	t-ratio	Coeff.	t-ratio
Whether child is aged:[a]												
6–11 months[b]	−0.205	−1.58	−0.331	−1.33	−0.089	−0.45	−0.342	−2.38	−0.294	−1.82	0.021	0.08
12–23 months[b]	−0.772	−6.47	−0.745	−3.57	−0.701	−3.62	−0.736	−5.12	−0.854	−5.77	−0.600	−2.43
24–35 months[b]	−0.498	−4.21	−0.519	−2.26	−0.426	−2.28	−0.530	−3.95	−0.578	−3.71	−0.333	−1.40
35–47 months[b]	−0.662	−5.61	−0.463	−1.97	−0.428	−2.37	−0.639	−4.87	−0.807	−5.72	−0.583	−2.43
48–59 months[b]	−0.735	−6.19	−0.656	−3.00	−0.625	−3.42	−0.761	−5.91	−0.817	−5.07	−0.541	−2.16
Whether child is female[b]	−0.078	−1.53	−0.169	−1.90	−0.145	−2.16	−0.083	−1.65	−0.025	−0.39	0.060	0.65
Birth order of child	−0.077	−3.36	−0.173	−4.46	−0.099	−3.31	−0.079	−2.86	−0.060	−1.83	−0.071	−1.98
Predicted log household expenditure per capita[c]	0.106	2.11	0.065	0.74	0.103	1.68	0.090	1.54	0.174	2.67	0.052	0.60
Whether child's father has:[d]												
Primary schooling[b]	0.137	1.02	0.416	1.55	0.269	1.49	0.090	0.60	−0.166	−0.62	−0.143	−0.43
Secondary schooling[b]	0.178	1.32	0.462	1.69	0.266	1.29	0.192	1.30	−0.037	−0.14	−0.196	−0.58
GCE O/L or equivalent[b]	0.178	1.17	0.498	1.62	0.200	0.92	0.229	1.29	−0.038	−0.13	−0.011	−0.03
GCE A/L or equivalent[b]	0.418	2.57	0.568	1.89	0.417	1.76	0.351	1.80	0.091	0.28	0.280	0.76
Whether child's mother has:[d]												
Primary schooling[b]	−0.034	−0.27	−0.068	−0.34	−0.093	−0.69	−0.059	−0.40	0.052	0.40	0.154	0.59
Secondary schooling[b]	0.045	0.35	−0.061	−0.29	−0.006	−0.05	−0.009	−0.06	0.163	1.37	0.189	0.74
GCE O/L or equivalent[b]	0.131	0.91	−0.009	−0.04	0.152	0.89	0.214	1.24	0.257	1.78	0.164	0.58
GCE A/L or equivalent[b]	0.239	1.52	0.061	0.26	0.149	0.84	0.210	0.99	0.462	2.36	0.448	1.48

	(1)		(2)		(3)		(4)		(5)		(6)	
No. of electrical connections per capita in province of residence	0.421	0.86	−0.131	−0.16	0.006	0.01	0.483	0.91	0.924	1.50	0.961	1.08
Whether household has flush toilet in home	**0.156**	2.35	0.150	1.33	**0.171**	1.93	**0.128**	2.04	**0.123**	1.81	0.046	0.38
Whether household has piped water	**0.180**	2.58	0.177	1.50	**0.181**	2.51	**0.177**	2.04	**0.227**	2.61	**0.356**	2.51
Whether household belongs to following ethnic group:[e]												
Sri Lankan Tamil	−0.125	−1.06	−0.196	−1.10	−0.120	−0.77	−0.099	−0.56	**−0.247**	−1.87	−0.316	−1.40
Indian Tamil	**−0.656**	−6.66	**−0.731**	−5.09	**−0.696**	−5.97	**−0.746**	−5.36	**−0.555**	−4.23	**−0.736**	−4.35
Moor, Malay, Burgher and other	0.178	1.82	**0.299**	2.17	0.107	1.04	0.116	0.97	0.088	0.85	−0.013	−0.07
Intercept	**−1.497**	−3.15	**−2.120**	−2.41	**−1.988**	−3.34	**−1.366**	−2.42	**−1.439**	−2.43	−0.080	−0.09
Number of observations	2,314		2,314									
	14.73											

Note: See notes to Table 4.4.
Source: Calculations from DCS–DHS (2000).

First, consider the weight results. The OLS estimates indicate strong age effects, with z-scores declining with age. While sex does not appear to significantly influence child weight, birth order does. Even after controlling for age, higher birth-order children have lower weights than lower birth-order children. This is consistent with evidence from other countries that 'first born' children often have a nutritional advantage compared to children, particularly girls, born later (Lewis and Britton 1998; Horton 1988).

Among the household-level variables, log expenditure per capita has a significant effect on weight, with a 1 per cent increase in per capita expenditure being associated with an increase of about 0.1 in the z-score. Both father's and mother's schooling have significant effects, but only at higher levels of schooling (typically completion of O or A levels or equivalent). The favourable association between maternal schooling and child malnutrition can be attributed to such factors as superior knowledge and practices concerning childcare, feeding practices, environmental health and household hygiene, all of which is consistent with prior literature. Access to piped water and electricity also has strong positive effects. Indian Tamils are at significantly higher risk of being undernourished relative to other groups.

The quantile regression results suggest important differences at different points in the conditional distribution of weight. At the lower end of the distribution, the coefficients on the sex variable are large, significant and negative; however, they are insignificant at the 0.75 and 0.95 quantiles. Insofar as the dependent variable is already standardized for sex differences and age differences, the result is indicative of intra-household gender discrimination (in the allocation of food) at the bottom of the conditional distribution of weight but not at the top.

Another interesting finding is the significance of birth order in the middle of the conditional distribution (the 0.25, 0.50 and 0.75 quantiles), but not at the very bottom (0.10) and the very top (0.90), of weight. It is unclear why this would be the case.

Yet another notable result is the complete absence of significant income (expenditure) effects on weight at all but the 0.90 quantile and above. The estimated coefficient on per capita expenditure is not only significant but also quite large at this point of the conditional weight distribution (0.19 standard deviation for a 1 per cent increase in household expenditure per capita). This result, while rather surprising and counterintuitive, has an important policy implication, namely, that policy interventions that aim to increase household incomes (for example, stronger economic growth and the income support component of the *Samurdhi* programme)[11] are unlikely to be effective in improving the weights of children at the lower end of the conditional weight distribution. Such findings may, for example, indicate a stronger policy bias towards, direct food consumption-based measures to ensure adequate nutrition intake among households and individuals, that is, programmes such as the *Thriposha* (triple nutrient) programme – a pre-cooked cereal-based food designed to supplement energy, protein and micronutrients among nutritionally vulnerable women and children – or school feeding programmes.[12]

The results with respect to parental schooling also suggest a similar story. Of the eight dummy variables included for father's and mother's schooling, only one has a significant coefficient at the 0.10 quantile. In contrast, four of the dummy variables have significant coefficients at the 0.90 quantile. Having a mother who has completed A level or an equivalent level of schooling is associated with no significant increase in the weight of a child at the 10th quantile and with increases of 0.27, 0.35, 0.39 and 1.12 standard deviations at the 0.25, 0.50, 0.75, and 0.90 quantiles, respectively. Thus, the 'beneficial' effect of maternal schooling on weight accrues disproportionately to children in the upper tail of the conditional weight distribution.[13]

The empirical results show access to electricity having significant effects on weight throughout the conditional weight distribution. However, as with expenditure per capita and parental schooling, electricity access has disproportionately larger nutritional effects at the upper than at the lower end of the conditional weight distribution. For instance, a one unit increase in the number of electricity connections per capita in a province is associated with an increase of 0.8 standard deviations in weight at the 0.10 quantile, 1.1 standard deviations at the 0.50 quantile, and 2.4 standard deviations at the 0.90 quantile. Thus, the effect of electricity access on child weight is three times as large at the 0.90 as at the 0.10 quantile.

The results with respect to child height are broadly similar, with the major difference being that electricity access appears to have no significant effect on child height at any quantile. On the other hand, access to a flush toilet has significant effects on height but not on weight. The effects of household expenditure per capita and parental schooling are generally less pronounced for height than for weight. The results also suggest that being Indian Tamil is more strongly negatively related with child height than with child weight at all points of the conditional weight distribution.

7   Concluding remarks and policy implications

The chapter considers the important issue of child malnutrition, high-lighting some of the key issues underpinning the reduction in child malnutrition. The chapter adopted a quantile regression approach, in exploring the effects of variables such as a child's age, sex and birth order; household expenditure per capita; parental schooling; and infra-structure on child weight and height at different points of the condi-tional distributions of weight and height. We find that OLS estimates of the determinants of child weight and height, which in effect estimate the effects of intervention variables at the mean, can be misleading. For instance, the OLS estimates do not indicate the presence of intra-household gender discrimination in the allocation of nutritional inputs; however, the quantile regressions show evidence of discrimination against girls at the lower end of the weight and height distribution. In other words, even though on average Sri Lankan girls are not nutrition-ally disadvantaged relative to boys, among children at the highest risk of malnutrition girls are disadvantaged relative to boys. Policy interven-tions to address child malnutrition need to be sensitive to this reality, and need especially to target girls at high risk of undernutrition.

Likewise, OLS estimates of the income effect on child weights and heights can also be misleading. While such estimates would lead one to believe that increases in income are associated with strong nutritional improvements, the quantile regressions indicate that this is gener-ally true only at the upper end of the conditional weight and height distributions (0.75 and 0.90 quantiles). Over much of the lower end of the distributions, household expenditure per capita is not a significant determinant of child weight or height. What this means is that income-generating interventions, although very important for a number of other social outcomes, are unlikely to be effective in raising the nutri-tional levels of those at the greatest risk of malnutrition.

Indeed, the quantile regressions show that most of the explanatory variables considered in this chapter tend to have larger and more sig-nificant effects on child weight and height at the higher quantiles than at the lower quantiles. Thus, for example, parental education, electricity access and even availability of piped water have larger effects on child weight and height at the upper quantiles than at the lower quantiles. The implication for policy is that since these general interventions – parental schooling, infrastructure and income growth – are not as effec-tive in raising the nutritional status of children in the lower tail of the conditional weight and height distributions, it may be important to target direct nutritional interventions, such as food supplementation programmes (which we have not considered in this chapter owing to lack of data), to at-risk children.[14]

However, from a general perspective, it is worth noting that an integrated package of maternal and child health services to address child malnutrition and promote child growth has been designed by the government. The package commences at conception and proceeds through foetal life, infancy and childhood, with the interventions including, for example, family planning to space and limit children, antenatal care to ensure foetal growth and wellbeing, breast-feeding, and promoting appropriate weaning. Such policies and programmes to reduce child malnutrition are also being complemented by health and nutrition education. However, few of these direct and indirect public nutritional interventions have been subjected to any rigorous evaluation. As such, little is known about their effectiveness and the extent to which they have contributed to a decline in child malnutrition.

Appendix: Derivation of log household expenditure per capita

The Demographic and Health Survey does not collect expenditure or income data. This problem was addressed by predicting log per capita expenditure for each household in the DHS sample based on the coefficients from a regression using household demographics, location variables, and housing and asset variables as explanatory variables on the sample of households from the Sri Lanka Integrated Survey (SLIS) 1999/2000 where the explanatory variables were identical to variables available in the DHS data (Table 4A.1).

The SLIS was carried out across all provinces of the country between October 1999 and the third quarter of 2000. It surveyed a total of 7,500 households in 500 urban, rural and estate communities using household, community and price questionnaires. The DHS covered all provinces except the Northern and Eastern provinces and was in the field from May to August of 2000 (DCS 2000). Thus, the assumption underlying the exercise – that the relationship between household consumption and other household variables is the same in both samples – is not unreasonable given that the survey periods – and geographical coverage – overlap.

Total household expenditure in SLIS was calculated by adding all monthly expenditure on food and non-food consumption items from sections 6 (expenditure and durable goods), 3 (housing) and *(to p.84)*

Table 4A.1: Regression of log annual consumption expenditure per capita, SLIS data

Independent variable	Coeff.	T-statistic
Intercept	7.834	49.72
Household size	–0.086	–12.6
No. of females aged 0–4 as % of HH size	0.001	0.72
No. of males aged 5–14 as % of HH size	0.002	1.84
No. of females aged 5–14 as % of HH size	0.002	2.41
No. of males aged 15–24 as % of HH size	0.002	2.49
No. of females aged 15–24 as % of HH size	0.004	4.11
No. of males aged 25–44 as % of HH size	0.005	5.49
No. of females aged 25–44 as % of HH size	0.003	2.79
No. of males aged 45–59 as % of HH size	0.005	4.58
No. of females aged 45–59 as % of HH size	0.003	2.85
No. of males aged 60 and over as % of HH size	0.003	3.12
No. of females aged 60 and over as % of HH size	0.003	2.61
No. of females aged 0–4 as % of HH size*head of HH is female	–0.003	–0.90
No. of males aged 5–14 as % of HH size*head of HH is female	0.001	0.29
No. of females aged 5–14 as % of HH size*head of HH is female	0.003	1.15
No. of males aged 15–24 as % of HH size*head of HH is female	0.003	1.33
No. of females aged 15–24 as % of HH size*head of HH is female	0.001	0.42
No. of males aged 25–44 as % of HH size*head of HH is female	0.002	0.83
No. of females aged 25–44 as % of HH size*head of HH is female	0.004	1.73
No. of males aged 45–59 as % of HH size*head of HH is female	0.005	1.83
No. of females aged 45–59 as % of HH size*head of HH is female	0.003	1.27
No. of males aged 60 and over as % of HH size*head of HH is female	0.003	1.06
No. of females aged 60 and over as % of HH size*head of HH is female	0.004	1.60
Head of HH is female	–0.212	–0.96
Household size*head of HH is female	–0.006	–0.60
Age of HH head	0.003	0.83
Age of HH head squared	0.000	–2.10
HH head is a widow	0.032	0.73
Head of household's highest level of schooling is:		
Middle school (grade 7–10)	–0.093	–1.58
O level or equivalent	–0.087	–1.06
A level or equivalent	0.009	0.08
Degree or above	–0.036	–0.15

(*continued*)

Table 4A.1: Continued

Independent variable	Coeff.	T-statistic
Head of household's highest level of schooling is:		
Primary school (grade 1–6)*age of head	0.003	3.48
Middle school (grade 7–10)*age of head	0.006	5.21
O level or equivalent*age of head	0.008	5.29
A level or equivalent*age of head	0.009	4.30
Degree or above*age of head	0.013	2.87
Head of household's highest level of schooling is:		
Primary school (grade 1–6)*HH is located in rural area	–0.110	–2.20
Middle school (grade 7–10)*HH is located in rural area	–0.116	–2.14
O level or equivalent*HH is located in rural area	–0.140	–2.32
A level or equivalent*HH is located in rural area	–0.201	–2.92
Degree or above*HH is located in rural area	–0.291	–2.78
HH size*HH is located in rural area	0.011	1.51
Head is female*HH is located in rural area	0.012	0.26
Age of HH head*HH is located in rural area	0.000	0.21
HH head is a widow*HH is located in rural area	–0.040	–0.82
Highest educational level of spouse of head is:		
Primary (grade 1–6)	–0.020	–1.05
Middle school (grade 7–10)	0.040	2.03
O level or equivalent	0.095	4.05
A level or equivalent	0.173	5.61
Degree or above	0.311	4.65
Drinking water source:		
Unprotected well	–0.159	–2.15
Tube well	0.174	1.99
Street tap	–0.048	–1.27
Tap in house	0.104	2.70
River/stream	–0.159	–0.77
Other	–0.076	–0.75
Toilet:		
Pour flush	0.219	3.56
Waterseal	0.032	0.59
Pit	–0.043	–0.50
Bucket	–0.062	–0.36
Other	1.419	3.48
Shared with other households	–0.080	–3.60
Fuel for cooking:		
Sawdust	–0.139	–1.12
Kerosene	–0.057	–1.15
Gas	0.355	12.67
Electricity	0.350	0.87
Other	–1.359	–7.46
Roof type:		
Asbestos	–0.080	–2.81
Tin	–0.135	–3.07

(*continued*)

82

Table 4A.1: Continued

Independent variable	Coeff.	T-statistic
Cadjan/palmyrah/straw	–0.128	–1.33
Other	–0.240	–4.07
Floor type:		
Cement	–0.357	–5.76
Wood	0.777	1.90
Prepared clay	–0.602	–7.06
Unprepared earth	–0.486	–4.11
Other	–0.247	–1.17
Wall type:		
Mud	–0.079	–1.01
Wood	–0.157	–2.60
Cadjan/palmyrah	–0.081	–0.41
Other	0.289	2.41
Drinking water source:		
Unprotected well*HH location is rural	0.088	1.15
Tube well*HH location is rural	–0.206	–2.25
Street tap*HH location is rural	0.056	1.31
Tap in house*HH location is rural	0.060	1.30
River/stream*HH location is rural	0.063	0.30
Other*HH location is rural	–0.049	–0.44
Toilet:		
Pour flush*HH location is rural	–0.042	–0.62
Waterseal*HH location is rural	0.001	0.01
Pit*HH location is rural	–0.035	–0.40
Bucket*HH location is rural	–0.081	–0.39
Other*HH location is rural	–1.340	–3.23
Fuel for cooking:		
Sawdust*HH location is rural	0.096	0.59
Kerosene*HH location is rural	0.227	2.41
Gas*HH location is rural	–0.010	–0.26
Electricity*HH location is rural	0.165	4.60
Other*HH location is rural	0.085	1.75
Roof type:		
Asbestos*HH location is rural	0.073	0.73
Tin*HH location is rural	0.247	3.24
Cadjan/palmyrah/straw*HH location is rural	–0.012	–0.14
Other*HH location is rural	–1.402	–2.96
Floor type:		
Cement*HH location is rural	0.096	0.91
Wood*HH location is rural	–0.034	–0.25
Prepared clay*HH location is rural	–0.078	–0.29
Unprepared earth*HH location is rural	0.048	0.59
Other*HH location is rural	0.046	0.56
Wall material:		
Mud*HH location is rural	0.028	0.13
Wood*HH location is rural	–0.155	–1.20

(*continued*)

Table 4A.1: Continued

Independent variable	Coeff.	T-statistic
Cadjan/palmyrah*HH location is rural	0.323	1.62
Other*HH location is rural	–0.276	–0.44
HH has a fridge	0.673	0.55
HH has a bicycle	–0.541	–0.78
HH has a motorbike	–0.383	–0.53
HH location is rural	–0.184	–1.27
Whether HH resident of the following district:		
Gampaha	–0.144	–2.51
Kalutara	–0.098	–2.01
Kandy	–0.235	–5.08
Matale	–0.192	–3.36
Nuwara Eliya	0.192	3.37
Galle	–0.302	–5.75
Matara	–0.332	–5.95
Hambantota	–0.125	–1.80
Kurunegala	0.017	0.27
Puttalam	–0.113	–1.76
Anuradapura	0.187	3.17
Polonnaruwa	0.101	0.93
Badulla	0.041	0.79
Monaragala	0.082	1.95
Ratnapura	–0.034	–0.51
Kegalle	–0.220	–3.10
Gampaha*HH location is rural	0.218	3.23
Kalutara*HH location is rural	0.000	0
Kandy*HH location is rural	–0.035	–0.58
Matale*HH location is rural	–0.004	–0.05
Nuwara Eliya*HH location is rural	–0.200	–2.81
Galle*HH location is rural	0.180	2.76
Matara*HH location is rural	0.202	2.93
Hambantota*HH location is rural	0.295	3.61
Kurunegala*HH location is rural	–0.009	–0.12
Puttalam*HH location is rural	0.246	3.21
Anuradapura*HH location is rural	0.008	0.11
Polonnaruwa*HH location is rural	0.122	1.04
Badulla*HH location is rural	0.006	0.09
Ratnapura*HH location is rural	0.099	1.28
Kegalle*HH location is rural	0.006	0.07
Adjusted R^2	0.527	
$F_{(145, 5465)}$	44.07	
Sample size	5,611	

Note: HH = household.
Source: Calculations from DCS–DHS (2000).

(*from p.79*) 4 (education) of the questionnaire for each household in the sample and adjusting by a spatial cost-of-living index. Per capita expenditure was defined as total household expenditure divided by the number of household members.

A set of variables common to both questionnaires was first identified and, based on these variables, several others were constructed, totalling 76. These included household age/sex composition; age, gender and marital status (namely, whether widow or widower) of household head; education of household head and the head's spouse; drinking water source; availability and type of toilet; quality of housing (namely, material of floor, roof, and wall); type of cooking fuel; presence of household 'assets' (such as refrigerator, bicycle and motorcycle); and location of the household (whether rural and the district in which the household is located). An additional 70 variables were generated using two-way interactions of the basic variables with the age and gender of the head and location (rural or otherwise). The complete list of common and constructed variables is shown in Table 4A.1, which also reports the regression results.

The regression model performed well with an adjusted R^2 of 0.53. The sample mean of log per capita expenditure was 7.4257 (indicating per capita expenditure of Rs 1,678.71), while the predicted value of the same from regression estimates was 7.4258 (per capita expenditure of Rs 1,678.53).

Acknowledgements

This chapter is a revised version of a paper presented at the UNU–WIDER conference on Advancing Health Equity, Helsinki, September 2006. We thank seminar participants at the Centre for Market and Public Organization, University of Bristol, and at the UNU–WIDER conference on Advancing Health Equity Conference, for their comments. Permission to use data from the Demographic and Health Survey Sri Lanka 2000 was obtained from the Department of Census and Statistics, Government of Sri Lanka.

Notes

1. See Behrman (1992) for an exhaustive survey of this literature. Studies that suggest direct labour productivity and/or wage effects of anthropometric indicators of health and nutrition include Strauss (1986), Deolalikar (1988), Sahn and Alderman (1988), Behrman and Deolalikar (1989b), and Haddad

and Bouis (1991). Behrman and Lavy (1994) also find effects on cognitive achievement.

2. See Behrman and Deolalikar (1988) and Strauss and Thomas (1995) for a review. Some of the individual studies include Akin et al. (1990), Barrera (1990a, 1990b), Behrman and Deolalikar (1989a), Behrman and Wolfe (1987), Cebu Study Team (1989), Christianensen and Alderman (2004), Haddad et al. (2003), Horton (1988), Lawson and Appleton (2007), Sahn (1989), Stifel and Alderman (2003), Strauss (1990), Thomas et al. (1990, 1991), Thomas et al. (1996), and Wolfe and Behrman (1987).

3. Naturally, the children at the lower end of the anthropometric scale will not always be those most at risk, since some children unlikely to be malnourished but having favourable values of observed predictors of health will get included in the lowest quantile. This issue is discussed in more detail later.

4. One possible explanation for the paradox is that infant mortality is largely a function of the utilization of preventive and curative health services, including immunization and maternal and child health services, while child nutrition depends additionally on food and dietary intake during infancy and early childhood. While Sri Lanka enjoys good medical infrastructure, feeding practices, especially for infants and young children, may be less than ideal. There is some evidence that supports this, for example, a large proportion of newborns are not provided colostrum (the milk produced by the mother's breasts in the first 2–3 days after childbirth), which contains important antibodies and provides the child's first form of immunization.

5. See the Appendix.

6. Throughout this report, data on child malnutrition rates are reported only for children aged 3 months or older. As seen in Table 4.2, child malnutrition in Sri Lanka, as in most other countries, only sets in after the age of 6 months, when children are weaned from exclusive breast-feeding.

7. The prevalence of underweight children fell from 38 per cent in 1993 to 29 per cent in 2000. The proportion of stunted children declined even more – from 25 per cent to 14 per cent. Thus, the underweight and stunting rates have declined at annual rates of 1.3 and 1.6 percentage points, respectively, over the period 1993–2000. Regionally Sri Lanka compares favourably to its neighbours in terms of the decline in the child malnutrition rate.

8. Interactions between the age dummies and sex were included but were generally not significant, suggesting that the age profile of z-scores does not differ significantly across boys and girls.

9. The DHS data do not collect expenditure or income data. We have made use of the availability of identical variables to those found in the DHS (household size and composition, housing characteristics, ownership of assets, and location) as well as expenditure data in the Sri Lanka Integrated Survey (SLIS) 1999–2000 to predict log expenditure per capita for the DHS sample using the estimated coefficients from a log per capita expenditure function estimated using the SLIS data. Details are given in the Appendix.

10. We recognize the focus of this chapter is on the malnourished, and not the obese, and that there might be a degree of non 'non-linearity' of health outcomes in respect to higher (lower) scores representing better (worse) outcomes are re-emphasized.

11. Under the *Samurdhi* programme, the government provides an income supplement of Rs 500–1,000, depending upon family size and household poverty level, which can be used to purchase food items, such as grains, cereals and legumes. In addition, the programme has officers trained in maternal and child nutrition and infant care who work with target groups, such as pregnant women, lactating mothers and undernourished children, to help improve nutrition levels.

12. *Thriposha* is given to pregnant and lactating women during the first 6 months and infants between 6–11 months of age. In addition, it is given to children between 12–60 months who are at risk, as shown by growth faltering or other measures and as certified by the Medical Officer of Health.

13. The finding that parental education has a positive effect is perhaps of little surprise, and leads to the interpretation that income and maternal education may raise health, but not of the most unhealthy. Further preliminary analysis also suggested that although income and maternal education affects child stunting and wasting, it potentially has no effect on the conditional height or weight of the malnourished.

14. One such intervention in Sri Lanka is the *Thriposha* (triple nutrient) programme. *Thriposha* is a pre-cooked cereal-based food designed to supplement energy, protein, and micronutrients among nutritionally vulnerable women and children. It is provided to pregnant and lactating women during the first six months and infants aged 6–11 months. In addition, it is given to children aged 12–60 months who are at risk, as shown by growth faltering or other measures and as certified by the medical officer of health. Another intervention is a school-feeding programme under which poor children are given a hot meal in school. The twin objectives of the school meal are to attract poor children to attend school and to provide these children with adequate nutrition to stay in school and do well in school work.

References

Akin, J., D. Guilkey and B. Popkin (1990) 'The Production of Infant Health: Gender Differences in Input Demand and Health Status', in T. P. Schultz (ed.), *Research in Population Economics* (Greenwich CT: JAI Press).

Barrera, A. (1990a) 'The Role of Maternal Schooling and Its Interaction with Public Health Programmes in Child Health Production', *Journal of Development Economics*, 32 (1): 69–92.

Barrera, A. (1990b) 'The Interactive Effects of Mother's Schooling and Unsupplemented Breastfeeding on Child Health', *Journal of Development Economics*, 34: 81–98.

Behrman, J. R. (1992) 'Intrahousehold Allocation of Nutrients and Gender Effects: A Survey of Structural and Reduced-form Estimates', in S. R. Osmani (ed.), *Nutrition and Poverty* (Oxford: Clarendon Press for UNU–WIDER), 287–320.

Behrman, J. R. and A. B. Deolalikar (1988) 'Health and Nutrition', in H. Chenery and T. N. Srinivasan (eds), *Handbook of Development Economics*, Vol. I (Amsterdam: North Holland; Elsevier Science Publishers B.V.), 631–711.

Behrman, J. R. and A. B. Deolalikar (1989a) 'Seasonal Demands for Nutrient Intakes and Health Status in Rural South India', in D. E. Sahn (ed.), *Causes and*

Implications of Seasonal Variability in Household Food Security (Baltimore: Johns Hopkins University Press), 66–78.

Behrman, J. R. and A. B. Deolalikar (1989b) 'Wages and Labor Supply in Rural India: The Role of Health, Nutrition and Seasonality', in D. E. Sahn (ed.), *Causes and Implications of Seasonal Variability in Household Food Security* (Baltimore: Johns Hopkins University Press), 107–118.

Behrman, J. R. and V. Lavy (1994) 'Child Health and Schooling Achievement: Association, Causality, and Household Allocations', Mimeo (Washington DC: World Bank).

Behrman, J. R. and B. L. Wolfe (1987) 'How Does Mother's Schooling Affect the Family's Health, Nutrition, Medical Care Usage, and Household Sanitation?', *Journal of Econometrics*, 36 (1–2): 185–204.

Buchinsky, M. (1994) 'Changes in the US Wage Structure 1963–1987: Application of Quantile Regression', *Econometrica*, 62 (2): 405–58.

Buchinsky, M. (1995) 'Quantile Regression, Box-Cox Transformation Model, and the US Wage Structure, 1963–1987', *Journal of Econometrics*, 65 (1): 109–54.

Cebu Study Team (1989) 'The Production of Child Health: Morbidity and Growth Differences Related to Gender of the Infant', Mimeo (Chapel Hill: University of North Carolina).

Chamberlain, G. (1994) 'Quantile Regression, Censoring and the Structure of Wage', in C. Sims and J. J. Laffont (eds), *Proceedings of the Sixth World Congress of the Econometric Society* (New York: Cambridge University Press).

Christiansen, L. and H. Alderman (2004) 'Child Malnutrition in Ethiopia: Can Maternal Knowledge Augment the Role of Income?', *Economic Development and Cultural Change*, 52: 287–312.

Deolalikar, A. (1988) 'Nutrition and Labour Productivity in Agriculture: Wage Equation and Farm Production Function Estimates for Rural India', *Review of Economics and Statistics*, 70 (3): 406–13.

DCS (Department of Census and Statistics) (2000) *Demographic and Health Survey, 2000* (Colombo: Government of Sri Lanka, Department of Census and Statistics).

Efron, B. (1979) 'Bootstrap Methods: Another Look at the Jacknife', *Annals of Statistics*, 7: 1–26.

Eide, E. and M. H. Showalter (1998) 'The Effect of School Quality on Student Performance: A Quantile Regression Approach', *Economics Letters*, 58: 345–50.

Folbre, N. (1984a) 'Comment on "Market Opportunities, Genetic Endowments, and Intrafamily Resource Distribution"', *American Economic Review*, 74 (June): 518–20.

Folbre, N. (1984b) 'Household Production in the Philippines: A Non-Neoclassical Approach', *Economic Development and Cultural Change*, 32 (2): 303–30.

Folbre, N. (1986) 'Cleaning House: New Perspectives on Households and Economic Development', *Journal of Development Economics*, 22 (1): 5–40.

Haddad, L. and H. Bouis (1991) 'The Impact of Nutritional Status on Agricultural Productivity: Wage Evidence from the Philippines', *Oxford Bulletin of Economics and Statistics*, 53 (1): 45–68.

Haddad, L., H. Alderman, S. Appleton, L. Song and Y. Yohannnes (2003) 'Reducing Malnutrition: How Far Can Income Growth Take Us?', *World Bank Economic Review*, 17 (1): 107–31.

Horton, S. (1988) 'Birth Order and Child Nutritional Status: Evidence on the Intrahousehold Allocation of Resources in the Philippines', *Economic Development and Cultural Change*, 36 (2): 341–54.

Koenker, R. and G. Bassett (1978) 'Regression Quantiles', *Econometrica*, 46 (1): 33–50.

Lawson, D. and S. Appleton (2007) 'Child Health in Uganda – Policy Determinants and Measurement', *European Journal of Development Research*, 19 (2): 210–33.

Lewis, S. A. and J. R. Britton (1998) 'Consistent Effects of High Socioeconomic Status and Low Birth Order, and the Modifying Effect of Maternal Smoking on the Risk of Allergic Disease During Childhood', *Respiratory Medicine*, 92 (10): 1237–44.

McElroy, M. B. and M. J. Horney (1981) 'Nash-Bargained Household Decisions: Toward a Generalization of the Theory of Demand', *International Economic Review*, 22 (2): 333–50.

Manser, M. and M. Brown (1980) 'Marriage and Household Decision-Making: A Bargaining Analysis', *International Economic Review*, 21 (1): 31–44.

Sahn, D. (ed.) (1989) *Causes and Implications of Seasonal Variability in Household Food Security* (Baltimore: Johns Hopkins University Press).

Sahn, D. E. and H. Alderman (1988) 'The Effect of Human Capital on Wages, and the Determinants of Labour Supply in a Developing Country', *Journal of Development Economics*, 29 (2): 157–84.

Stifel, D. and H. Alderman (2003) 'The "Glass of Milk" Subsidy Programme and Malnutrition in Peru', WB Policy Research Working Paper 3089 (Washington DC: World Bank).

Strauss, J. (1986) 'Does Better Nutrition Raise Farm Productivity?', *Journal of Political Economy*, 94 (April): 297–320.

Strauss, J. (1990) 'Households, Communities and Preschool Children's Nutrition Outcomes: Evidence from Rural Côte d'Ivoire', *Economic Development and Cultural Change*, 38 (2): 231–61.

Strauss, J. and D. Thomas (1995) 'Human Resources: Empirical Modelling of Household and Family Decisions', in J. R. Behrman and T. N. Srinivasan (eds), *Handbook of Development Economics*, Vol. 3 (Amsterdam: North-Holland).

Thomas, D., J. Strauss and M. H. Henriques (1990) 'Child Survival, Height for Age and Household Characteristics in Brazil', *Journal of Development Economics*, 33 (2): 197–234.

Thomas, D., J. Strauss and M. H. Henriques (1991) 'How Does Mother's Education Affect Child Height?', *Journal of Human Resources*, 26 (2): 183–211.

Thomas, D., V. Lavy and J. Strauss (1996) 'Public Policy and Anthropometric Outcomes in the Côte d'Ivoire'. *Journal of Public Economics*, 61 (2): 155–92.

UNDP (United Nations Development Programme) (2002) *Human Development Report 2002: Deepening Democracy in a Fragmented World* (New York: UNDP).

Wolfe, B. L. and J. R. Behrman (1987) 'Women's Schooling and Children's Health: Are the Effects Robust with Adult Sibling Control for the Women's Childhood Background?' *Journal of Health Economics*, 6 (3): 239–54.

5
Environmental Determinants of Child Mortality in Kenya

Clive J. Mutunga

1 Introduction

Child mortality is perhaps one of the most crucial and avoidable global health concerns. The issue is commonly on the agenda of public health and international development agencies and has received renewed attention as a part of the United Nations' Millennium Development Goals (MDG). Approximately 10 million infants and children under five years of age die each year, with large variations in under-five mortality rates across regions and countries (WHO 2004). In many low-income countries, 10-20 per cent of children die before reaching five years (Moser et al. 2005).

Childhood mortality rates have declined all over the world in the last 55 years. Between the mid-1940s and early 1970s, even the child death rates in developing countries reduced significantly (see, for example, Baker 1999). A great deal of these gains were achieved through interventions targeted at communicable diseases (diarrhoea, respiratory infections, malaria, measles and other immunizable childhood infections).

However, these health gains, or more specifically, the rate of improvement, was not sustained. In the mid-1970s and early 1980s infant mortality rates rose in Africa, because disease-oriented vertical programmes were not effective and the economic woes from HIV/AIDS impacted. Maternal, environmental, behavioural and socioeconomic factors were recognized as additional important determinants of infant survival. According to UNICEF (1999), the decline in child mortality in Africa has been slower since 1980 than it was in the 1960s and 1970s. Of the 20 countries with the world's highest child mortality rates, 19 are in sub-Saharan Africa (WHO 2003). The region's under-five mortality in 2007 was 148 per 1,000 live births (UNICEF 2009), compared with the minimum goal of 70/1,000 adopted internationally at the 1990 World Summit for Children. Causes of infant mortality are multi-factorial, especially in developing countries, where there are great variations between social, economic and demographic groups of people even inside one country.

Although an enormous literature exists on child mortality, evidence on why infant and child mortality rates remain high in many sub-Saharan African countries despite action plans and interventions made is still relatively scanty, especially on environmentally related risk factors, which account for about one-fifth of the total burden of disease in low-income countries according to recent estimates (World Bank 2001). WHO (2002) reports that, among the 10 identified leading mortality risks in high-mortality developing countries, unsafe water, sanitation and hygiene ranked second, while indoor smoke from solid fuels ranked fourth. About 3 per cent of these deaths (1.7 million) are attributable to environmental risk factors, and child deaths account for about 90 per cent of the total.

According to Shyamsundar (2002), environmental health risks fall into two broad categories. The first are the traditional hazards related to poverty and lack of development, such as lack of safe water, inadequate sanitation and waste disposal, indoor air pollution and vector-borne diseases. The second category comprises modern hazards such as rural air pollution and exposure to agro-industrial chemicals and wastes caused by development that lacks environmental safeguards.

As the world enters the 21st century, the debate on childhood mortality remains a big issue for developing countries. Their commitment is reflected in their desire to reduce the level of child mortality by two-thirds of its 1990 levels by the year 2015, as expressed in the MDGs. To achieve this goal, it is imperative to determine what factors contribute to the high levels of child mortality in developing countries.

Several studies have been conducted on infant and child mortality in Kenya, most of which have used indirect methods such as the Trussell's technique to estimate child mortality. Some of these studies have also employed multivariate linear and logistic regression to identify the determinants of infant child mortality. However, ordinary least squares (OLS) or binary dependent variable regression models cannot handle the aspect of child mortality very well because the occurrence of the transition event is the dependent variable, owing to problems of censoring (and truncation), time-varying covariates and structural modelling (Jenkins 2003). This study introduces survival analysis into child mortality modelling in Kenya. Duration models are the most suited for such analysis because they account for problems such as right-censoring, structural modelling and time-varying covariates, which traditional econometric techniques cannot handle adequately.

2 Background

Although accurate information on cause of death is lacking, the leading causes of under-five mortality in Kenya, like most countries in sub-Saharan Africa (SSA) are HIV/AIDS, pneumonia, malaria, measles and diarrhoeal disease (WHO 2004). Kenya experienced a dramatic fall in child mortality in the late 1940s and early 1960s. Until around 1980, the under-five mortality rate fell at an annual rate of about 4 per cent per annum. This rate of decline slowed in the early 1980s to about 2 per cent per annum (Murray and Lopez 1996). Data from the 1998 Kenya Demographic and Health Survey (KDHS) show that, far from declining, the under-five mortality rate increased by 25 per cent from the late 1980s to the mid-1990s (National Council for Population and Development, Central Bureau of Statistics, and Macro International 1989). The recent Kenya Demographic and Health Survey (CBS, MOH and ORC Macro 2004) shows that under-five mortality rate is 115 deaths per 1,000 live births (see Table 5.1).

Table 5.1 shows the infant and under-five mortality rates for each of the three five-year periods preceding the 1998 KDHS and the 2003 KDHS. The use of rates for five-year periods conceals any year-to-year fluctuations in early childhood mortality. For the most recent five-year period preceding the survey, infant mortality is 77 deaths per 1,000 live births, and under-five mortality is 115 deaths per 1,000 live births. This means that one in every nine children born in Kenya dies before attaining his or her fifth birthday. This pattern shows that 29 per cent

Table 5.1: Levels and trends of childhood mortality in Kenya

Years preceding the survey	Neonatal mortality	Post-neonatal mortality	Infant mortality	Child mortality	Under-five mortality
0–4	33	44	77	41	115
5–9	32	41	73	40	110
10–14	31	42	73	35	105

Notes: All rates are expressed per 1,000 live births, except for child mortality, which is expressed per 1,000 children surviving to 12 months of age.
Source: CBS, MOH and ORC Macro (2004).

of deaths under the age of five occur during the neonatal period and 38 per cent occur during the post-neonatal period. In general, both infant and under-five mortality rates are increasing, with the increases being more pronounced during the period between the mid-1980s and the mid-1990s.

Statement of the problem

The environment, which sustains human life, is also a profound source of ill-health for many of the world's people. In the least developed countries, one in five children do not live to see their fifth birthday, mostly because of avoidable environmental threats to health. This translates into approximately 11 million avoidable childhood deaths each year (WRI 1999; World Bank 2004). Hundreds of millions of others, both children and adults, suffer ill-health and disability that undermine their quality of life and hopes for the future. These environmental health threats, arguably the most serious environmental health threats facing the world's population today, stem mostly from traditional problems long since solved in the wealthier countries, such as a lack of clean water, sanitation, adequate housing and protection from mosquitoes and other insect and animal disease vectors.

Poverty also influences health because it largely determines an individual's environmental risks, as well as access to resources to deal with those risks. Throughout the developing world, the greatest environmental health threats tend to be those closest to home. Many in these countries live in situations that imperil their health through steady exposure to biological pathogens in the immediate environment. More than 1 billion people in developing countries live without adequate shelter or in unacceptable housing. A further 1.4 billion lack access to safe water, and another 2.9 billion people have no access to adequate sanitation (World Bank 2004), all of which are essential for good hygiene. Unable to afford clean fuels, the poor largely rely on biomass fuels for cooking and heating. Inside the smoky dwellings of developing countries, air pollution is often higher than outdoors in the world's most congested cities.

As already mentioned, infant mortality rates in Kenya are still very high compared with other countries and increased by 30 per cent between 1989 and 2003. Reducing child mortality is the fourth MDG, whose target is to reduce the under-five mortality rate by two-thirds between 1990 and 2015. Despite numerous interventions and action plans, very little evidence exists on why the infant and child mortality rates are increasing in Kenya. If Kenya is committed to achieving the MDG on child mortality, it is prudent to understand clearly the factors that are contributing to the high levels of mortality. This study therefore explores the household's environmental and socioeconomic characteristics and their effect on child and infant mortality in Kenya.

Objectives of the study

The general aim of the study is to explore the relationship between households' environmental and socioeconomic characteristics and child mortality. The specific objectives are to assess the relationship between the environment and child mortality in Kenya and to identify the environmental determinants of child mortality, controlling for other covariates.

3 Literature review

Theoretical literature

There is a relatively large literature that focuses on the determinants of child mortality (for a survey, see Wolpin 1997). Theoretical frameworks are often presented as health production functions, which capture the structural relation between health outcomes and the household's behavioural variables, such as nutrition, breastfeeding, and child spacing (see Schultz 1984). In the framework of a health production function, child mortality risks depend on both observed health inputs and unobserved biological endowments or frailty. Not properly taking account of these unobserved characteristics or the relation between children within a family may lead to inconsistent and inefficient estimators (for example, see Ridder and Tunali 1999).

There are a number of different analytical frameworks through which to view the effects of different determinants on childhood mortality. Demographic research by Mosley and Chen (1984) and by Schultz (1984) made the distinction between variables considered to be exogenous or socioeconomic (that is, cultural, social, economic, community and regional factors) and endogenous or biomedical factors (that is, breastfeeding patterns, hygiene, sanitary measures and nutrition). The effects of the exogenous variables are considered indirect because they operate through the endogenous biomedical factors. Likewise, the biomedical factors are called intermediate variables or proximate determinants because they constitute the middle step between the exogenous variables and child mortality (Jain 1988; Mosley and Chen 1984; Schultz 1984; United Nations 1985).

Mosley and Chen (1984) were among the first to study the intermediate biomedical factors affecting child mortality, labelled 'proximate determinants'. They distinguished 14 proximate determinants and categorized them into four groups: maternal (fertility) factors; environmental sanitation factors; availability of nutrients to the foetus and infant; and injuries and personal illness control factors.

Empirical literature

Several studies have been carried out on infant and child mortality using census and survey data. In Kenya, all of these studies have used indirect methods, mostly Trussell's technique, the Preston method and the Coale–Demeny model life table to estimate child mortality.

For instance, Jada (1992) and Okumbe (1996) combine the Trussell's technique for estimating child mortality based on the Coale–Demeny model life table with multivariate linear regression; Wanjohi (1996) employs the Trussell–Preston methods and multivariate regression analysis to calculate mortality indices for each woman; Omariba (1993) utilizes the Coale and Trussell technique as well as multiple regression analysis using census data to estimate mortality in Kajiado district; De-Gita (1996) and Ouma (1991) also employ Trussell's technique; while Kamau (1998) uses cross-tabulation and regression analysis. All these studies, which use either the KDHS or census data to measure the effect of socioeconomic, environmental or demographic covariates on child mortality, find demographic, socioeconomic and environmental factors (type of toilet facility, type of bathing facility, source of drinking water) to be significantly related to infant and child mortality.

In Malawi, Baker (1999) and Espo (2002) use indirect methods to estimate levels and trends of mortality. Although the results from the former study indicate that owning a pit latrine does not have a significant effect on child mortality (which is explained by the argument that just because a household has sanitation facilities it does not mean that they will be used hygienically or by all members of the household), the latter's results indicate that source of drinking water and sanitation facilities are strong predictors of infant mortality.

Woldemicael (1988) employs a logistic regression to examine the effect of some environmental and socioeconomic factors on childhood diarrhoea in Eritrea, using data from the 1995 Eritrea Demographic and Health Survey (EDHS). The results show that the type of floor material, household economic status, and place of residence are significant predictors of diarrhoea.[1] Similarly Timaeus and Lush (1995), in a comparative study of rural areas of Ghana, Egypt, Brazil and Thailand, find that children's health is affected by environmental conditions and the economic status of the household.

Duration modelling is applied by Hala (2002) to assess the impacts of water and sanitation on child mortality in Egypt. Results show that access to municipal water decreases the risk, and sanitation is found to have a more pronounced impact on mortality than water.

The hazard rate framework is elegantly utilized by Van der Klaauw and Wang (2003), in which a flexible parametric framework for analysing infant and child mortality is developed. Their model predicts that a significant number of deaths of children under five years can be averted by providing access to electricity, improving the education of women, providing sanitation facilities, and reducing indoor air pollution. In particular, reducing indoor air pollution and increasing the educational level of women might have substantial impacts on child mortality. In a related study, Jacoby and Wang (2003) examine the linkages between child mortality and morbidity and the quality of the household and community environment in rural China using a competing risks approach. The key findings are that: (1) the use of unclean cooking fuels (wood and coal) significantly reduces the neonatal survival probability in rural areas; (2) access to safe water or sanitation reduces child mortality risks by about 34 per cent in rural areas; (3) a higher maternal education level reduces child mortality and female education has strong health externalities; (4) access to safe water/sanitation and immunization reduces the incidence of diarrhoea in rural areas, and access to modern sanitation facilities (flush toilets) reduces the prevalence of diarrhoea in rural areas; (5) significant linkages between the incidence of acute respiratory infections and the use of unclean cooking fuels are found using the city-level data constructed from the survey.

Wang (2003), using the results from the 2000 Ethiopia Demographic and Health Survey, examines the environmental determinants of child mortality by constructing three hazard models (the Weibull, the piecewise Weibull and the Cox model) to examine three age-specific mortality rates – neonatal, infant and under-five mortality – by location (urban/rural), female education attainment, religious affiliation, income quintile, and access to basic environmental services (water, sanitation and electricity). The estimation results show a strong statistical association between child mortality rates and poor environmental conditions.

Overview of the literature

There is general consensus in the literature that a household's socioeconomic and environmental characteristics do have significant effects on child and infant mortality. This is true for studies which employ both direct and indirect techniques to estimate infant and child mortality.

As observed in most studies, a household's income has a significant effect on the survival prospects of children. Higher mortality rates are experienced in low-income households compared with their affluent counterparts.

The mother's level of education is strongly linked to child survival. Higher levels of educational attainment are generally associated with lower mortality rates, since education exposes mothers to information about better nutrition, about the use of contraceptives to space births, and about childhood illnesses and treatment. Larger differences have been found to exist between the mortality of children of women who have attained secondary education and above and those with primary level of education or less.

On the household's environmental characteristics, a safe drinking water supply has a significantly negative effect on child mortality. The same holds true for those with sanitation, which in most cases is taken to be access to a flush toilet or a ventilated improved pit latrine.

Differentials by urban/rural residence have commonly been observed, with urban areas having more advantages and therefore better child survival prospects.

As regards the demographic variables, the patterns of mortality by maternal age and birth order are typically U-shaped. Children born to both relatively old and young women have higher mortality rates than others; the interpretation of the effect of maternal age at birth on infant mortality must be biological, that is, it depends on reproductive maturity. Moreover, first and higher-order births also have higher mortality rates since the birth order reflects the components of the child's biological endowment. As for the child's gender, it is widely believed that male mortality is higher owing to biological disadvantages. Twins face a higher mortality risk.

4 Methods

Theoretical model

In this section, we present the model for estimating child mortality. Our study employs survival analysis, whose main concepts are the failure function (also known as hazard function) and the survivor function. Our interest is to estimate the probability of a child dying within the next day after surviving for t months, as a result of environmental factors, among others. We focus on children that are born alive and model their mortality probabilities until reaching the age of five. We use duration models to specify these mortality probabilities (see Van den Berg 2001, for a recent survey on duration models).

The length of a spell for a child is a realization of a continuous random variable T with a cumulative distribution function, failure function $F(t)$, and probability density function, $f(t)$. The failure function is given as:

$$F(t) = \Pr(T \leq t),\qquad(5.1)$$

where T is the length of a completed spell and t is the elapsed time since entry to the state at time 0.

The survivor function is obtained from the failure function and is given as:

$$S(t) \equiv 1 - F(t).\qquad(5.2)$$

Thus,

$$\Pr(T > t) = 1 - F(t) \equiv S(t).\qquad(5.3)$$

The survivor function $S(t)$ and the failure function $F(t)$ are each probabilities, and therefore inherit the properties of probabilities. The survivor function lies between 0 and 1, and is a strictly decreasing function of t. The survivor function is equal to 1 at the start of the spell ($t = 0$) and is 0 at infinity.

Closely related is the concept of hazard rate, which is given as:

$$\theta(t) = \frac{f(t)}{1 - F(t)} = \frac{f(t)}{S(t)}.\qquad(5.4)$$

There is a one-to-one relationship between a specification for the hazard rate and the survivor function, which after some manipulation is given as:

$$S(t) = \exp[-H(t)],\qquad(5.5)$$

where

$$H(t) = \int_0^t \theta(u)\,du = -\mathrm{Ln}[S(t)] \geq 0\qquad(5.6)$$

is the integrated hazard function.

The important result is that, whatever functional form is chosen for (*t*), one can derive $S(t)$ and $F(t)$ from it (and also $f(t)$ and $H(t)$), and vice versa.

Empirical model

Our aim is to estimate the hazard ratio of the probability of a child dying within the next day after surviving for *t* days, as a result of environmental factors, among others. In the context of child mortality, the hazard rate is often referred to as the child mortality rate (Ridder and Tunali 1999). The child mortality rate at age *t* can be interpreted as the probability at which a child dies at this age, given that the child survived until age *t*. We focus on children who are born alive and model their mortality probabilities up to the age of five.

To check robustness, we implement two models, a parametric (Weibull) and a semi-parametric model (Cox). In the former model, we assume that child mortality decreases monotically with age while in the latter the baseline hazard function is assumed not to take any particular parametric form.

Weibull model

The literature contains an abundance of choices for parametric models, but we adopt a popular one, the Weibull model. The hazard function of the Weibull model is defined as $h(t) = \alpha \lambda t^{\alpha-1}$ where $\lambda = \exp(\beta'X)$. α is a scale parameter with $\alpha < 1$ indicating that the hazard falls continuously over time, while $\alpha > 1$ indicates the opposite (see Greene 2000).

The hazard function $h(t/X)$ will be estimated using maximum likelihood estimation (MLE). The likelihood function is given as:

$$L = \frac{f_1(t)f_2(t), \ldots, f_n(t)}{t, X, \beta, \alpha}, \tag{5.7}$$

where $f_i(t)$ $i = 1, \ldots, n$ is the probability distribution

$$f(t) = S(t) \text{ if dead} = \{_0^1 \therefore f(t) = S(t) \tag{5.8}$$

$$L = \prod_{i=1}^{n} [h(t)S(t)][S(t)] $$

$$= \prod_{i=1}^{n} [h(t)S(t)] \tag{5.9}$$

The log-likelihood function is expressed as:

$$\log L = \sum_{i=1}^{n} \log h_i(t) + \sum_{i=1}^{n} \log S_i(t). \tag{5.10}$$

The log of $h(t)S(t)$ is the individual contribution of the likelihood function that we intend to maximize.

Cox model

The distinguishing feature of Cox's proportional hazard model, sometimes simply referred to as the Cox model, is its demonstration that one could estimate the relationship between the hazard rate and the explanatory variables without having to make any assumptions about the shape of the baseline hazard function. Hence the Cox model is sometimes referred to as a semi-parametric model. The result derives from innovative use of the proportional hazard assumption together with several other insights and assumptions, and a partial likelihood method of estimation rather than maximum likelihood.

The Cox model is given as follows:

$$h(t \mid X) = h(t) \exp(X_1\beta_1 + \cdots + X_m X_m) \tag{5.11}$$

The model makes no assumptions about the form of $h(t)$ (the nonparametric part) of the model but assumes a parametric form of the effects of the predictors on the hazard.

Parameter estimates in the model are obtained by maximizing the partial likelihood as opposed to the likelihood. The partial likelihood is given by:

$$L(\beta) = \prod_{Y_i \text{uncensored}} \frac{\exp(X_i\beta)}{\sum Y_j \geq Y_i \exp(X_j\beta)}. \tag{5.12}$$

The log partial likelihood is given by:

$$l(\beta) = \log L(\beta) = \prod_{Y_i \text{uncensored}} \left\{ X_i\beta - \log\left[\sum_{Y_j \geq Y_i} \exp(X_j\beta) \right] \right\}. \tag{5.13}$$

The partial log-likelihood can be treated as an ordinary log-likelihood to derive valid (partial) MLEs of β (see Cox 1972). However, one of the problems here is the possible existence of unobserved heterogeneity[2] between children from different families, since they potentially have a different duration distribution and the control for the effect of the related explanatory variables is incomplete. The result that holds generally about heterogeneity is that it leads to a downward biased estimate of duration dependence. Gail et al. (1984) showed that the unobserved heterogeneity tends to attenuate the estimated coefficients toward 0. On the other hand, standard errors and test statistics are not biased. For this reason, a correction for the unobserved heterogeneity based on the gamma distribution of heterogeneity with mean 1 and variance θ is used.

Data

The data used in the empirical analysis were obtained from the *Kenya Demographic and Health Survey 2003* (KDHS) compiled by CBS, MOH and ORC Macro (2004). The KDHS provides information on fertility, mortality, health issues, and socioeconomic and environmental conditions. The KDHS 2003 is a nationally representative sample of 8,195 women aged 15 to 49 and 3,578 men aged 15 to 54 selected from 400 clusters (sample points) throughout the eight provinces in Kenya.

As is often the case with data on child mortality, information comes from surveys among women. A special survey questionnaire for women, called the women's questionnaire, is administered to capture data on women's birth history. For each live-born child, the month of birth is recorded and whether or not the child is still alive at the time of the interview. If a child died during the observation period, the age at which the child died is asked. The age of death is observed within intervals: if a child died within a month after birth, the age of death is recorded in days; if the child died between one month and two years, it is recorded in months; and otherwise it is recorded in years. We use these data to model the child mortality rate. Because we are interested only in child mortality until age five, we will artificially right-censor at this age. Right-censoring can also occur if a child is alive at the moment of the interview and younger than five years old.

The KDHS also collects information on asset ownership, such as of a car, radio, television or refrigerator. Asset ownership is a proxy for wealth and economic status (see, for example, Filmer and Pritchett 2001). In low-income countries, where household income is often difficult to measure (particularly in rural areas), consumption expenditures are often used in determining poverty (see, for example, Deaton 1997). Although asset ownership is less sensitive to short-term fluctuations than consumption expenditures, asset ownership and consumption expenditures are strongly correlated. Additionally, the KDHS provides information on livestock and land ownership, which are indicators of both the economic and the social status of a household. Land owner-ship is also an indicator of income from agriculture.

Limitations of the data

The KDHS data are recorded retrospectively and can therefore suffer from misreporting; for example, a child who died at a very young age might not be reported. Several DHS studies show evidence of downward bias in reporting child deaths (Jacoby and Wang 2003); that is, the longer the recall period, the more likely the possibility that the respond-ents will misreport the case. The quality of mortality estimates calcu-lated from retrospective birth histories depends upon the completeness with which births and deaths are reported and recorded. Potentially the most serious data quality problem is the selective omission of the birth histories of those who did not survive, which can lead to underestima-tion of mortality rates. Other potential problems include displacement of birth dates, which may cause a distortion of mortality trends, and misreporting of the age at death, which may distort the age pattern of mortality. When selective omission of childhood death occurs, it is usu-ally most severe for deaths in early infancy. If early neonatal deaths are selectively underreported, the result is an unusually low ratio of deaths occurring within seven days to all neonatal deaths, and an unusually low ratio of neonatal to infant deaths. Underreporting of early infant deaths is most commonly observed for births that occurred long before the survey. An examination of the ratios shows no significant number of deaths omitted in the 2003 KDHS.

Definition of variables

The variables used in the estimations are defined in this section. The hazard rate, or in our case the child mortality rate, is the dependent variable and is defined as the probability per time unit that a child who has survived to the beginning of the respective interval will fail (die) in that interval.

The explanatory variables are classified into three groups: environ-mental, socioeconomic and demographic. The choice of these variables was guided by the determinants of the child mortality literature. The main focus of this study is, however, on the environmental variables.

Measurement of variables

Household income is proxied by wealth indices, which are calculated by the KDHS on the basis of ownership of household assets. We categorize

Table 5.2: Variable summary

Variable	Estimation	Obs	Mean	Std dev.	Min	Max	Frequency (%)
Socioeconomic							
Household size	hhsize	5,949	5.98	2.54	1	24	
Mother has education	m_educ	4,739					79.66
Mother has education	m_noeduc	1,210					20.34
Household has electricity	has_elec	766					12.88
Household is poor	poor	3,693					62.08
Household is rich	rich	2,256					37.92
Demographic							
The child is male	male	3,015					50.68
The child is a twin	twin	201					3.38
Mother's age	mage	5,949	28.16	6.65	15	49	
Mother's age squared	mage2	5,949	837.34	403.50	225	2401	
Environmental							
Household has safe water	saf_water	4,453					74.85
Household has unsafe water	unsaf_water	1,496					25.15
Household uses low-polluting fuel	fuelLP	767					12.89
Household uses high-polluting fuel	fuelHP	5,182					87.11
Household has sanitation	has_sani	4,366					73.39
Household has no sanitation	no_sani	1,583					26.61

all the households into rich (richest, rich and medium) and poor (poor and poorest).

Two dummies are constructed for mother's education. These are mothers with education and those without. The former are those having at least primary education.

In this study, households with access to private or public tap water, as well as covered well water, are considered to have safe water. Similarly, households that have either a flush toilet or a pit latrine, whether private or shared, are regarded as having sanitation, as opposed to those without any facility.

The households' main source of cooking fuel is categorized thus: households using liquefied petroleum gas, electricity, kerosene and biogas are considered users of low-polluting fuels; those using charcoal, firewood and coal are regarded as users of high-polluting fuels.

5　Results

Descriptive statistics

This sub-section contains a discussion of the characteristics of the study variables.

Table 5.2 shows that the youngest woman was 15 while the oldest was 49 years of age, resulting in a mean age of 28 years. The mean household size was six members. With regard to educational attainment, about 80 per cent of the women had at least primary education. About 13 per cent of the households had electricity, while 62 per cent of them were considered poor. Out of the sample, 3.4 per cent of the children were twins, and 50.7 per cent of them were males. Out of the women interviewed, 73.4 per cent were from a household with a flush toilet or a pit latrine and hence considered to have sanitation. In addition, 74.9 per cent met the study's qualification of having safe water. The majority (87.1 per cent) of the households use high-polluting sources of fuels for their cooking.

Empirical results

Table 5.3 indicates both the Weibull and Cox models' coefficient and hazard rate estimates for child mortality in Kenya. The hazard ratios show the marginal impact of the variable on child mortality. The standard errors are robust and have been adjusted to clustering on the clusters.

All the variables in both the estimated Weibull and Cox models are significant and have the expected signs. A child born a twin has

Table 5.3: Coefficient and hazard ratio estimates for Weibull and Cox models

Variable	Weibull model				Cox model			
	Coefficient	Z-value	Hazard ratio	Z-value	Coefficient	Z-value	Hazard ratio	Z-value
The child is male	0.285*** (0.090)	3.160	1.330*** (0.120)	3.160	0.291*** (0.090)	3.222	1.338*** (0.121)	3.222
The child is a twin	1.182*** (0.159)	7.429	3.260*** (0.519)	7.429	1.171*** (0.159)	7.360	3.225*** (0.513)	7.360
Household size	-0.146*** (0.023)	-6.319	0.864*** (0.020)	-6.319	-0.146*** (0.023)	-6.312	0.864*** (0.020)	-6.312
Mother's age	-0.094* (0.049)	-1.915	0.910* (0.045)	-1.915	-0.086* (0.049)	-1.745	0.918* (0.045)	-1.745
Mother's age squared	0.002** (0.001)	2.350	1.002** (0.001)	2.350	0.002** (0.001)	2.219	1.002** (0.001)	2.219
Mother has no education	0.154*** (0.046)	3.368	1.166*** (0.135)	3.368	0.147*** (0.046)	3.231	1.159*** (0.134)	3.231
Household has safe water	-0.148*** (0.034)	-4.395	0.863*** (0.092)	-4.395	-0.151*** (0.034)	-4.498	0.860*** (0.091)	-4.498
Household has sanitation	-0.259 (0.127)	-2.045***	0.772*** (0.121)	-2.045	-0.230 (0.127)	-1.816*	0.794*** (0.125)	-1.816
Household has electricity	-0.312 (0.102)	-3.048***	0.732*** (0.149)	-3.048	-0.296*** (0.102)	-2.900	0.743*** (0.151)	-2.900

Household uses low polluting fuel	-0.095** (0.042)	-2.247	0.909** (0.169)	-2.247	-0.091** (0.042)	-2.149	0.913** (0.170)	-2.149
Household is rich	-0.111*** (0.041)	-2.690	0.895*** (0.105)	-2.690	-0.108*** (0.041)	-2.626	0.897*** (0.105)	-2.626
Constant	-1.363* (0.743)	-1.836						
P	0.327 (0.014)	23.454	0.327 (0.014)	23.454				
LogL	-2710.2	-4198.1						
No. of observations	5949	5949						
No. of failures	502	502						
Wald χ^2	90.1	93.1						

Notes: Standard errors in parentheses.
* significant at 10%; ** significant at 5%; *** significant at 1%.
Source: Authors' own analysis.

a significantly lower survival probability than a single born, mainly owing to biological factors. Male children (boys) have lower survival prospects than female children (girls). There is U-shaped pattern relationship between mother's age and childhood mortality, with children of the youngest and oldest women experiencing the highest risk of death.

With regard to the socioeconomic variables, household size is negatively related to child mortality, meaning that higher child survival prospects are experienced in larger households in Kenya. Lower mortality is experienced in affluent households because they have better child survival prospects. These households have better housing conditions, better nutrition, better education and hence more empowerment and are able to afford better medical attention and care, thus significantly enhancing the survival probability of all their members, including the children.

Households with access to safe water have significantly lower mortality rates. Access to sanitation facilities is also significantly related to child mortality. Children born in households with either flush toilets or pit latrines have a lower mortality rate than those born in households without any toilet facility.

With regard to the source of cooking fuel, children born in households using high-polluting fuels as their main source of cooking fuel have higher mortality rates compared with those using low-polluting fuels. A higher incidence of respiratory infections that are responsible for child deaths is expected in households which use 'dirty' fuels as opposed to those using clean cooking fuels.

All these findings are consistent with Hala (2002), Woldemicael (1988), Van der Klaauw and Wang (2003), and Jacoby and Wang (2003).

From the Weibull model estimates, the shape parameter α, which is shown as ρ in STATA, has a value of 0.3, which implies that the hazard rate is decreasing continuously over time; in other words, there is negative time dependence. This means that children face a higher hazard (mortality rate) in the initial days after birth than in later periods. The same is shown by the plotted graph of the hazard function (Figure 5.1).

6   Conclusions and policy implications

The chapter has considered the issue of child mortality and empirically examined the environmental determinants of child mortality in Kenya, using survival analysis. For purposes of robustness, two models have been implemented. Estimation results from both the Weibull and Cox models have shown that households' socioeconomic and environmental characteristics do have a significant impact on child mortality.

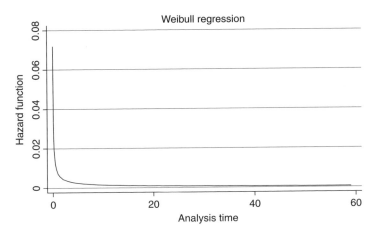

Figure 5.1: Weibull hazard function
Source: Authors' own analysis.

As regards the demographic variables, children born twins, male children, and children born of the youngest and oldest women experience high risks of death. All of these are mainly due to biological factors. As for the socioeconomic variables, better survival prospects are found to exist for children born in wealthier families. Lower mortality rates have also been found in households with electricity. Household size is negatively related to child mortality, meaning that lower child survival prospects are experienced in smaller households.

As expected, environmental characteristics of the household have been found to be significantly related to child mortality. Lower mortality rates are experienced in households that have access to safe drinking water, those with access to sanitation facilities, and those using low-polluting fuels as their main source for cooking.

From a policy perspective these are potentially interesting conclusions. Considering that Kenya has committed to the MDGs, the fourth of which is the reduction of child mortality, the country should be relentless in its efforts to meet these goals. Of particular importance will be the mainstreaming of the MDGs into the current national policy of an economic recovery strategy. Closely related to this should be the pursuit of pro-poor development strategies, as recognized in various government sessional papers. Sectoral programmes such as the Integrated Mother and Childhood Illnesses programme should also be emphasized in the same regard, particularly given the wealthier household dimension to the above findings.

Greater efforts need to be put in place to ensure provision of basic services such as water for all. Availability of safe sources of drinking water would significantly reduce child mortality and therefore investments in this sector will be rewarding. Access to sanitation facilities such as toilets entails a private cost but does have significant social benefits. The government should work closely with both the private sector and civil society to ensure that households have universal access to sanitation facilities as this will to a great extent reduce the number of infant deaths. In addition, the proposed housing policy should make it mandatory for each housing unit to have a sanitation facility such that all households have access to sanitation facilities.

Government policy should be focused towards promoting the use of low-polluting fuels and in particular discouraging the use of firewood and charcoal, which cause deforestation and other environmental problems. Through the use of economic instruments, incentives should be created for the promotion of cleaner fuel sources. This would also create employment opportunities, which translate into increased earnings and reduced poverty.

Acknowledgements

This study is a revised version of a paper presented at the UNU–WIDER conference on Advancing Health Equity, Helsinki, 29–30 September 2006.

Notes

1. Woldemicael (1988) also found an important relationship between diarrhoeal morbidity and age of child and number of children living in the house with particularly high prevalence of diarrhoea at the age of weaning and in households with large number of living children. However, the effects of toilet facility and maternal education are not found to be statistically significant when other factors are held constant.
2. Most empirical studies assume that health inputs have constant impacts on child mortality over the age of the child. We will relax these assumptions by accounting for unobserved heterogeneity.

References

Baker, R. (1999) 'Differential in Child Mortality in Malawi', Social Networks Project Working Papers, No. 3, University of Pennsylvania.
CBS (Central Bureau of Statistics) [Kenya], MOH (Ministry of Health) [Kenya], and ORC Macro (2004) *Kenya Demographic and Health Survey 2003* (Calverton, MD: CBS, MOH and ORC Macro).

Cox, D. R. (1972) 'Regression Models and Life-Tables', *Journal of the Royal Statistical Society*, Series B, 74: 187–220.

Deaton, A. (1997) *The Analysis of Household Surveys: A Microeconometric Approach to Development Policy* (Baltimore: Johns Hopkins University Press).

De-Gita, S. K. (1996) 'The Socio-Economic Differentials of Infant and Child Mortality in Kenya: Evidence from Kenya Demographic and Health Survey (KDHS) 1993 Data', MA thesis, Population Studies and Research Institute, University of Nairobi, Kenya.

Espo, M. (2002) 'Infant Mortality and its Underlying Determinants in Rural Malawi', Dissertation, University of Tampere Medical School, Finland.

Filmer, D. and L. H. Pritchett (2001) 'Estimating Wealth Effects without Expenditure Data – or Tears: An Application to Educational Enrollments in States of India', *Demography*, 38: 115–32.

Gail, M. H., S. Wieand and S. Piantadosi (1984) 'Biased Estimates of Treatment Effect in Randomized Experiments with Nonlinear Regression and Omitted Covariates'. *Biometrika*, 71: 431–44.

Greene, W. H. (2000) *Econometric Analysis*, 4th edn (London: Prentice-Hall).

Hala, A. (2002) 'The Effect of Water and Sanitation on Child Mortality in Egypt', Environmental Economics Unit, Department of Economics, Gothenburg University, Sweden.

Jacoby, H. and L. Wang (2003) 'Environmental Determinants of Child Mortality in Rural China: A Competing Risks Approach' (Washington DC: World Bank).

Jada, L. F. (1992) 'Determinants of Levels and Differentials of Early Childhood Mortality in Kenya Based on Kenya Demographic and Health Survey (KDHS) 1989', MA thesis, Population Studies and Research Institute, University of Nairobi, Kenya.

Jain, A. (1988) 'Determinants of Regional Variations in Infant Mortality in Rural India', in A. Jain and L. Visaria (eds), *Infant Mortality in India: Differentials and Determinants* (Bombay: Sage Publications).

Jenkins, S. P. (2003) 'Survival Analysis', Lecture notes, University of Essex.

Kamau, D. N. (1998) 'Child Survival Determinants in the Arid and Semi-Arid Lands: A Study of Machakos, Kilifi and Taita-Taveta Districts', MA thesis, Population Studies and Research Institute, University of Nairobi, Kenya.

Moser, K., D. Leon and D. Gwatkin (2005) 'How Does Progress Towards the Child Mortality Millennium Development Goal Affect Inequalities Between the Poorest and Least Poor? Analysis of Demographic and Health Survey Data', *British Medical Journal*, 331: 1180–82 (19 November).

Mosley, W., and L. Chen (1984) 'An Analytical Framework for the Study of Child Survival in Developing Countries', *Population and Development Review*, 10: 25–45.

Murray, C. J. L. and A. Lopez (1996) *The Global Burden of Disease: A Comprehensive Assessment of Mortality from Diseases, Injuries and Risk Factors in 1990 and Projected to 2020* (Cambridge MA: Harvard University Press).

National Council for Population and Development (NCPD), Central Bureau of Statistics (CBS), Office of the Vice President and Ministry of Planning and National Development [Kenya], and Macro International (MI) (1989) *Kenya Demographic and Health Survey 1989* (Calverton MD: NCPD, CBS and MI).

Okumbe, J. (1996) 'Demographic and Socio-Economic Correlates of Neonatal Mortality in Kenya', MA thesis, Population Studies and Research Institute, University of Nairobi, Kenya.

Omariba, D. W. R. (1993) 'Socio-Economic Determinants of Child Survival in Upper Matasia Sub-Location, Kajiado District, Kenya', MA thesis, Population Studies and Research Institute, University of Nairobi, Kenya.

Ouma, F. O. (1991) 'Environmental Risk and Socio-Economic Factors Influencing Infant and Child Mortality in Siaya District: A Case Study of Jera Sub-Location', MA thesis, Population Studies and Research Institute, University of Nairobi, Kenya.

Ridder, G., and I. Tunali (1999) 'Stratified Partial Likelihood Estimation', *Journal of Econometrics*, 92: 193–232.

Schultz, T. (1984) 'Studying the Impact of Household Economic and Community Variables on Child Mortality', *Population and Development Review*, 10: 215–35.

Shyamsundar, P. (2002) 'Poverty-Environment Indicators', World Bank Environmental Department Paper (Washington DC: World Bank).

Timaeus, I. M. and L. Lush (1995) 'Intra-Urban Differentials in Child Health', *Health Transition Review*, 5 (2): 163–90.

United Nations (1985) *Socio-Economic Differentials in Child Mortality in Developing Countries* (New York: United Nations).

UNICEF (United Nations Children's Fund) (2009) UNICEF On-line Database. Available at: www.unicef.org/statistics/index_24183.html.

UNICEF (1999) *The State of the World's Children 1999* (New York: UNICEF).

Van den Berg, G. J. (2001). 'Duration Models: Specification, Identification, and Multiple Durations', in J. J. Heckman and E. Leamer (eds), *Handbook of Econometrics*, Vol.V (Amsterdam: North Holland).

Van der Klaauw, B. and L. Wang (2003) 'Child Mortality in Rural India', World Bank Working Paper (Washington DC: World Bank).

Wang, L. (2003) 'Environmental Determinants of Child Mortality: Empirical Results from the 2000 Ethiopia DHS' (Washington DC: World Bank).

Wanjohi, K. P. (1996) 'The Influence of Environmental Factors on Infant and Child Mortality: A Study of Six Districts in Kenya', MA thesis, Population Studies and Research Institute, University of Nairobi, Kenya.

Woldemicael, G. (1988) 'Diarrhoeal Morbidity among Young Children in Eritrea: Environmental and Socio-Economic Determinants', Department of Statistics and Demography, University of Asmara, Eritrea.

Wolpin, K. (1997) 'Determinants and Consequences of the Mortality and Health of Infants and Children', in M. Rosenzweig and O. Stark (eds), *Handbook of Population and Family Economics* (Amsterdam: Elsevier Science B.V.).

World Bank (2001) 'Health and Environment', Background paper for the World Bank Environment Strategy (Washington DC: World Bank).

World Bank (2004) World Development Indicators (WDI), *The World Bank Online Database* (Washington DC: World Bank), at http://data.worldbank.org/data-catalog.

WHO (World Health Organization) (2002) *The World Health Report 2002: Reducing Risks, Promoting Healthy Life* (Geneva: World Health Organization).

WHO (World Health Organization) (2003) *The World Health Report 2003: Shaping the Future* (Geneva: World Health Organization).

WHO (World Health Organization) (2004) *The Global Burden of Disease: 2004 Update* (Geneva: World Health Organization).

WRI (World Resources Institute) (1999) *World Resources (1998–99): Environmental Change and Human Health* (Washington DC: World Bank).

6
How Growth and Related Instabilities Lower Child Survival

Patrick Guillaumont, Catherine Korachais and Julie Subervie

1 Introduction

The reduction of under-five mortality is one of the most universally accepted Millennium Development Goals (MDGs). Yet a significant debate appeared regarding the means of reaching it and its realism with respect to most African countries (Sahn and Stifel 2003). The measures recommended for the achievement of this objective are mainly medical ones (Sachs 2002). However, without underestimating the importance of these measures, vaccinations in particular, it seems obvious that the reduction in the rate of child mortality is mainly determined by the evolution of the macroeconomic environment (see Grigoriou 2005 for an overview of quantitative work on the determinants of under-five mortality).

The influence of per capita income level on mortality is frequently underlined. However, the same income growth does not have the same effect on child survival if it is stable or unstable. Here we assume that income rises and falls have asymmetrical effects on mortality. The goal of this analysis is thus to show how growth instability influences the evolution of under-five mortality. Because income instability is itself mainly determined by exogenous factors of instability, such as world prices or climatic instabilities, also defined as 'primary instabilities' (Guillaumont et al. 1999), we are also particularly interested in their impact on child survival.

Naturally, the analysis of the impact of instabilities on under-five mortality implies an accurate identification of the channels through which instabilities act. One of them is the effect of growth instability on average economic growth, which is itself a significant factor of lower mortality. But beyond this channel, which is based on a well-established literature, there are two other channels. We assume that they result either from the impact of instabilities on the evolution of income distribution for a given growth, or, more directly, from irreversible effects of negative shocks on mortality. Thus, since under-five mortality represents the most reliable and universal indicator of poverty, it enables a general impact of instabilities on poverty to be captured. This issue appears to be on particular importance with regard to the present economic crisis.

Using the GMM (generalized method of moments) system estimator on a panel sample of 97 developing countries covering four five-year periods from 1980 to 1999, we first examine the effect of exogenous shocks through income instability. We then explore more deeply the relation through primary instabilities: world agricultural commodity price instability; instability of exports of goods and services; and instability of agricultural production. After examining how instabilities affect child survival, we present the methodology and data and the results.

2 Three ways that instabilities affect child survival

Negative shocks on income, or political shocks, are likely to involve mortality rises, as is explained in various studies (Gakusi et al. 2005; Cornia and Paniccià 2000; Shkolnikov et al. 1998). Here, we are interested in the rarely studied effect of instability, that is, the effect of the succession of positive and negative shocks. Instability thus defined (instability of income, exports, terms of trade, climate) generally has two types of effects: ex ante risk effects and ex post asymmetry effects owing to different responses to falls and rises in income, exports and so on (Guillaumont 2006). Asymmetry effects are easier to highlight and, as with their impact on mortality, probably prevail. This is what we hypothesize in examining the three main channels through which instabilities affect child survival.

Effect resulting from a lower growth

Developing countries are often characterized by strong macroeconomic instability. This observation has led to a significant literature on the relation between instabilities and growth (for an overview, see Guillaumont 2006). Many works have tested either the negative effect of income growth instability (Ramey and Ramey 1995; Hnatkovska and Loayza 2005; Norrbin and Yigit 2005) or the effect of 'primary instabilities' (export, climatic, terms of trade instabilities) on income growth (for a simultaneous treatment of several instabilities, see, for example, Guillaumont et al. 1999). The most abundant and oldest stream of literature refers to the effects of export instability. In these various works, the authors assume an effect of instability either through uncertainty and innovation, or asymmetric responses to positive and negative shocks.[1] Moreover, several of these works examine the factors conditioning the impact of instabilities on growth through interactive variables (see Hnatkovska and Loayza 2005 for institution quality, financial depth and trade openness; Guillaumont 1994 and Combes and Guillaumont 2002 for openness policy).

Since instabilities have an effect on the average income level, they must influence mortality through this channel. The relation between average income level and mortality indicators has been studied for a long time (Preston 1975) and in many works. The existence of the relation between average income level and child survival rate is not questioned, but its functional form has been recently discussed (Grigoriou 2005): taking into account the bounded character of child survival, the logistic form is preferred to the logarithmic one that is traditionally used.

In this study, we focus on the effects of instability that do not result from a lower average income. We do not revisit the relation between instability and income growth and thus we do not need to consider the relation between average income and mortality. Nevertheless, we will see that the functional form of the relation between average income and mortality has implications concerning the effects of instability on mortality.

Effect resulting from a lower contribution of growth to poverty reduction

While there are many works relating to the effects of income growth on poverty (Ravallion and Chen 1997; Dollar and Kraay 2002; Bourguignon 2003; Adams 2004), only a few deal with the effects of income instability on poverty (and consequently on mortality). Even though the effect of shocks on poverty is considered often in the literature, particularly in microeconomic literature, the relation between income instability and poverty reduction for a given growth has rarely been tested directly (see, however, Guillaumont 2006; Guillaumont and Korachais 2010). It is indeed reasonable to assume that, for a given income growth, instability affects the poverty level, measured either by its incidence or by its depth: instability has permanent asymmetrical effects on the living conditions of the poor (people below the poverty line) and the 'almost poor' (people close to the poverty line). The poor and 'almost poor' are particularly exposed to negative shocks, the effects of which are not compensated by positive ones. Macroeconomic instability can thus affect the standard of living of the poorest without modifying the average income level. For instance, parents' decisions regarding their children's school attendance,

loss of human capital associated with layoff or productive assets liqui-
dation are asymmetrical in the sense that they are not easily reversible.
This idea is directly inherited from the microeconomic literature on the
poverty trap, which is difficult to escape because of microeconomic and
macroeconomic conditions.

Since instability influences income distribution, it has an effect on
poverty that does not pass through to the average income level. This
complex and changing effect has been the subject of some rare cross-
country econometric analyses (Breen and Garcia-Peñalosa 2005; Laursen
and Mahajan 2005). Referring to microeconomic results (see, for example, Dercon 2006), Agénor (2004) as well as Laursen and Mahajan (2005)
examine the main reasons why the poor are more vulnerable than the
non-poor: the poor have few sources to diversify income; they are poorly
qualified and less mobile between sectors and areas; they have limited
access to credit and insurance markets; and they depend more on public
transfers and social services. However, analyses of the instability effects
among income groups show that the next to last quintile – instead of
the last one – appears to be the most severely affected. That is why we
can assume that the 'almost poor' may become 'durably poor' under
unstable conditions.

The effect of instabilities on income distribution and monetary poverty is likely to have consequences on mortality insofar as the survival
function of each country is concave: since instability makes income
distribution more unequal, it is likely to cause an increase in average
mortality for a given average income level. Indeed, it has been shown
that the relationship between child survival and income should be
logistic (which means first convex then concave). But, as child survival
is above 500 per 1,000 in all countries, this amounts to saying that we
study only the concave part of the relationship. That involves a negative effect of inequality on survival, for a given average income level
(Figure 6.1). It should be noted that the effect of instability on income
distribution mainly occurs in the medium or long term.

A direct asymmetry effect or irreversibility effect

Macroeconomic instability can affect child survival without necessarily modifying either the average income level or its distribution.
Indeed, negative economic shocks can have negative effects on child
health, which cannot be compensated for by a subsequent positive
shock. Sharp falls in income involve rises in child mortality owing
to the deterioration of physical or mental health. This deterioration
can come from a reduction in access to food, drugs or medical care
or from suddenly unhealthier living conditions. This was the case in

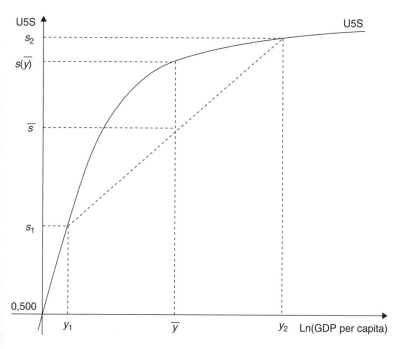

Figure 6.1: The survival level associated with an equal (stable) income is higher than the survival level associated with an unequal (unstable) income: $s(\bar{y}) > \bar{s}$

acute circumstances such as famines (Sen 1983) or the transition of some former Soviet Union countries (Cornia and Paniccià 2000), but is also likely to occur in less critical situations, in particular among poor people. Moreover, health deterioration leads to rises in child mortality that cannot be compensated by a positive shock: when economic conditions change and become more favourable, child mortality does not decrease sufficiently to ensure compensation. This effect is perceptible in the short term (covering the duration of a two-phase cycle), but the deterioration of child health can also have irreversible effects on child mortality in the longer term.

This effect, too, follows from the concavity of the survival function: for a given average income level, the average survival level is higher if income is stable than if unstable. Here, we refer again to Figure 6.1. However the 'distribution effect' differs from the irreversibility effect. First, because it is less direct, the 'distribution effect' resulting from instability may be lower than the irreversibility effect. Second, the direct effect of irreversibility is rather short-term, whereas the effects that are likely to modify income distribution mainly work in a longer term.

We must also examine the implications of the change in concavity with the average income level: for a survival rate higher than 500 per 1,000, concavity first increases then decreases, tending to disappear.[2] As a result, the irreversibility effect of instability on survival successively increases then decreases with the average income level, and the maximum is reached when the third derivative of the survival function is null. However, this point is reached for an extremely low level of income, so that the countries of the sample are all located beyond this point. Thus, the direct effect of instability is expected to be decreasing in our sample (Figure 6.2), that is, it is likely to be higher in the low-income countries than in other countries (see below for details).

When we consider the relation over several periods, we must also take into account the fact that the relation varies over time: the curve moves up because of technical progress, that is, the improvement and dissemination of knowledge. Since the function is logistic, this curve's movement implies a stronger concavity. The result is that the more significant the technical progress, the stronger is the effect of the instability on the average survival level, and the greater the decline of this effect with the increase in the average income level.

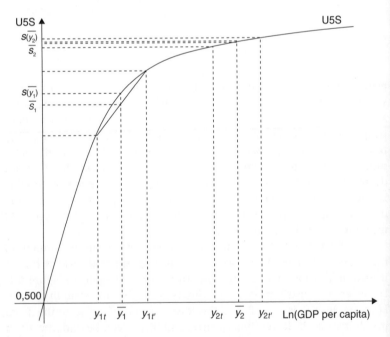

Figure 6.2:   Instability is likely to be higher in low-income countries

Thus, macroeconomic instability can reduce under-five survival in three ways: by reducing average income growth and making it more unequal – these two indirect effects contribute to a lower reduction in child mortality – but also by directly increasing child mortality in an irreversible manner, when the living conditions of the poor temporarily worsen.

The survival level associated with a stable income is higher than the survival level associated with an unstable income, and all the more so as the average income is weak (as long as we are located in the zone where concavity decreases).

3 Methodology

Definitions of the variable to be estimated and the variable of interest

Since the under-five survival indicator is limited asymptotically, and an increase in this indicator does not represent the same performance when its initial level is weak or high, the best functional form to examine is that where the variable is expressed as a logit, as Grigoriou (2005) underlined (Figure 6.3). We choose the under-five survival indicator

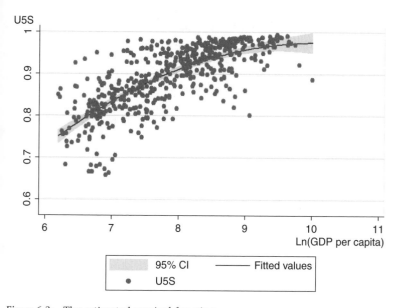

Figure 6.3: The estimated survival function
Source: Author's calculations.

(U5S) in preference to the under-five mortality indicator (U5M), so that an increase in the indicator reflects an improvement, that is to say:

$$S = \text{logit U5S} = \ln\left(\frac{\text{U5S}}{1-\text{U5S}}\right) = \ln(\text{U5S}) - \ln(\text{U5M}),$$

where U5M is the under-five mortality rate ranging between 0 and 1 and U5S = 1 − U5M.

The under-five survival indicator is extracted from the under-five mortality data of the Demographic Health Surveys supplemented by the estimates of the World Health Organization (Ahmad et al. 2000). This database corresponds to the most recent update, complete and homogeneous, of the various works already carried out by UNICEF, the World Bank and the United Nations, since it provides estimates of the average under-five mortality rate over five-year periods between 1955 and 1999 for 171 of the 191 member states of the World Health Organization (WHO).

The instability of a variable is always measured relative to a reference value. It is often measured by the standard deviation of the growth rate, that is, relative to the average growth rate. But measuring the deviation from the trend is preferred. The problem then lies in the choice of this trend value. Insofar as the series may be neither purely deterministic nor purely stochastic, the reference value can be estimated from a mixed adjustment, concurrently combining a deterministic element and a stochastic element – the method used in various works of the Centre d'Etudes et de Recherches sur le Développement International (CERDI) and chosen by the Committee for Development Policy (United Nations) for the measurement of the economic vulnerability index. The indicator thus selected is the average of the quadratic deviation relative to the mixed trend.[3]

$$Ins_{quadra} = 100\sqrt{\frac{1}{n+1}\sum_{k=0}^{n}\left(\frac{Y_{t+k}-\hat{Y}_{t+k}}{\hat{Y}_{t+k}}\right)^2},$$

where $\hat{Y}_t = \exp(\ln Y_t')$ and $\ln Y_t' = \hat{a} + \hat{b}.\ln Y_{t-1} + \hat{c}.t$.

The model

The relation between income instability and under-five survival

The model that allows us to test the effect of income instability on under-five survival while controlling for the average income level is as follows:

$$S_{it} = \alpha_0 + \alpha_1.Ins_{it} + \alpha_2.y_{it} + \alpha_3.X_{it} + \mu_i + \eta_{it}, \tag{6.1}$$

where S_{it} is the logit of the under-five survival rate over a five-year period, y_{it} is the average per capita income over the period expressed in logarithms, X_{it} is a vector of control variables such as the importance of vaccinations or women's education (expressed in logarithms), μ_i represents country-specific effects, and η_{it} is the error term. Here, income instability (Ins_{it}) influences the average child survival rate independently of the average income level. By this way, the coefficient of the instability captures both the repartition effect and the direct asymmetry effect analysed above.[4]

We first choose to measure the instability of per capita income over the same period t. This 'present instability' is measured with regard to a four-decade mixed trend (1960–2000) as explained above. Then, we also measure instability over the previous period, in order to capture the effects likely to act in the longer term (in particular, some effects likely to modify income distribution). 'Past instability' captures the effect of shocks occurring between 1975 and 1979 on child survival during the period 1980–84, between 1980 and 1984 on child survival during the period 1985–89, and so on. Finally, we use a measure of instability covering 12 years, that is, both the past and present periods. In other words, 'overall instability' takes into account shocks occurring between 1972 and 1984 for the period 1980–84, between 1977 and 1989 for the period 1985–89, and so on.

The relation between primary instabilities and under-five survival

We also analyse the effect of primary instabilities on child survival because we assume they are the main sources of income instability. As low-income countries are often characterized by a significant share of primary commodities in their exports and by strong exposure to natural disasters, the incidence of instability in global agricultural commodity prices and climatic shocks is hypothesized to be higher in these countries than in the developed nations (IMF 2003). In order to test the effect of primary instabilities, we introduce successively into the model the instability of exports of goods and services in constant dollars (in this sense, the exports measure is a 'volume' measure), the instability of agricultural production per capita which is taken as a proxy of climatic instability, and the instability of world agricultural commodity prices.[5] The econometric models, which allow us to test the effects of primary instabilities on child survival for a given income level, are similar to the previous model.[6]

Data, variables and sample

The econometric analysis is based on a panel of 97 developing countries over the periods 1980–84, 1985–89, 1990–94 and 1995–99. Table 6.1

Table 6.1:   Composition of the sample

* Algeria	Eritrea	* Mozambique
Angola	Ethiopia	Namibia
* Argentina	* Fiji	* Nepal
* Bangladesh	Gabon	* Nicaragua
Belize	* Gambia	* Niger
* Benin	* Ghana	Nigeria
* Bolivia	* Guatemala	Oman
* Botswana	Guinea	* Pakistan
* Brazil	Guinea-Bissau	* Papua New Guinea
Burkina Faso	* Guyana	* Paraguay
* Burundi	* Haiti	* Peru
Cambodia	* Honduras	* Philippines
* Cameroon	* India	* Rwanda
Cape Verde	* Indonesia	Samoa
* Central African Republic	* Iran, Islamic Rep.	Saudi Arabia
Chad	* Jamaica	* Senegal
* Chile	* Jordan	* Sierra Leone
* China	* Kenya	Solomon Islands
* Colombia	Lao PDR	* South Africa
Comoros	Lebanon	* Sri Lanka
* Congo, Dem. Rep.	* Lesotho	* Sudan
* Congo, Rep.	Madagascar	* Swaziland
* Costa Rica	* Malawi	* Syrian Arab Republic
Côte d'Ivoire	* Malaysia	Tanzania
Djibouti	Mali	Thailand
Dominican Republic	Mauritania	Togo
Ecuador	Mauritius	Trinidad and Tobago
Egypt, Arab Rep.	Mexico	Tunisia
El Salvador	Mongolia	Turkey
Equatorial Guinea	Morocco	Uganda
		Uruguay
		Vanuatu
		Venezuela
		Vietnam
		Yemen, Republic of
		Zambia
		Zimbabwe

Note: * Refers to the small sample (Table 6.3, Column 2).
Source: Authors' estimates.

displays the composition of the sample. In order to control for country-specific effects, the potential endogeneity of the regressors and the omitted variable bias, we use the GMM system estimator. We introduce into each model two important control variables, although their availability is relatively limited (which implies a reduction in the sample): the rate of diphtheria–pertussis–tetanus (DPT) vaccination of children less than one year of age (WDI 2005) and the average years of schooling for women over 25 years (Barro and Lee 2000).

For the instability variables, average income is measured by GDP per capita expressed in constant dollars for the base year 2000 (WDI 2005). The variable of export instability is measured from total exports of goods and services in constant dollars for the base year 2000 (WDI 2005). The variable of climatic instability is measured from the agricultural production index per capita (FAOSTAT 2006). The world agricultural commodity price index is of the Deaton–Miller type,[7] constructed from price series in dollars (IFS 2005), converted into local currency, deflated by the export unit value of the developed countries.

4 Results

Descriptive statistics

As mentioned above, the econometric analysis is based on a panel of 97 developing countries for which four observations are available: 1980–84, 1985–89, 1990–94 and 1995–99. The panel is not balanced. Moreover, the sample can vary noticeably with the introduction of some variables.[8]

Table 6.2 gives the statistical description of the variables. It reveals some heterogeneity within the sample: the under-five mortality rate is multiplied by 3.2 between the first and the third quartile, the rate of vaccination by almost 2 and the level of education by 3.4. We also observe that some heterogeneity in the levels of income instability, export instability, agricultural production instability and world agricultural commodity price instability is not particularly striking between the quartiles (instability is multiplied by approximately 2 between the first quartile and the third quartile). Furthermore, if income instability and climatic instability remain moderate on average (respectively 4.14 per cent and 6.22 per cent), the average instability of exports and of world prices (which are dependent) prove rather important since they respectively reach 10.83 per cent and 16.63 per cent.

The effects of instability on child survival

The effects of instability on child survival have been tested with a semi-logarithmic model. Indeed, the effects depend on whether the initial level of instability is weak or high. The variable of interest is thus not expressed in logarithms, unlike the control variables.

Table 6.2:   Descriptive statistics

	U5S	U5M	GDP	VACCIN	EDUC
Min	0.67	0.01	494.11	1.00	0.10
Max	0.99	0.33	18323.86	99.00	8.18
Mean	0.89	0.11	3358.55	61.23	3.12
1st quartile	0.84	0.05	1283.18	42.25	1.37
2nd quartile	0.90	0.10	2563.61	65.60	2.86
3rd quartile	0.95	0.16	4636.39	82.20	4.68
No. of countries	97	97	97	97	67

	INS(GDP)	INS(X)	INS(AGRI)	INS(Pw)
Min	0.36	0.97	0.96	2.30
Max	18.54	62.65	22.57	124.72
Mean	4.14	10.83	6.22	16.63
1st quartile	2.34	5.87	3.22	8.94
2nd quartile	3.58	8.81	4.71	12.75
3rd quartile	5.38	13.12	8.54	17.96
No. of countries	97	82	92	43

Notes:
U5M   Under-five mortality rate, bounded by 0 and 1;
U5S   Under-five survival rate, bounded by 0 and 1 (U5S = 1 − U5M);
GDP   Gross domestic product per capita, based on purchasing power parity, constant international dollars, base year 2000;
VACCIN   Rate of DPT vaccination of children under the age of one year;
EDUC   Average number of schooling years of women over 25 years of age;
INS(GDP)   Instability of per capita income, constant dollars, base year 2000;
INS(X)   Instability of exports of goods and services, constant dollars, base year 2000;
INS(AGRI)   Instability of agricultural production per capita;
INS(Pw)   Instability of international agricultural prices.
Source: Authors' estimates.

Table 6.3 displays the results of the estimate of the effect of 'present instability' (measured by the average of the quadratic deviation relative to a mixed trend) on the logit of child survival, using the GMM system estimator. In order to enlarge the sample, we also choose to run regressions without including the education variable, which drops many observations. The effect of average income instability on child survival proves to be significant at a threshold of 1 per cent for the two samples. In addition, primary instabilities appear to be significant (only on the small sample for export instability). Moreover, the effect of income instability on child survival has been tested with two other instability measurements (the standard deviation of annual growth rate and the average of the absolute deviation relative to the mixed trend). The results also prove to be significant (not presented here).

	INS(GDP)		INS(X)		INS(AGRI)		INS(Pw)	
	1	2	3	4	5	6	7	8
Instability	-0.061***	-0.039***	-0.005	-0.010**	-0.042***	-0.020*	-0.008***	-0.010***
	0.012	0.014	0.004	0.005	0.012	0.012	0.003	0.004
GDP pc	0.881***	0.749***	0.825***	1.007***	0.920***	1.094***	0.846***	0.806***
	0.106	0.124	0.108	0.273	0.127	0.247	0.087	0.205
Vaccination	0.160***	0.122*	0.208***	0.357***	0.175***	0.370***	0.283***	0.246**
	0.055	0.066	0.062	0.13	0.049	0.117	0.075	0.113
Education		0.215**		-0.107		-0.133		0.078
		0.103		0.245		0.203		0.163
Constant	-4.935***	-3.995***	-4.883***	-6.780***	-5.278***	-7.436***	-5.217***	-4.821***
	0.769	0.964	0.787	2.27	0.958	2.06	0.692	1.766
No. of obs	353	254	293	225	345	247	168	134
No. of countries	97	67	82	61	92	65	43	35
Hansen	0.071	0.141	0.034	0.119	0.088	0.069	0.109	0.226
AR1	0.004	0.002	0.000	0.001	0.082	0.000	0.073	0.045
AR2	0.803	0.119	0.826	0.869	0.116	0.190	0.069	0.069

Notes:
Standard errors, corrected for heteroscedasticity, appear below the coefficients.
Estimator: GMM system;
Dependent variable: logit of under-five survival rate (S);
INS(GDP): Instability of per capita income, constant dollars, base year 2000;
INS(X): Instability of exports of goods and services, constant dollars, base year 2000;
INS(AGRI): Instability of agricultural production per capita;
INS(Pw): Instability of international agricultural prices;
Instability is measured on each period t;
All variables are expressed in logarithms except instability;
Periods: 1980–84, 1985–89, 1990–94, 1995–99
* significant at 10%, ** significant at 5%, *** significant at 1%.
The Hansen statistic, which is the minimized value of the two-step GMM criterion function, generally indicates that instruments are exogenous.
AR(1) and AR(2) tests generally indicate that there is no problem of autocorrelation in the model.
Source: Authors' estimates.

We also run regressions including an interactive term ($Ins_{it}*y_{it}$) in order to capture the likely decreasing effect of instability with income level. The results are not significant (not presented here). In fact, although the effect of instability seems to decrease with income level, this phenomenon does not appear very pronounced in our sample. This can be highlighted by the examination of the estimated logistic function. From results displayed in Table 6.3, column 1, we get the following relationship (for the mean value of the vaccination variable):

$$Logit\ U5S = 0.9\ ln(GDP) - 4.5, \tag{6.2}$$

which is equivalent to:

$$U5S = \frac{1}{1 + \exp^{-(0.9 ln(GDP) - 4.5)}} \tag{6.3}$$

From this equation, we get the second derivative function. It is negative and increasing, which means that the curve is concave and that concavity diminishes as income increases. Nevertheless, we note that the decrease in the effect of instability may not be very strong since many observations are located on the right part of the logistic curve where concavity does not vary much (the minimum income level equals 500 PPP$). This may explain the lack of significance of the results concerning an effect of instability expected to decrease with income.

Table 6.5 gives the marginal impact of instability (measured from the calculations provided in Table 6.4) according to several values of child survival:[9] when income instability increases by 5 points, the average child survival rate decreases by 0.018 units (0.024 units for the first quartile of child survival). In other words, the average mortality rate is strongly affected since it changes from 110 to 128 per 1,000 (from 160 to 184 per 1,000 for the first quartile of child survival). Moreover, the

Table 6.4: Impact of instability (*Ins*) on under-five survival (*s*) according to a semi-logistic specification

Specification	Derivative	$\dfrac{ds}{dIns}$	Interpretation
$\ln\left(\dfrac{s}{1-s}\right) = \alpha + \beta.Ins$	$\dfrac{1}{s.(1-s)}.ds = \beta.dIns$	$\beta.s.(1-s)$	Marginal impact depending on β and on $s.(1-s)$

Source: Following the analysis of Grigoriou (2005).

Table 6.5: Marginal impact of 'present instability' on child survival

	INS(GDP)	INS(X)	INS(AGRI)	INS(Pw)
Mean of U5S	–0.0036	–0.0009	–0.0019	–0.0010
First quartile of U5S	–0.0047	–0.0012	–0.0025	–0.0013
Second quartile of U5S	–0.0032	–0.0008	–0.0017	–0.0009
Third quartile of U5S	–0.0017	–0.0004	–0.0009	–0.0004

Source: Calculated from the coefficients of instability obtained in Columns 2, 4, 6, and 8 of Table 6.3 at different levels of under-five survival (mean of the sample, first, second and third quartile of the sample).

marginal impact of income instability is 2.8 times stronger for the first quartile of child survival than for the third.

The results concerning the effects of instability in exports, climate, and world prices can be analysed in a similar way: when export instability increases by 10 points, the average mortality rate changes from 110 to 119 per 1,000 (from 160 to 172 per 1,000 for the first quartile of child survival). In the same way, when agricultural production instability increases 10 points, the average mortality rate goes from 110 per 1,000 to 129 per 1,000 (from 160 to 185 per 1,000 for the first quartile of child survival). Lastly, when the instability of the world agricultural commodity prices increases 10 points, the average mortality rate rises from 110 to 120 per 1,000 (from 160 to 173 per 1,000 for the first quartile of child survival).

Table 6.6 presents the effect of 'past instability' (income instability then primary instabilities), which appears significant on the two samples. Table 6.8 gives the marginal impact of 'past instability' according to several values of child survival: when income instability increases by 5 points, the average child survival rate decreases by 0.0155 units (0.0205 units for the first quartile of child survival). In other words, the average mortality rate changes from 110 to 125 per 1,000 (from 160 to 180 per 1,000 for the first quartile of child survival).

Table 6.7 also shows a significant effect of 'overall instability' (except for export instability, which is significant only on the large sample). Note that the coefficients of 'overall instability' are larger than the coefficients of 'past instability' (Table 6.6) and of 'present instability' (Table 6.3). Indeed, 'overall instability' may reflect both the irreversibility effect, which is likely to occur over the period, and the effect of instability over the previous years. Table 6.9 gives the marginal impact of 'overall instability' on child survival: when income instability increases 5 points, the average child survival rate decreases by 0.037 units (0.049 units for the first quartile of child survival). So, the average mortality rate is strongly *(to p.128)*

Table 6.6: Effect of 'past instability' on child survival

	INS(GDP)		INS(X)		INS(AGRI)		INS(Pw)	
	1	2	3	4	5	6	7	8
Instability	-0.035**	-0.034*	-0.006***	-0.014*	-0.051***	-0.027*	-0.001***	-0.001*
	0.018	0.021	0.002	0.008	0.013	0.016	0.000	0.000
GDP per capita	1.038***	0.865***	0.934***	0.644***	0.853***	1.190***	0.909***	0.771***
	0.168	0.201	0.104	0.132	0.137	0.272	0.087	0.199
Vaccination	0.295***	0.296***	0.204***	0.127*	0.210***	0.438***	0.143**	0.276**
	0.085	0.099	0.068	0.073	0.053	0.141	0.057	0.107
Education		0.056		0.340***		-0.231		0.086
		0.166		0.112		0.228		0.157
Constant	-6.843***	-5.519***	-5.758***	-3.375***	-4.895***	-8.372***	-5.264***	-4.824***
	1.214	1.663	0.753	1.063	1.008	2.366	0.643	1.685
No. of observations	339	251	267	218	349	251	168	134
No. of countries	95	67	79	63	93	66	43	35
Hansen	0.024	0.013	0.054	0.312	0.174	0.366	0.374	0.103
AR1	0.000	0.001	0.000	0.001	0.035	0.001	0.005	0.000
AR2	0.496	0.240	0.306	0.115	0.419	0.544	0.408	0.464

Notes: Standard errors, corrected for heteroscedasticity, appear below the coefficients.
Estimator: GMM system;
Dependent variable: logit of under-five survival rate (S);
INS(GDP): Instability of per capita income, constant dollars, base year 2000;
INS(X): Instability of exports of goods and services, constant dollars, base year 2000;
INS(AGRI): Instability of agricultural production per capita;
INS(Pw): Instability of international agricultural prices;
Instability is measured on each period $(t-1)$;
All variables are expressed in logarithms except instability;
Periods: 1980–84, 1985–89, 1990–94, 1995–99
* significant at 10%, ** significant at 5%, *** significant at 1%.
The Hansen statistic, which is the minimized value of the two-step GMM criterion function, generally indicates that instruments are exogenous. AR(1) and AR(2) tests generally indicate that there is no problem of autocorrelation in the model

	INS(GDP)		INS(X)		INS(AGRI)		INS(Pw)	
	1	2	3	4	5	6	7	8
Instability	-0.096***	-0.082**	-0.006**	-0.018	-0.085***	-0.052**	-0.014**	-0.012**
	0.024	0.035	0.003	0.011	0.027	0.024	0.006	0.006
GDP per capita	0.868***	0.789***	0.845***	0.677***	0.800***	1.064***	0.828***	0.764***
	0.104	0.208	0.108	0.177	0.127	0.230	0.087	0.220
Vaccination	0.135**	0.202***	0.212***	0.280***	0.229***	0.402***	0.302***	0.242*
	0.061	0.083	0.068	0.091	0.052	0.123	0.078	0.127
Education		0.110		0.154		-0.153		0.118
		0.159		0.144		0.199		0.187
Constant	-4.560***	-4.350***	-5.080***	-4.009***	-4.264***	-7.104***	-5.043***	-4.450**
	0.743	1.591	0.773	1.403	0.961	1.978	0.690	1.962
No. of observations	328	248	262	214	349	251	168	134
No. of countries	94	67	77	62	93	66	43	35
Hansen	0.030	0.068	0.085	0.047	0.082	0.293	0.253	0.283
AR1	0.000	0.000	0.000	0.000	0.001	0.000	0.007	0.001
AR2	0.883	0.554	0.610	0.867	0.247	0.318	0.263	0.127

Notes: Standard errors, corrected for heteroscedasticity, appear below the coefficients.
Estimator: GMM system;
Dependent variable: logit of under-five survival rate (S);
INS(GDP): Instability of per capita income, constant dollars, base year 2000;
INS(X): Instability of exports of goods and services, constant dollars, base year 2000;
INS(AGRI): Instability of agricultural production per capita;
INS(Pw): Instability of international agricultural prices;
Instability is measured on each period (on $(t-1)$ and t);
All variables are expressed in logarithms except instability;
Periods: 1980–84, 1985–89, 1990–94, 1995–99
* significant at 10%, ** significant at 5%, *** significant at 1%.
The Hansen statistic, which is the minimized value of the two-step GMM criterion function, generally indicates that instruments are exogenous. AR(1) and AR(2) tests generally indicate that there is no problem of autocorrelation in the model.
Source: Authors' estimates.

Table 6.8:   Marginal impact of 'past instability'

	INS(PIB)	INS(X)	INS(AGRI)	INS(Pw)
Mean of U5S	–0.0031	–0.0013	–0.0025	–0.0001
First quartile of U5S	–0.0041	–0.0017	–0.0033	–0.0001
Second quartile of U5S	–0.0028	–0.0012	–0.0022	–0.0001
Third quartile of U5S	–0.0014	–0.0006	–0.0011	0.0000

Source: Calculated from the coefficients of instability obtained in Columns 2, 4, 6, and 8 of Table 6.6 at different levels of under five survival (mean of the sample, first, second and third quartile of the sample).

Table 6.9:   Marginal impact of 'overall instability'

	INS(PIB)	INS(X)	INS(AGRI)	INS(Pw)
Mean of U5S	–0.0074	–0.0016	–0.0047	–0.0012
First quartile of U5S	–0.0098	–0.0021	–0.0064	–0.0016
Second quartile of U5S	–0.0066	–0.0014	–0.0043	–0.0011
Third quartile of U5S	–0.0034	–0.0008	–0.0021	–0.0005

Source: Calculated from the coefficients of instability obtained in Columns 2, 4, 6, and 8 of Table 6.7 at different levels of under five survival (mean of the sample, first, second and third quartile of the sample).

(from p.125) affected since it expands from 110 to 147 per 1,000 (from 160 to 209 per 1,000 for the first quartile of child survival).

5   Conclusion

In this chapter, we extend the earlier micro-based chapters of the book to consider how the broader but potentially equally important issue of macroeconomic instabilities are likely to affect under-five survival beyond their effect through lower economic growth. First, they have an irreversible influence on child mortality owing to asymmetry in the reaction of child health to the ups and downs in economic variables. Moreover, they may involve a stronger income inequality (because the 'almost poor' people are more likely to suffer from income shocks), which reduces the average child survival rate.

Our econometric analysis made it possible, controlling for the impact of average income, to establish several results concerning the relation between instabilities and under-five survival: average income instability – as well as primary instabilities (relating to climate, world commodity prices, exports) that are the main exogenous sources of income instability – appears to have a direct effect ('present instability') on child survival in the developing countries of the sample. This effect proved to be of quite a large scale, since increasing income instability by 5 points is likely to involve a 16 per cent increase in the mortality rate. Moreover, income instability also appears to have an effect on child survival in the longer run ('past instability'), although of lesser magnitude. Although provisional, these results suggest that addressing the issue of macro-economic instability is a significant way to improve health level in developing countries.

The analysis presented here could be extended in several directions. One is to work out a specification of the relation, making it possible to test the existence of thresholds and other non-linearities. Is there a minimum level of instability above which the effect matters? Is there a level of per capita income beyond which the effect of instability is no longer significant? What are the factors conditioning the effect of instability? It would also be interesting to compare the direct effects of macroeconomic instability on child survival with those resulting from lower economic growth.

Notes

1. Note that the assumption of asymmetry is more particularly used in the analysis of the effects of primary instabilities.
2. Null at the inflection point located at 500 per 1,000, the second derivative of the survival function is then negative. Moreover, on this interval, it is first decreasing then increasing.
3. This measurement seems to be best adapted to our study. However, tests of robustness have been carried out with alternative measurements, such as the standard deviation of the annual growth rate and the average of the absolute deviation relative to the mixed trend: $Ins_{absolu} = \dfrac{100}{n+1} \displaystyle\sum_{k=0}^{n} \dfrac{\left| Y_{t+k} - \hat{Y}_{t+k} \right|}{\hat{Y}_{t+k}}$.
4. It did not appear relevant to introduce the Gini coefficient in the regression in order to isolate the direct asymmetry effect since the latter is likely to also affect the Gini coefficient.
5. It is also possible to combine these two primary instabilities in an index of exogenous shocks, via a simple or weighted average. The results obtained did not prove to be conclusive.
6. Political instability is not considered as such in the model. It cannot be treated as a primary instability since it itself depends on the primary instabilities listed above.
7. The Deaton–Miller index is a geometrically weighted index. Here, the price of each commodity is weighted by its share in the total value of agricultural production in 1990: $P_{it} = \prod_{j} P_{jt}^{Wi0}$.
8. In particular, the estimate of the effect of the instability of world agricultural prices on child survival is carried out on a sample reduced to the agricultural commodity-exporting countries, that is, the countries whose exports of agricultural commodities constitute 50 per cent or more of total commodity exports.

9. Indeed, the response of child survival to instability depends on the child survival level, owing to the logistic form applied to the child survival variable.

References

Adams, R. J. (2004) 'Economic Growth, Inequality and Poverty: Estimating the Growth Elasticity of Poverty', *World Development*, 32 (12): 1989–2014.

Agénor, P. (2002) 'Macroeconomic Adjustment and the Poor, Analytical Issues and Cross-Country Evidence', *Journal of Economic Surveys*, 18 (3): 1467–6419.

Ahmad, O. B., A. D. Lopez and M. Inoue (2000) 'The Decline in Child Mortality: A Reappraisal', *Bulletin of the World Health Organization*, 78 (10): 1175–91.

Barro, R. J., and J.-W. Lee (2000) 'International Data on Educational Attainment Updates and Implications', NBER Working Paper 7911 (Cambridge MA: National Bureau of Economic Research).

Bourguignon, F. (2003) 'The Growth Elasticity of Poverty Reduction: Explaining Heterogeneity across Countries and Time Periods', in T. Eicher and S. Turnovski (eds), *Inequality and Growth: Theory and Policy Implications* (Cambridge MA: MIT Press).

Breen, R. and C. Garcia-Peñalosa (2005) 'Income Inequality and Macroeconomic Volatility: An Empirical Investigation', *Review of Development Economics*, 9 (3): 380–98.

Combes, J. and P. Guillaumont (2002) 'Commodity Price Volatility, Vulnerability and Development', *Development Policy Review*, 20 (1): 25.

Cornia, G. A. and R. Paniccià (2000) *The Mortality Crisis in Transitional Economies* (Oxford: Oxford University Press for UNU–WIDER).

Dercon, S. (2006) 'Vulnerability: A Micro Perspective', in F. Bourguignon, B. Pleskovic and J. van der Gaag (eds), *Securing Development in an Unstable World* – Annual Bank Conference on Development Economics, Amsterdam, 117–46.

Dollar, D. and A. Kraay (2002) 'Growth Is Good for the Poor', *Journal of Economic Growth*, 7 (3): 195–225.

FAOSTAT (2006) Food and Agricultural Organization of United Nations, Rome (Italy), at: http://faostat.fao.org.

Gakusi, A., M. Garenne and G. Gaullier (2005) 'Chocs externes, gestions de l'état et mortalité des enfants en Zambie de 1964 à 1998', *African Development Review*, 17 (1): 70.

Grigoriou, C. (2005) 'Essais sur la vulnérabilité des enfants dans les pays en développement: L'impact de la politique économique', Thesis, Université d'Auvergne, Centre d'Etudes et de Recherches sur le Développement International, Clermont-Ferrand.

Guillaumont, P. (1994) 'Politique d'ouverture et croissance économique: Les effets de la croissance et de l'instabilité des exportations', *Revue d'économie du développement*, 1: 91–114.

Guillaumont, P. (2006) 'Macro Vulnerability in Low-Income Countries and Aid Responses', in F. Bourguignon, B. Pleskovic and J. van der Gaag (eds), *Securing Development in an Unstable World*, Annual Bank Conference on Development Economics, Amsterdam, 65–108.

Guillaumont, P. and C. Korachais (2010) 'When Unstable, Growth Is Less Pro-poor', UNU–WIDER Working Paper No. 2010/77.

Guillaumont, P., S. Guillaumont Jeanneney and J. Brun (1999) 'How Instability Lowers African Growth', *Journal of African Economies*, 8 (1): 87–107.

Hnatkovska, V. and N. Loayza (2005) 'Volatility and Growth', in J. Aizenman and B. Pinto (eds), *Managing Economic Volatility and Crises: A Practitioner's Guide* (Cambridge: Cambridge University Press), 65–100.

IFS (2005) International Financial Statistics (Washington DC: IMF Group), at: www.imfstatistics.org/IMF/expired.asp

IMF (International Monetary Fund) (2003) 'Fund Assistance for Countries Facing Exogenous Shocks', Technical Report, Policy Development and Review Department, IMF, Washington DC.

Laursen, T. and S. Mahajan (2005) 'Volatility, Income Distribution, and Poverty', in J. Aizenman and B. Pinto (eds), *Managing Volatility and Crisis: A Practitioner's Guide* (Cambridge: Cambridge University Press), 101–36.

Norrbin, S. C. and F. P. Yigit (2005) 'The Robustness of the Link between Volatility and Growth of Output', *Review of World Economics*, 141 (2): 343–56.

Preston, S. (1975) 'The Changing Relation between Mortality and Level of Economic Development', *Population Studies*, 29 (2): 231–48.

Ramey, G. and V. Ramey (1995) 'Cross-Country Evidence on the Link between Volatility and Growth', *American Economic Review*, 85 (5): 1138–51.

Ravallion, M. and S. Chen (1997) 'What Can New Survey Data Tell Us about Recent Changes in Distribution and Poverty?', *World Bank Economic Review*, 11 (2): 357–82.

Sachs, J. D. (2002) 'Macroeconomics and Health: Investing in Health for Economic Development', Technical Report (Geneva: Commission on Macroeconomics and Health, World Health Organization).

Sahn, D. E. and D. C. Stifel (2003) 'Progress Toward the Millennium Development Goals in Africa', *World Development*, 31 (1): 23–52.

Sen, A. (1983) *Poverty and Famines: An Essay on Entitlement and Deprivation* (Oxford: Oxford University Press for UNU–WIDER).

Shkolnikov, V. M., G. A. Cornia, D. A. Leon and F. Mesle (1998) 'Causes of the Russian Mortality Crisis: Evidence and Interpretations', *World Development*, 26 (11): 1995–2011.

WDI (2005) World Development Indicators (Washington DC: World Bank Group), at: www.columbia.edu/cgi-bin/cul/resolve?AUQ2574

7
Intra-Household Arrangements and Adult Health Satisfaction: Evidence from Mexico

Mariano Rojas

1 Introduction

This chapter deals with the impact of household arrangements on an individual's health satisfaction, through a subjective wellbeing approach. It thus provides both a unique methodological complement to the earlier papers in the series, and extends the child-based analysis to come with the key intrahousehold allocations issues that are vital to understanding the development process.

The literature on household arrangements is vast. Some authors have proposed that the family is basically a communitarian organization, where all – and not merely economic – household resources are pooled together into a common pot from which all family members can benefit equally. On the other hand, other authors approach the family as a cooperative equilibrium outcome, so that individualistically motivated adults remain in the group as long as they attain benefits. Under the cooperative bargaining models, the benefits from household resources, for example, pooling income, emotional support, investment in relational and economic goods, division of household tasks and responsibilities, confidence and trust, are distributed on the basis of a bargaining process. Extreme situations may include altruistic behaviour, where some members make sacrifices for the benefit of others, or a totally individualistic household, where members act as partners, with separate budgets, personal relations, and so on.

The literature on intra-household arrangements has stressed that the family is a black box that may entail communitarianism, altruism, cooperation, bargaining and conflict (Bergstrom 1997; Hart 1990; Vogel 2003). This chapter argues that the nature of household arrangements is relevant for the study of health satisfaction. Whether a person has equal access to the health benefits from his[1] household resources depends on the nature of the intra-household arrangement. Hence, the intra-household distribution of these resources for satisfactory health is determined by the nature of household arrangements, making the distribution of health satisfaction within the household a relevant area of research. In particular, this chapter is interested in studying the household arrangements of low-income families, where an unequal distribution of relevant health satisfaction resources is assumed to be more pernicious for some household members.

The status of a person within the family and his position as breadwinner are used as proxies for his social and economic power within the family. Under a cooperative bargaining model, the distribution of health satisfaction follows closely the status allocation as breadwinner and family status, while no similar relationship is expected in a communitarian model.

This investigation also examines which income proxy is more relevant in explaining health satisfaction. The explanatory power of alternative income proxies, such as household income, personal income, household per capita income, and household equivalent income, is analysed. In an effort to determine which income proxy is better for explaining the health satisfaction of a person, I address two relevant issues:

(i) whether household economic resources are pooled together to generate health satisfaction;[2] and
(ii) whether there are family-size depletion effects in utilizing these economic resources to generate health satisfaction.[3]

The investigation follows a subjective wellbeing approach (Headey et al. 1985; Headey and Wearing 1992; Veenhoven 1996; Van Praag et al. 2003; Van Praag and Ferrer-i-Carbonell 2004; Rojas 2005, 2006a, 2006b). It is argued that health satisfaction, as declared by the person, provides useful information that cannot be captured fully by objective health indicators alone. Health satisfaction captures information not only on the occurrence of illness but also about the social and family context within which these illnesses affect wellbeing. For example, the fact of being ill is not enough to assess a person's wellbeing, since that particular observation overlooks such relevant factors as the existence and nature of family support, the quality of medical attention (human and therapeutic), the role of social stigmas and social expectations, modification of activities by the patient (household chores or recreational pastime), and the existence and support of friends. In other words, being ill is not the same as suffering from an illness. Some variation in suffering is to be expected among those afflicted with the same illness. Thus, health satisfaction encompasses information not only on being ill but also about related conditions influencing the degree of suffering.

The chapter is structured as follows. First, I introduce the literature on theories of the family, highlighting the relevance of household arrangements in studying health satisfaction. I then present the database and discuss the construction of a health satisfaction indicator. The following section discusses the income proxies related to health satisfaction, and shows that household income has greater explanatory power than personal income and that no adjustment for family size is required. After studying the relationship between health satisfaction and a person's status within the family, I examine the relationship between health satisfaction and the breadwinner status, with a particular focus on the situation in low-income groups. I then examine the role of intra-household bargaining power in health satisfaction, and, finally, present the major conclusions of the investigation.

2 Household arrangements and intra-household health satisfaction

Most people live in a variety of family arrangements. They share responsibilities and long-run life projects as well as emotional support and economic resources. They also produce relational and economic goods under an institutional framework known as the family. Family arrangements deal with the intra-family distribution of economic and relational resources that generate life satisfaction and, in particular, health satisfaction; hence they are crucial in the study of the wellbeing of a person. In his work on the family, Vogel (2003: 393) states that: 'In the case of the family the principle is reciprocity and an informal contract between family members concerning responsibilities for the welfare of family members'. There is a contract between spouses, between parents and their children, between adults and their elderly parents, and between adults and further relatives.

In his pioneer work on the economic approach to the study of the family, Becker (1973, 1974, 1981) assumes that some family members – usually the head of the family – behave altruistically, while others behave selfishly. Thus, Becker combines communitarian and individualistic characteristics within his analysis of the family. He assumes that altruistic members are concerned with the wellbeing of the rest of the family, although not necessarily as much as they are concerned about their own wellbeing. In consequence, the wellbeing of other members is incorporated in the utility function of altruistic members. Selfish members are concerned just with their own circumstances, and they have no interest in the wellbeing of the rest of the family. The altruistic behaviour of income earners implies that health satisfaction is not closely related to their breadwinner or family status within the household. From an economic point of view, in a perfectly communitarian family (Rojas 2007a), the relationship between health satisfaction and the household-income proxy of a person should be the same for all household members, regardless of role as breadwinner or status within the family.

Recent studies consider the family as a cooperative arrangement in which members, particularly spouses and adult members, exhibit selfish behaviour; they are concerned only about their own utility and they act unilaterally. Thus, a cooperative equilibrium (a marriage or a family) emerges because it is convenient to all household members. This approach, known as the 'cooperative bargaining model of the family' (Manser and Brown 1980; McElroy 1985, 1990; Lundberg and Pollak 1993, 1996; Pollak 1994, 2002), explains intra-family decisions as the result of a collective-choice process that takes place on the basis of selfish and unilateral interests, leading to cooperative household equilibriums. Hence, family members remain in the household as long as the arrangement is to their advantage.

According to cooperative bargaining models, the distribution of bargaining power within the family influences the kind of cooperative equilibrium that emerges as well as its corresponding intra-household distribution of gains (Binmore 1987). Asymmetries in the access to household income develop from the differences in the bargaining power of family members. For example, Lundberg et al. (1997) find that an increase in a person's income raises his decision-making power within the family. Thus, according to cooperative bargaining models, these asymmetries should be reflected in the intra-household distribution of health satisfaction.

The present investigation tests, on the basis of a person's breadwinner and family status, whether an asymmetric arrangement in health satisfaction exists in Mexico.[4] Being the main or a secondary breadwinner within the family should provide more bargaining power, which the person could transform into a cooperative equilibrium that raises his health satisfaction relative to other family members. Status within the family is another important variable associated with bargaining power because of the advantage of influencing the internal division of labour at the household level. This means that a person, for example the mother or grandparent, who may not be earning income could hold substantial bargaining power as a consequence of their place within the family's division of labour. Hence, if family arrangements are based on cooperative bargaining models, then family members with greater bargaining power should also enjoy greater health satisfaction.

Rojas (2007a) makes a distinction between communitarian and individualistic families on the basis of the altruistic and cooperative bargaining models. In a perfectly communitarian family, the subjective wellbeing of the person should depend on his household income but still be independent of his breadwinning role and family status. Likewise, earning a large share of the household's income or no share at all should not matter for a person's wellbeing in a communitarian/altruistic household. On the contrary, in an individualistic family, which develops because cooperative equilibrium is convenient for each member, an individual's breadwinning and family status should affect his relative wellbeing. Family members with greater bargaining power should have greater wellbeing benefits from a given endowment of household resources (household income and other relevant resources). Furthermore, in an individualistic family, access to resources that contribute to wellbeing is expected to be strongly related to a person's share in generating household income. This chapter focuses on health satisfaction, and uses the subjective wellbeing approach to explore how household arrangements influence the relationship between health satisfaction and household income.[5]

It is clear that household arrangements have important implications for health satisfaction. These household arrangements matter for the allocation of relevant health-satisfaction resources among household members. These relevant resources refer to expenditure in health care, such as medicines and vaccines, doctor visits, laboratory analyses and hospital therapy. They also refer to the allocation of time resources by family members in care-giving and undertaking of health-threatening activities. Substantial intra-household asymmetries in the access to relevant resources for health satisfaction suggest that there may be relatively healthy persons in low-income families as well as relatively unhealthy persons in high-income families. If this is the case, then household income is not a good proxy for the health satisfaction of each household member. On the other hand, if family arrangements are basically communitarian, then household income becomes a good proxy for every household member's health satisfaction.

3   The database

The survey

A survey was conducted in five states of central and south Mexico, as well as in the Federal District (Mexico City), during October and November of 2001.[6] A stratified-random sample was balanced by household income, gender and urban/rural areas. As 1,540 questionnaires were properly completed, the sample size was considered acceptable for inference in central Mexico. It is important to note that only adult people were interviewed, and so the health satisfaction of children and teenagers (less than 18 years old) in the family was not considered in this investigation. Furthermore, the unit of study in the survey was the person, not the family. It would have been preferable to interview all adult members in a household, but financial constraints did not allow the construction of such a database.

The variables

The survey collected information on the following quantitative and qualitative variables:

Demographic and social variables: education, age, gender, marital status, household composition (age and number of household-income-dependent persons), family status (father, mother, daughter or son, grandparent, other), and breadwinning status (main breadwinner, secondary breadwinner, marginal breadwinner, no breadwinner).

Economic variables: current household income and current personal income.

Health satisfaction: the question asked was: 'How satisfied are you with your current health?'

The verbal answer had a seven-option scale, ranging from extremely unsatisfied to extremely satisfied. Health satisfaction was considered as an ordinal variable. Table 7.1 presents the frequency for the health satisfaction variable.

Table 7.1: Frequency for health satisfaction variable

Health satisfaction	Per cent
Extremely unsatisfied	0.20
Very unsatisfied	0.98
Unsatisfied	8.74
Neither satisfied nor unsatisfied	7.50
Satisfied	52.51
Very satisfied	24.46
Extremely satisfied	5.61
Total	100.00

Source: Authors' own calculations based on own database.

4   What income proxy to use?

Studies on the relationship between health satisfaction and income must take into consideration that income is merely a proxy of the capacity to purchase goods and services in order to satisfy one's health needs. Therefore, it must first be decided what constitutes the best income proxy for approximating a person's command over resources that satisfy his health needs. A relevant characteristic of a household arrangement is the size of the group and its demographic structure, and the common practice is to adjust income by family size and the age structure of its members.[7] Thus, the following income proxies were considered: household income, personal income and family-size adjusted income measures (household per capita income and household equivalent income calculated with the OECD equivalence scale).

Household income can constitute a good proxy for a person's command over the resources useful for satisfying one's health needs if the family is basically communitarian and there are no family-size depletion effects. Personal income, on the other hand, is an individualistic proxy of the command over resources and can be a good proxy in an individualistic family but not in a communitarian family, in which a person may have access to resources even without being an income earner. Household income per capita and household equivalent income adjust to the number (and sometimes the age structure) of family members,[8] making them relevant proxies in communitarian families and if family-size depletion effects exist.

Several regressions were run with health satisfaction as the explained variable and the logarithm of different incomes proxies[9] as the explanatory variable to determine which income proxy has the greatest explanatory power on health satisfaction. Table 7.2 shows the goodness of fit for each regression, as well as the estimated coefficient and its significance test.

According to Table 7.2, indicators that stress personal command over economic resources (such as personal income) are not good explanatory variables of health satisfaction. Thus, the health satisfaction of a person is strongly related to his household command over economic resources, rather than to personal command over economic resources. In addition, results from Table 7.2 also indicate that family-size adjusted indicators (such as household income per capita and household equivalent income) do not provide greater explanatory power than the non-adjusted household income indicator.

Table 7.2: Statistics from regression analyses: health satisfaction as explained variable, different income proxies as explanatory variables; results from ordered probit regressions

Explanatory variable	Pseudo-R^{2a}	Coefficient	Significance
Ln household income	0.035	0.211	0.00
Ln personal income	0.012	0.039	0.00
Ln household per capita income	0.029	0.167	0.00
Ln household equivalent income (OECD scale)	0.033	0.198	0.00

Note: [a] Refers to Cox and Snell pseudo-R^2.
Source: Author's own calculations based on own database.

Table 7.3: Income groups and frequency of observations

Income group[a]	Range in monthly income (Mexican pesos[b])	Frequency (%)
Low	$3,350 \geq Y \geq 0$	30.0
Middle	$7,000 \geq Y > 3,350$	33.8
High	$Y > 7,000$	36.2

Notes:
[a] On the basis of household income.
[b] Exchange rate in 2001: 9.30 Mexican pesos equivalent to approximately US\$1.
Source: Author's own calculations based on own database.

Thus, it seems that Mexican families, in utilizing their economic resources to satisfy health needs, do not behave in an extreme 'housemate way'. Furthermore, family-size depletion effects seem to be small. Consequently, the present investigation uses household income as proxy for a person's command over economic resources to satisfy his health requirements.

Three income groups were constructed on the basis of household income of the person. These are shown in Table 7.3, along with the frequency of observations in each group. The low-income group refers to families with a daily household income of approximately US\$12. The middle-income group refers to families with daily household income ranging between US\$12 and US\$25, while high-income families have household income exceeding approximately US$25. The sample is distributed more or less uniformly across the income groups.

5   Family status and health satisfaction

Family statuses

Family status is an intra-family feature and it constitutes a proxy for a person's bargaining power within the family. Cultural factors have established a family hierarchy within which the father and mother are expected to have more decisionmaking power. However, in some cultures, grandparents are highly respected and they have decision power, while in other cultures children have attained great bargaining power. Six categories for family status were distinguished: father, mother, son, daughter, grandparent and other. Table 7.4 shows the distribution of household members in the sample according to their family status.

The role of family status in health satisfaction

As is shown in Table 7.4, there are substantial differences in average health satisfaction based on family status. Health satisfaction is greater for son, daughter and father. Being a mother, grandparent or other is associated with lower health satisfaction. These differences could be a reflection of the family status or other sociodemographic and economic characteristics that are correlated with the person's family status. Hence, the following regression was conducted to study the role of a person's family status in his health satisfaction after controlling for other relevant characteristics that may be directly related to health and health satisfaction, such as age, education, income and marital status. Father was the category of reference.

Table 7.4:   Family status frequency and corresponding average health satisfaction

Family status	Percentage in sample	Average health satisfaction
Father	31.6	58.6
Mother	27.6	55.3
Son	18.8	62.1
Daughter	15.6	60.0
Grandparent	2.0	48.6
Other	4.4	57.1
Total number of observations	1,535	

Source: Author's own calculations based on own database.

$$HS = \beta_0 + \beta_1 FS_{mother} + \beta_2 FS_{son} + \beta_3 FS_{daughter} + \beta_4 FS_{grandpa}$$
$$+ \beta_5 FS_{other} + \beta_6 \ln Y + \phi X_{control} + \mu \qquad (7.1)$$

where:

HS	refers to *health* satisfaction, a categorical variable;
FS_{mother}	is a dichotomous variable with the value of 1 if the person has the status of *mother* within the family, and 0 otherwise;
FS_{son}	is a dichotomous variable with value of 1 if the person has the status of *son* within the family, and a value of 0 otherwise;
$FS_{daughter}$	is a dichotomous variable with value of 1 if the person has the status of a *daughter* within the family, and 0 otherwise;
$FS_{grandpa}$	is a dichotomous variable with value of 1 if the person has a *grandparent* status within the family, and a value of 0 otherwise;
FS_{other}	is a dichotomous variable with value of 1 if the person has *other* family status within the family, and a value of 0 otherwise;
$\ln Y$	refers to the logarithm of household income;
$X_{control}$	is a vector of the following control variables (ϕ is a vector of parameters):

Education: education in levels;

Age: age in years;

Marital status: vector of dichotomous variables about marital status, *single* was the category of reference.

The existence of substantial intra-household disparities in health satisfaction in low-income families is the main focus of this investigation. It has been argued that large disparities can be a reflection of the fact that some household members are being marginalized from access to household resources, and that this marginalization in low-income families could have pernicious effects on health satisfaction. Regression (7.1) was run for each income group subsample (defined in the previous section). Table 7.5 shows the results from the exercise by income group and for the whole sample.

The results indicate that there are important differences in the relationship between breadwinner status and health satisfaction across income groups. In low-income families, sons and fathers have very similar health satisfaction levels. Mothers enjoy slightly lower health satisfaction than fathers and sons, although the difference is not statistically significant. There is some suggestion that daughters have much lower health satisfaction than fathers or sons. Hence, it seems that daughters of low-income families have a greater probability than other family members of having poor health satisfaction. Their situation is of great

Table 7.5: Health satisfaction and family status, by income group: ordered probit regression

	Low income		Middle income		High income		Whole sample	
	Coefficient	Signif.	Coefficient	Signif.	Coefficient	Signif.	Coefficient	Signif.
Mother	-0.117	0.36	**-0.287**	0.03	**-0.381**	0.00	-0.256	0.00
Daughter	-0.353	0.18	-0.339	0.21	-0.118	0.68	-0.259	0.09
Son	-0.058	0.83	-0.433	0.10	-0.030	0.91	-0.177	0.23
Grandparent	0.164	0.62	-0.381	0.29	-0.340	0.56	-0.161	0.47
Other	-0.246	0.40	-0.323	0.30	-0.003	0.99	-0.208	0.25
Ln Y	-0.068	0.33	0.255	0.34	-0.056	0.54	**0.087**	0.01
Age	-0.015	0.00	-0.015	0.00	-0.012	0.02	-0.014	0.00
Education	0.093	0.05	0.103	0.01	0.114	0.00	0.114	0.00
Married	0.022	0.91	-0.253	0.29	0.168	0.52	-0.021	0.87
Stable partner	-0.210	0.44	-0.504	0.12	-0.076	0.82	-0.259	0.14
Separated	0.064	0.84	-0.439	0.20	0.157	0.65	-0.053	0.78
Divorced	-0.003	0.99	0.369	0.39	0.283	0.43	0.264	0.24
Widowed	-0.333	0.23	0.517	0.16	0.119	0.81	0.011	0.96
Cox and Snell pseudo-R^2	0.084		0.082		0.056		0.097	

Source: Author's own calculations based on own database.

concern: their health satisfaction is at risk not only because of their low household income but also because of their family status.

It is interesting to compare the situation of low-income families with that of high-income households. High-income family mothers have significantly less health satisfaction than fathers. The health satisfaction of the daughters and sons does not substantially differ from that of the fathers in low-income families.

The observed relationship between family status and health satisfaction can perhaps be explained by cultural patterns regarding the role of women (mothers and daughters) and men (fathers and sons). These cultural roles vary across income groups.

As Table 7.5 indicates, education has a positive impact on the probability of having excellent health satisfaction, and health satisfaction declines with age. These findings are evident across all income groups. Marital status does not seem to make a big difference in health satisfaction, with a likely exception for persons in a stable relationship or the divorced. On the basis of the results from the whole sample, it is clear that health satisfaction increases with income.

6   Breadwinner status and health satisfaction

Breadwinner status

The survey gathered information on personal self-reported breadwinner status, which is another relevant intra-household characteristic. Four categories were used: main breadwinner, secondary breadwinner, marginal breadwinner and no breadwinner. This variable provides information on a person's status with respect to his role in generating household income. Table 7.6 gives the breakdown according to breadwinner status and the corresponding average health satisfaction.

The role of breadwinner status in health satisfaction

As is observable in Table 7.6, differences in average health satisfaction across breadwinner status are relatively small. These differences – or their absence – could emerge because of the status itself or because of other sociodemographic and economic characteristics that are correlated to a person's breadwinner status. Hence, the following regression was carried out to study the role of breadwinner status on health satisfaction:

$$HS = \beta_0 + \beta_1 S_B + \beta_2 M_B + \beta_3 N_B + \beta_4 \ln Y + \phi X_{control} + \mu \qquad (7.2)$$

Table 7.6: Breadwinner status frequency and corresponding average health satisfaction

Breadwinner status	Percentage in sample	Average health satisfaction
Main breadwinner	46.5	58.5
Secondary breadwinner	22.9	59.9
Marginal breadwinner	18.0	56.3
No breadwinner	12.6	57.7
Total number of observations	1,535	

Source: Author's own calculations based on own database.

where:

HS refers to *health* satisfaction, a categorical variable;

S_B is a dichotomous variable, with a value of 1 if the person is a secondary breadwinner, and a value of 0 otherwise;

M_B is a dichotomous variable, with a value of 1 if the person is a marginal breadwinner, and a value of 0 otherwise;

N_B is a dichotomous variable, with a value of 1 if the person is no breadwinner, and a value of 0 otherwise;

$\ln Y$ refers to the logarithm of household income;

$X_{control}$ is a vector of the following control variables (ϕ is a vector of parameters):

Education: education in levels;

Age: age in years;

Marital status: vector of dichotomous variables about marital status, *single* was category of reference;

Gender: with a value of 1 for males and 0 for females.

The category of reference corresponds to *main* breadwinner.

The existence of substantial intra-household disparities in the health satisfaction of low-income families is a main concern of this investigation. It has been argued that large disparities could indicate that some household members are being marginalized from access to household resources, and that this marginalization could have pernicious effects on health satisfaction if household income is low.

If there are substantial intra-household disparities in health satisfaction in low-income (economically poor) families, then wellbeing inferences made on the basis of a household income would be inaccurate.[10]

Regression (7.2) is run for each income group subsample to further explore the relevance of breadwinner status in the relationship between household income and personal health satisfaction.[11] Table 7.7 shows

Table 7.7: Health satisfaction and breadwinner status, by income group: ordered probit regression, main breadwinner as reference category

	Low income		Middle income		High income		Whole sample	
	Coefficient	Signif.	Coefficient	Signif.	Coefficient	Signif.	Coefficient	Signif.
Secondary breadwinner	-0.280	0.09	-0.049	0.72	-0.056	0.67	-0.070	0.38
Marginal breadwinner	-0.243	0.08	-0.234	0.15	-0.314	0.05	-0.235	0.01
No breadwinner	-0.180	0.31	-0.353	0.03	-0.307	0.12	-0.290	0.00
Ln Y	-0.067	0.34	0.239	0.38	-0.050	0.58	**0.083**	0.02
Gender	0.029	0.80	0.130	0.25	0.189	0.08	0.125	0.05
Age	-0.015	0.00	-0.016	0.00	-0.015	0.01	-0.014	0.00
Education	0.086	0.06	0.099	0.01	0.111	0.01	0.114	0.00
Married	0.123	0.34	-0.071	0.57	0.001	0.99	0.017	0.81
Stable partner	-0.127	0.58	-0.308	0.23	-0.295	0.25	-0.223	0.11
Separated	0.128	0.66	-0.347	0.27	-0.020	0.95	-0.071	0.69
Divorced	0.012	0.98	0.502	0.19	0.105	0.76	0.232	0.28
Widowed	-0.204	0.39	0.622	0.07	0.100	0.82	0.035	0.84
Cox and Snell pseudo-R^2	0.088		0.090		0.061		0.104	

Source: Author's own calculations based on own database.

the results from the ordered-probit econometric exercise for each income group, as well as for the whole sample. It is noted that secondary and marginal breadwinners have a lower probability of being satisfied with their health with respect to the main breadwinner in low-income families. Secondary breadwinners have similar health satisfaction with respect to the main breadwinner in middle- and high-income families.

These findings indicate the possible existence of cooperative bargaining arrangements in low-income families. The next section explores further the relationship between a person's contribution to the household income and his health satisfaction.

The results in Table 7.7 also show that the impact of gender becomes more relevant as household income increases. Women enjoy similar health satisfaction to men in low-income families, but this is not the case in middle- or in high-income families, in particular.

7   Share in the household income

The previous section used self-reported breadwinner status to explore whether there is a difference in the relationship between health satisfaction and household income on the basis of a person's breadwinner role. The same issue can be addressed on the basis of the person's share in the household income. Let the share be defined as the ratio of the respondent's personal income (Y_{per}) over household income (Y_H):

$$S_{per/H} = \left(\frac{Y_{per}}{Y_H}\right) * 100. \tag{7.3}$$

Table 7.8 provides some basic statistics for $S_{per/H}$. As can be observed, the mean value for the share of a person's income in the household income is 58 per cent. One-fifth of the people in the survey have a nil share, meaning that they make no contribution to their household income. On the other hand, 37 per cent of the people in the survey have a 100 per cent share, indicating that they earn the totality of the household income.

Based on the cooperative bargaining family models, a person's greater share in income generation is associated with greater bargaining power within the household and subsequently attaining a cooperative equilibrium that is more favourable to him individually. Thus, if breadwinner status is of importance, then the health satisfaction of the person should rise as his share of personal income increases in the household income.

Table 7.8: Descriptive statistics: share of personal income in household income

Range	Percentage
$S_{per/H} = 0$	19.7
$50.0 \geq S_{per/H} > 0$	24.7
$100 > S_{per/H} > 50.0$	18.5
$S_{per/H} = 100$	37.1
Mean value for $S_{per/H}$	58.0

Source: Author's own calculations based on own database.

The following regression was run to determine whether health satisfaction is related to a person's share in the generation of household income:

$$HS = \varphi_0 + \varphi_1 \ln Y + \varphi_2 S_{per/H} + \omega X_{control} + \mu \qquad (7.4)$$

All the variables in regression (7.4) have already been defined. Table 7.9 shows the estimated parameters by income group as well as for the whole sample.

A person's share in the generation of his household income does have a significant impact in middle-income families, and the probability of that person enjoying high health satisfaction rises with his share. The relationship between a person's share in the generation of household income and his health satisfaction is slightly significant in low-income families. There is no relationship at all between these two variables in high-income families.

Hence, the results in Table 7.9 indicate that some cooperative bargaining elements with respect to the allocation of relevant resources for health satisfaction could be present in low- and middle-income families. It seems that major breadwinners can easily afford to be altruistic in high-income families.

8 Conclusion

As noted in the introductory chapter of this volume, a significant proportion of the health-related literature focuses on reported health.[12] This investigation addressed the issue of the kinds of intra-household arrangements that prevail with respect to health satisfaction. Using the case of Mexico, we argue that health satisfaction provides useful

Table 7.9: Health satisfaction and share in household income generation, by income group: ordered probit regression

	Low income		Middle income		High income		Whole sample	
	Coefficient	Signif.	Coefficient	Signif.	Coefficient	Signif.	Coefficient	Signif.
Share in household income	**0.002**	**0.10**	**0.004**	**0.01**	**0.000**	**0.84**	**0.002**	**0.04**
$\text{Ln} Y$	-0.152	0.13	0.294	0.28	-0.077	0.41	**0.101**	**0.01**
Gender	0.094	0.40	0.105	0.34	0.240	0.02	0.151	0.01
Age	-0.013	0.00	-0.016	0.00	-0.013	0.02	-0.014	0.00
Education	0.085	0.06	0.089	0.02	0.110	0.01	0.105	0.00
Married	0.153	0.25	-0.090	0.47	0.092	0.47	0.041	0.57
Stable partner	-0.096	0.67	-0.331	0.20	-0.165	0.52	-0.199	0.15
Separated	0.143	0.62	-0.300	0.34	0.107	0.73	-0.024	0.89
Divorced	0.055	0.89	0.451	0.24	0.247	0.48	0.262	0.22
Widowed	-0.210	0.38	0.696	0.05	-0.255	0.58	0.040	0.82
Cox and Snell pseudo-R^2	0.081		0.096		0.052		0.096	

Source: Author's own calculations based on own database.

information about a person's health, since it is not the same to be ill as it is to suffer from an illness. Family arrangements matter not only for the likelihood of a person becoming ill but also for the effect the illness has on a person's satisfaction. Subjective wellbeing places the health status of a person within his particular personal circumstances.

The intra-household distribution of health satisfaction is studied on the basis of testing the health satisfaction implications of alternative theories of the family, that is, communitarian or cooperative bargaining theories. Family status (being a father, mother, son, daughter, grand-parent or other) and breadwinner status (main, secondary, marginal and no breadwinner) are used as proxies for a person's bargaining power within the household. Then it is possible to test the communitarian versus cooperative bargaining theory of the family on the basis of whether the distribution of health satisfaction follows its expected pattern according to the person's bargaining power.

The main finding from the investigation is that household income has a larger explanatory capability than personal income in health satisfaction. This result hints that Mexican families do not exhibit extreme partnership arrangements with respect to allocating resources for health satisfaction.

Household income has larger explanatory power than household income per capita or household equivalent income. Thus, family-size depletion effects seem to be small in income having the capacity to generate health satisfaction. What matters for the health satisfaction of a person is the household income, not the family-size adjusted proxy. Consequently, it seems that there is some pooling of household resources within Mexican households, and that this pool of resources is available to everybody within the household as needed.

However, there are some disparities in health satisfaction within the family that could be associated with either cultural patterns or the intra-household distribution of power. Gender is noted to make a difference in health satisfaction, with women enjoying lower health satisfaction than men. In low-income families, daughters enjoy lower health satisfaction than fathers or sons, while mothers have lower health satisfaction in high-income families. This gender disparity could be explained by cultural patterns in the intra-household distribution of roles, or aspects such as ability to enter the labour market – topics which are covered in the next two chapters.

There are also some disparities in health satisfaction on the basis of the breadwinner status of the person and on the basis of his contribution to household income. These could indicate that some cooperative bargaining elements are present in low- and middle-income families in Mexico.

This investigation has shown that income-based poverty measures are very limited in serving as a proxy for some relevant wellbeing aspects, such as health satisfaction. The limitations of income-based poverty measures with respect to health satisfaction are many. First, these measures usually rely on household income per capita, whereas it has been shown that the relevant variable for health satisfaction is household income. Second, health satisfaction is not distributed uniformly within a household; thus, for a given household income, there are important intra-household disparities. Third, these intra-household disparities in health satisfaction can be explained by cultural patterns that discriminate against women, and by the cooperative bargaining elements present in family arrangements. However, the nature and intensity of these disparities vary across income groups.

The family is a fundamental institution in any society, but its nature varies across and within nations. Some nations may have more communitarian – and even altruistic – family arrangements, whereas in others more individualistic family arrangements based on cooperative bargaining equilibrium are common. The nature of these household arrangements does matter for the study of health. This chapter has shown that values and cultural patterns need to be incorporated into the analysis of social problems and in the design of social programmes that aim to enhance people's wellbeing.

Acknowledgements

This study was financially supported by an unrestricted educational grant from the Merck Company Foundation, the philanthropic arm of Merck and Company Inc., Whitehouse Station, New Jersey, USA. This chapter is a revised version of a paper presented at the UNU–WIDER conference on Advancing Health Equity, Helsinki, 29–30 September 2006.

Notes

1. This investigation uses a gender-biased language for simplicity of exposition; there is no intention to offend or marginalize either gender.
2. If resources are really pooled together, as is expected in a communitarian family, then household income should be a more relevant variable than personal income in explaining health satisfaction.

3. If there are no depletion effects, then household income should be a more relevant variable than household income per capita or household equivalent income in explaining health satisfaction. If this were the case, it could imply that any household member is fully insured by the household group, and that he can have access to all household resources in case of need.

4. The investigation restricts itself to the health domain. It is possible that, in cooperative bargaining families, bargaining power asymmetries make an impact in other life domains, for example the economic or consumption domain, but not in the health domain. Thus, the chapter studies the existence of communitarian or cooperative bargaining families with respect to the allocation of resources for health satisfaction only.

5. A vast literature has used the so-called objective indicators to study household arrangements and intra-household allocation of resources. See Lazear and Michael (1988), Carlin (1991), Bourguignon et al. (1994), Thomas (1990, 1993, 1997), and Haddad et al. (1997). These studies are not based on self-reported satisfaction measures and are basically interested in standards of living.

6. I am grateful to CONACYT, Mexico, for a grant that supported this survey.

7. See Rojas (2007b) for an in-depth study of equivalence scales.

8. Household income per capita does not take into consideration the fact that economies of scale may exist at the household level. It also presumes equal weights for all household members, regardless of their age. Household equivalent income measures, on the other hand, assume arbitrarily defined weights and scale economies.

9. Income is measured in Mexican pesos. One peso was added to each figure in order to avoid zero-value incomes, which would be problematic for logarithm calculations.

10. The low goodness of fit of regressions between health satisfaction and income indicates that income does not provide a good approximation of a person's subjective health situation, even if no inequality exists in the intra-household allocation of resources for health satisfaction. However, this investigation focuses on the intra-household distribution of health satisfaction at different income levels; it does not stress the issue of low goodness-of-fit coefficients and the possibility that the average relationship between health satisfaction and income might not be representative for all persons.

11. A further economic analysis would hypothesize that allocating household resources to the pursuit of greater health satisfaction for main and secondary breadwinners could be a rational household decision since their health is more valuable in economic (income-generating) terms for all household members. According to an alternative explanation, persons who are ill or in poor health are less likely to participate actively in the labour force and are consequently less likely to be main or secondary breadwinners. This explanation introduces endogeneity to the analysis and necessitates panel data to address the issue.

12. They also bring with them an array of issues associated with statistical reporting bias – elements of which are reported on and discussed in Chapter 1.

References

Becker, G. S. (1973) 'A Theory of Marriage: Part I', *Journal of Political Economy*, 81 (4): 813–46.

Becker, G. S. (1974) 'A Theory of Marriage: Part II'. *Journal of Political Economy*, 82 (2): S11–S26.

Becker, G. S. (1981) *A Treatise on the Family* (Cambridge MA: Harvard University Press).

Bergstrom, T. (1997) 'A Survey of Theories of the Family', in M. Rosenzweig and O. Stark (eds), *Handbook of Family and Population Economics* (Amsterdam: North Holland).

Binmore, K. (1987) *The Economics of Bargaining* (Cambridge MA: Blackwell).

Bourguignon, F., M. Browning, P. A. Chiappori and V. Lechene (1994) 'Intrahousehold Allocation of Consumption: Some Evidence on Canadian Data', *Journal of Political Economy*, 1002 (6): 1067–96.

Carlin, P. (1991) 'Intra-family Bargaining and Time Allocation', in T. P. Schultz (ed.), *Research in Population Economics*, Vol. 7 (Greenwich CT: JAI Press), 215–43.

Haddad, L., J. Hoddinott and H. Alderman (eds) (1997), *Intrahousehold Resource Allocation in Developing Countries: Models, Methods and Policy* (Baltimore: Johns Hopkins University Press).

Hart, G. (1990) 'Imagined Unities: Constructions of "the Household" in Economic Theory', in S. Ortiz (ed.), *Understanding Economic Theories* (Lanham: University Press of America).

Headey, B. and A. Wearing (1992) *Understanding Happiness: A Theory of Subjective Wellbeing* (Melbourne: Longman Cheshire).

Headey, B., E. Holmstrom and A. J. Wearing (1985) 'Models of Wellbeing and Ill-Being', *Social Indicators Research*, 17: 211–34.

Lazear, E. P. and R. T. Michael (1988) *Allocation of Income within the Household* (Chicago: University of Chicago Press).

Lundberg, S. and R. Pollak (1993) 'Separate Spheres Bargaining and the Marriage Market', *Journal of Political Economy*, 101 (2): 988–1010.

Lundberg, S. and R. Pollak (1996) 'Bargaining and Distribution in Marriage', *Journal of Economic Perspectives*, 10 (4): 139–58.

Lundberg, S., R. Pollak and T. Wales (1997) 'Do Husbands and Wives Pool Their Resources? Evidence from the UK Child Benefit', *Journal of Human Resources*, 32 (3): 463–80.

McElroy, M. B. (1985) 'The Joint Determination of Household Membership and Market Work: The Case of Young Men', *Journal of Labor Economics*, 3 (3): 293–316.

McElroy, M. B. (1990) 'The Empirical Content of Nash-Bargained Household Behaviour', *Journal of Human Resources*, 25 (4): 559–83.

Manser, M. and M. Brown (1980) 'Marriage and Household Decision-Making: A Bargaining Analysis', *International Economic Review*, 21 (1): 31–44.

Pollak, R. A. (1994) 'For Better of Worse: The Roles of Power in Models of Distribution within Marriage', *American Economic Review*, 84 (2): 148–52.

Pollak, R. A. (2002) 'Gary Becker's Contributions to Family and Household Economics'. NBER Working Paper W9232 (Cambridge MA: National Bureau of Economic Research).

Rojas, M. (2005) 'A Conceptual-Referent Theory of Happiness: Heterogeneity and Its Consequences', *Social Indicators Research*, 74 (2): 261–94.

Rojas, M. (2006a) 'The Complexity of Wellbeing: A Life-Satisfaction Conception and a Domains-of-Life Approach', in I. Gough and A. McGregor (eds), *Researching Wellbeing in Developing Countries* (Cambridge: Cambridge University Press).

Rojas, M. (2006b) 'Wellbeing and the Complexity of Poverty: A Subjective Wellbeing Approach', in M. McGillivray and M. Clarke (eds), *Understanding Human Wellbeing* (Tokyo: United Nations University Press).

Rojas, M. (2007a) 'Communitarian versus Individualistic Arrangements in the Family: What and Whose Income Matters for Happiness?', in R. J. Estes (ed.), *Advancing Quality of Life in a Turbulent World* (Guildford: Springer Verlag).

Rojas, M. (2007b) 'Estimating Equivalence Scales in Mexico: A Subjective Wellbeing Approach', *Oxford Development Studies*, 35 (3): 272–93.

Thomas, D. (1990) 'Intra-Household Resource Allocation: An Inferential Approach', *Journal of Human Resources*, 25 (4): 635–64.

Thomas, D. (1993) 'The Distribution of Income and Expenditure within the Household', *Annales d'économie et de Statistiques*, 29: 109–36.

Thomas, D. (1997) 'Incomes, Expenditures, and Health Outcomes: Evidence on Intrahousehold Resource Allocation', *Intrahousehold Resource Allocation in Developing Countries: Models, Methods and Policy* (Baltimore: Johns Hopkins University Press).

Van Praag, B. M. S. and A. Ferrer-i-Carbonell (2004) *Happiness Quantified: A Satisfaction Calculus Approach* (New York: Oxford University Press).

Van Praag, B. M. S., P. Frijters and A. Ferrer-i-Carbonell (2003) 'The Anatomy of Subjective Wellbeing', *Journal of Economic Behaviour & Organization*, 51 (1): 29–49.

Veenhoven, R. (1996) 'Developments in Satisfaction Research', *Social Indicators Research*, 37: 1–45.

Vogel, J. (2003) 'The Family', *Social Indicators Research*, 64: 393–435.

8
Individual and Collective Resources and Women's Health in Morocco

Marie-Claude Martin

1 Introduction

Poverty reduction policies are considered to help improve the health status of poor populations. Indeed, individual level of income is thought to be associated with the capacity to adopt and choose a life-style and environment favourable to health; it is generally accepted that a decent level of income provides the protection necessary to maintain and produce an adequate level of health. However, on a more aggregate level, matters are different. For example, the relationship between the public resources available at the municipal or regional level and the health of the individuals in the municipality or region is not as well understood and is the subject of some debate. Some questions therefore seem to be in order: Can the protective effect on health provided by an individual's income be reproduced instead (or in addition) by the level of collective resources?[1] Can the individual's capacity to produce health be increased or constrained by the presence or absence of appropriate collective resources given the level of individual resources? If yes, under which conditions?

In the literature, these questions tend not to be dealt with or are at best raised only indirectly. Several studies do measure the importance of place ('neighbourhood effect') by introducing measures of composition, that is measures that reflect the distribution and concentration of individual characteristics in a given environment (Macintyre et al. 1993, 2002). Very often these include such measures as level of poverty or income inequality, employment levels or racial profile (Pickett and Pearl 2001; Wilkinson et al. 1998; Kawachi et al. 1999; Kennedy et al. 1996; Townsend et al. 1988; Marmot et al. 1991; Deaton 1999, 2001a, 2001b). Less often, policy variables that reflect the level and type of social and economic services and infrastructures offered in a community or a region (Lynch 2000) are introduced directly. Studies of developing countries are even rarer and are generally limited to analysing the effects of infrastructures directly related to the risk of disease transmission, especially those involving potable water, sanitation and, to some extent, electricity and health services (Wang 2003; Thomas et al. 1996; Lavy et al. 1996; Rosenzweig and Wolpin 1982; Van der Klaauw and Wang 2004; Shi 2000).

In developing countries, some communities, regions and segments of the population are particularly disadvantaged in terms of access to public resources, and the uneven availability of such resources may contribute to the development of health disparities. It may also act as a modifying factor with respect to the (accepted) associations between health and socioeconomic status as measured, for example, by income and education. It therefore seems worthwhile to consider the interactions between available collective and individual resources and capabilities in the production of health.

In exploring these questions of the contribution of public resources to women's capacity to produce better health and of the potential interactions between collective and individual resources and vulnerability factors, this chapter makes use of the theoretical proposals and analytic tools favoured by the human development approach (UNDP 1990; Ranis and Stewart 2000), social epidemiology and determinants of health (Frenk et al. 1994), health production models (Grossman 1972, 2000), and Sen's body of theoretical work on capabilities (1987). The capability approach provides a unique perspective since it recognizes the importance of considering the freedom that individuals have to convert public and private resources and instrumental capabilities, such as education, into health and other benefits. It makes the distinction between access to resources and the freedom and the capacity to use them to achieve a set of functionings. The production approach derived from Grossman's perspective (1972) enables us in addition to explore and formalize questions of productivity, technical effectiveness, and interdependence between the two types of resources considered as inputs in the production of health.

2 Resources and health

There are deemed to be two pathways by which collective resources (public services and infrastructure) are associated with health status. The first is indirect: access to and use of the resources make it possible to increase the productivity of individual health production factors, particularly the level of education and income. The second pathway is direct: collective resources, which are associated with a community's level of social and economic development, create a 'health-promoting' environment. In Morocco, for example, a project to improve access to water is reported to have yielded direct health benefits by significantly reducing the prevalence of diarrhoeal diseases among children less than five years of age.[2] It also had indirect and certainly longer-term benefits by considerably increasing school registration and retention rates for girls (Klees et al. 1999).

I have adopted a production approach in order to estimate the capacity of women at given levels of vulnerability to produce health with both their own resources and the collective ones available to them.

3   The model

The model is formulated such that the production of individual health, H_{ij}, depends on a vector of independent variables of individual and family resources – education (I_{ij}) and a measure of wealth (Y_{ij}) – and on the availability of collective resources in a given region j along with other population attributes (z_j). The production of health also depends on initial conditions, represented by a vector of independent individual-vulnerability variables A_{ij}, which affect the capacity of women to convert their own resources into health. The collective resources vector (z_j) affects health production by increasing the productivity of individual resources, for example, through the introduction of a technological advance. For a given quantity of individual resources, the presence of collective resources thus increases the production of health. An individual's 'production technology' may then be written as:

$$H_{ij} = A_{ij} \, f_{ij} \, (I_{ij} \, (z_j), \, Y_{ij} \, (z_j)),$$

where f_{ij} may have a different functional form for each woman i.

The model thus points out the relative contributions of individual and collective characteristics and resources in the production of women's health, given individual vulnerability factors, and considers that the effectiveness of collective resources will depend on how well they fit with individual characteristics.

The variables in the model

The variable of interest in the model, H_{ij}, is health status as perceived by Moroccan women. Because of their vulnerability factors (A_{ij}) – age,[3] number of children and diagnosed morbidity – which may affect the productivity of other inputs,[4] women do not all have the same ability to be healthy and to transform their resources into health.

Individual and family resources are captured by the socioeconomic status of women and households; the two measures used are education (I_{ij}) and their standard of living (Y_{ij}). The inclusion of more than one measure of individual socioeconomic status allows for a more robust estimation of the relationship between collective (or purely contextual) resources and health status (Pickett and Pearl 2001).

Being educated is instrumental to achieve a given level of health. The higher the level of education, the better an individual can adopt or change to a healthy lifestyle, understand the risks associated with different behaviours, assimilate information of a medical nature, and follow prescriptions properly (Strauss and Thomas 1995; Caldwell 1979). As a direct input, education is a measure of knowledge, power and control (of lifestyle, fertility and so on). Education is also an indirect input: it measures the capacity to seek out and use an optimal combination of inputs and resources conducive to health (Drèze and Sen 1989) and to lower the price associated with investment in health through greater productivity (Leibowitz 2004).

The second dimension of socioeconomic status, standard of living, captures the financial capacity to obtain goods and services that may be used to ensure, maintain, or enhance a healthy environment, adequate nutrition, the seeking of care and so on (Sastry 1996; Strauss and Thomas 1995; Case 2002). It is generally accepted that there is a gradient between health and income, at least for women in developing countries and particularly in a middle-income country such as Morocco (Gwatkin et al. 2000). Standard of living, like education, is also considered an indirect input in health production, since it affects access to and use of the various collective resources available.

I have selected a measure that reflects long-term wealth, as determined by household possessions, rather than one that captures seasonal or annual income and so may vary over a short span of time. The choice of such a measure is also warranted by the issue of endogeneity: a measure of possessions or wealth may be considered exogenous and thus not to vary as a function of women's health except in the event of a catastrophe in which a household would have to dispose of its assets to finance emergency care.[5]

The standard-of-living measure is based on a factor analysis. A composite index is derived from different measures of possessions (telephone, kitchen range and so on), housing characteristics (roofing and flooring materials), and the socioeconomic status of the head of household. This type of index is widely used in the literature on the subject (Filmer and Pritchett 1998; Lindelow 2004).

Since we are studying the hypothesis of a relationship between the availability of collective resources (z_j) and health, the model uses measures of the availability (rather than the use) of public goods and services. The measures are density of primary schools and of health centres per capita. Their proximity (or subsidized access) encourages their use by reducing the costs entailed.

The other collective resources – such as water, electricity and sanitation infrastructures, means of transport, institutions of law and order – are incorporated in a comprehensive measure of the development of the *commune* (the municipality). This indicator captures both the potential of a health-promoting environment (direct pathway) and the opportunities it offers for improving individual health production capabilities (indirect pathway). Like women's standard of living, the level of development of the commune is a synthetic index based on a factor analysis.

Collective resources are associated with health independently of a commune's compositional characteristics, which are the result of the aggregation of individual characteristics. The model also estimates the effects of collective characteristics that are not 'purely' contextual. I have introduced two such compositional measures: the incidence of poverty, as measured by the percentage of the population living below the rural poverty line, and a measure of income distribution in the commune.

The data are drawn from three sources: Ministère de la Santé Publique, Royaume du Maroc (1999), and Direction de la Statistique (2000a, 2000b), which lay out the public and private infrastructure for each of Morocco's municipalities. The characteristics of the sample and the distribution of the variables in the model are presented in Table 8.1.

4   Calculations

In light of the hierarchical structure of the databases, I have used a multilevel analysis for my empirical calculations for the model (Goldstein 1995; Snijders and Bosker 1999; Rice and Jones 1997). The reconstituted database spans five hierarchically arranged levels: women, households, communes, provinces and regions. However, the model uses a three-level structure: women (i), communes (j) and regions (k). The first two and the last two units of observation were merged, and the structure of the observations was thus preserved.

Table 8.1: Characteristics of sample and variables

	Reference category (frequency)	Contrast category (frequency)
Dependent variable: health status (HS)		
Good (*n* = 551; 21.1%)	Fair (*n* = 1,434; 55%)	Poor (*n* = 623; 23.9%)
Independent variables		
Variables (distribution)		
Women (*n* = 2,608)		
Age (mean = 32.5; SD = 9.0)	21+ years (*n* = 2,338; 89.6%)	15–20 years (*n* = 270; 10.4%)
Children (mean = 4.2; SD = 3.2)	1+ children (*n* = 2,306; 88.4%)	No children (*n* = 302; 11.6%)
Education (literate or not)	No (*n* = 2,371; 90.9%)	Yes (*n* = 237; 9.1%)
Reported morbidity	None (*n* = 2,014; 77.2%)	At least 1 (*n* = 594; 22.8%)
Households (*n* = 2,170)		
Standard of living (SoL)	Lowest (*n* = 790; 36.4%)	Low (*n* = 877; 40.4%)
		Middle (*n* = 336; 15.5%)
		High (*n* = 117; 5.4%)
		Highest (*n* = 50; 2.3%)
Communes (*n* = 94)		
Primary schools per 100,000 inhabitants (mean = 118; SD = 64)	>150 schools (*n* = 23; 24.5%)	86–150: (*n* = 40; 42.6%)
		<86: (*n* = 31; 33%)
Health centres and dispensaries per 100,000 inhabitants (mean = 12.5; SD = 9.6)	>17 dispensaries (*n* = 19; 20.2%)	8–17: (*n* = 44; 46.8%)
		<8: (*n* = 31; 33%)
Level of development	High (*n* = 29; 30.9%)	Low (*n* = 65; 69.1%)
Provinces (*n* = 44)		
Poverty incidence (mean = 19.6; SD = 13.6)	Low (*n* = 16; 36.3%)	High (*n* = 28; 63.7%)

Source: See text.

Given the nature of the dependent variable, I have used an ordered multinomial logistic regression (Fielding 2002; Fielding et al. 2003) to respect the underlying order in the scale of the women's responses, namely good, fair or poor perceived health.

All the calculations are based on a restricted iterative generalized least squares (RIGLS) procedure and a second-order approximation by penalized quasi-likelihood. The calculations were made using Version 1.1 of MlwiN (including the MULTICAT programme for ordered multinomial models). The descriptive analyses were carried out with SPSS for Windows 11.5.

5   Results

Two series of results are presented here. The first deals with the complete sample and explores the associations between vulnerability, individual and collective resources, and the perceived health status of women. The second explores more particularly the question of the interactions between the characteristics of the women and those of the communes in which they live.

Table 8.2 sets out the results of the ordered multinomial model in five stages. The empty model includes only one random scale parameter with levels 2 and 3 to measure variations in health status between communes and regions. Models 1, 2 and 3 provide estimates of the fixed effects of individual (and household) variables and the presence of morbidity. Model 4 shows the fixed effects of the community variables, and model 5 is the final model. The coefficients, standard deviations and odds ratios are provided for each of the variables. The bold odds ratios are associated with coefficients significant at a level of $p < 0.5$

The reference population for all the models is uneducated women over 20 years of age who have children, whose relative standard of living is more than one half standard deviation below the mean, and who have no reported morbidity. The reference population lives in communes with more than 150 primary schools per 100,000 inhabitants and more than 17 primary healthcare facilities per 100,000 inhabitants. The incidence of poverty in these communes is under 30 per cent and the level of development is higher than the mean.

According to the results of the empty model, the median proportion of women reporting they are in good health (HS_g) is 18 per cent. Prevalence varies significantly between communes and between regions, thus warranting the three-level analysis.

Models 1 to 3 confirm the expected associations between the individual variables and perception of health. The vulnerability factors – age, number of children and reported morbidity – are strongly associated with the perception women have of their state of health. Controlling for the three vulnerability factors and education, which is also associated with the perception of good health, a strong relationship emerges between health and standard of living.[6] The women high on the scale of the composite standard-of-living index (mean + three standard deviations) report they are in good health more frequently (OR: 2.48; 95 per cent CI: 1.35 to 4.56) than the other groups.[7]

Models 4 and 5 suggest that the density of primary schools is significantly associated with a perception of good health. Communes with a very low school density, fewer than 86 schools per 100,000 inhabitants, seem to differ from the high-density reference communes. No model, though, shows an association between perception of health and density of health centres and dispensaries or the other communal variables, such as the communal development index, incidence of poverty, or inequality of income. I shall discuss this result in more depth later.

The random part of the multinomial model confirms that a not insignificant part of the variation in health in rural Morocco is associated with characteristics other than individual ones. The intra-class correlation (ICC) coefficients are 0.05 and 0.12 for the communes and regions respectively. Given the structure of the estimation model, these coefficients must be interpreted cautiously, but they may suggest that 5 per cent and 12 per cent of the variance in health status stems from the variation between communes and regions.

The final multinomial model gives us correlation coefficients of 4 per cent and 9 per cent respectively, with the proportion of explained variance at 12 per cent. The unexplained proportion is 88 per cent, of which 73 per cent comes from individual characteristics. It is not surprising that this should be the case, since it is primarily individual factors, such as genetics, that are the most important source of heterogeneity in health (Wagstaff et al. 2001). Such factors often go unobserved in this type of analysis.

6   Interactions between individual and collective resources

In the second set of calculations, I explore the hypothesis not only that the characteristics of the communes in which the women live are associated with their health but also that the association varies to some extent

Table 8.2: Ordered multinomial model of self-rated health

	Empty model			Model 1			Model 2	
	Coeff.	s.e.	Cum. P	Coeff.	s.e.	Cum. P	Coeff.	s.e
Responses								
HS_g	−1.52	0.20	0.18	−2.15	0.22	0.10	−1.34	0.1
HS_f	1.29	0.20	0.78	0.83	0.22	0.70	1.55	0.1
	Coeff.	s.e.	OR	Coeff.	s.e.	OR	Coeff.	s.e
Variables								
Age = 20 years (ref: > 20)				0.96	0.15	**2.61**		
0 children (ref: 1 child or +)				0.95	0.14	**2.59**		
Educated (ref: uneducated)				0.58	0.15	**1.79**		
Standard of living (ref: SoL = μ − 0.5 sd)								
SoL = μ + 3sd				0.85	0.31	**2.34**		
μ + 1.5sd < SoL < μ + 3sd				0.67	0.21	**1.95**		
μ + 0.5sd = SoL = μ + 1.5sd				0.57	0.14	**1.77**		
μ − 0.5sd < SoL < μ + 0.5sd				0.25	0.1	**1.28**		
1 morbidity (ref: none)							−1.01	
Density of schools (ref: D = 150 schools per 100,000 inhabitants)								
86 < D < 150								
D = 86								
Development index low (ref: high)								
Incidence of poverty high (ref: low)								
Variances								
Level 2	0.21	0.06		0.19	0.05		0.2	
Level 3	0.46	0.21		0.49	0.22		0.38	
Like	4757.2			4160.7				
Intra-class correlation								
ICC communes	0.05							
ICC regions	0.12							
Explained variance								
Unexplained variance								

Source: Author's calculations.

	Model 3			Model 4			Model 5		
Cum. P	Coeff.	s.e.	Cum. P	Coeff	s.e.	Cum. P	Coeff.	s.e.	Cum. P
0.21	−1.96	0.21	0.12	−1.1	0.26	0.25	−1.69	0.23	0.16
0.82	1.01	0.21	0.73	1.11	0.26	0.75	1.35	0.23	0.79
OR	Coeff.	s.e.	OR	Coeff	s.e.	OR	Coeff.	s.e.	OR
	0.87	0.15	**2.39**				0.86	0.15	**2.36**
	0.88	0.14	**2.41**				0.88	0.14	**2.41**
	0.56	0.15	**1.75**				0.56	0.15	**1.75**
	0.91	0.31	**2.48**				0.95	0.31	**2.59**
	0.67	0.21	**1.95**				0.69	0.22	**1.99**
	0.55	0.14	**1.73**				0.56	0.14	**1.75**
	0.27	0.1	**1.31**				0.29	0.1	**1.34**
0.36	−0.89	0.10	**0.41**				−0.87	0.10	**0.42**
				−0.3	0.18	0.74	−0.23	0.17	0.79
				−0.41	0.19	**0.66**	−0.39	0.17	**0.68**
				−0.22	0.13	0.80	−0.19	0.13	0.83
				−0.2	0.15	0.82			
	0.16	0.05		0.19	0.05		0.15	0.05	
	0.41	0.18		0.42	0.19		0.34	0.16	
	3939.7			4752.6			3927.8		
	0.04						0.04		
	0.11						0.09		
							0.12		
							0.88		

with the level of the individual resources the women have at their disposal and their own capacity to use the available resources to achieve a desirable level of health. In other words, there are interactions between characteristics of the individual and those of the collectivity, especially access to public resources. For example, the poorest women may derive relatively greater benefit from the available collective resources than the wealthiest women if the resources are such that the poor can use and understand them. However, if the collective resources are too specialized or obviously too expensive, it is the more educated or wealthier women who will derive relatively greater benefit from them. To test this hypothesis, I disaggregated the total sample, breaking it down into four subsamples defined by the composite standard-of-living index. I then ran the calculations for the complete sample, adding the interaction terms associated with the key variables tested with the subsamples.

On the whole, in rural Morocco 21 per cent of women reported that their health status was good. The most affluent did so in a greater proportion than did women with the lowest standard of living; 35 per cent of the former and fewer than 14 per cent of the latter said their health is good, even though the incidence of morbidity for both groups is very similar. The proportion knowing how to read and write differs greatly depending on standard of living: 73 per cent of the wealthiest women are educated in contrast to only 2 per cent of the most disadvantaged ones. The proportion of women under 20 is the same in both groups, but there is a substantial difference between the wealthiest and poorest women in terms of the number who have no children. In addition, fewer than 3 per cent of women from the highest standard-of-living segment but nearly 45 per cent of the poorest women live in the 32 communes considered to have a low level of development. If we further refine the disaggregation of communes in terms of level of development and consider the six least developed of the 32 communes, 93 per cent of their inhabitants fall into the most disadvantaged segment of the population.

Table 8.3 lays out the results of the ordered multinomial analysis of self-rated health by standard-of-living segment.[8] Morbidity is the only individual variable that presents a significant association with health for all segments. Still, the odds ratios demonstrate a marked spread from 0.85 for the wealthiest segment to 0.41 for the poorest. The odds ratios for the two other vulnerability variables, age and number of children, also display a wide spread: they are more than twice as high for the poorest segments as for the wealthiest ones. The negative effects of age and number of children seem to increase as standard of living falls.

Table 8.3: Multinomial model of self-rated health stratified by standard of living

	Stratum 1 'wealthy'			Stratum 2			Stratum 3			Stratum 4 'poor'			Total population		
Responses	Coeff.	s.e.	Cum. P	Coeff.	s.e.	Cum. P	Coeff.	s.e.	Cum. P	Coeff.	s.e.	Cum. P	Coeff.	s.e.	Cum. P
HS_g	0.35	0.06	0.59	-0.45	0.32	0.39	-1.1	0.28	0.25	-1.56	0.24	0.17	-1.07	0.18	0.26
HS_f	0.86	0.06	0.70	2.39	0.35	0.92	2	0.28	0.88	1.69	0.24	0.84	1.93	0.19	0.87
	Coeff.	s.e.	OR	Coeff.	s.e.	OR	Coeff.	s.e.	OR	Coeff.	s.e.	OR	Coeff.	s.e.	OR
Variables															
Age ≤ 20 years (ref: > 20)	0.13	0.08	1.14	0.75	0.4	2.12	0.98	0.22	2.66	0.75	0.27	2.12	0.85	0.15	2.34
0 children (ref: 1+ child)	0.05	0.07	1.05	0.72	0.35	2.05	0.98	0.21	2.66	0.95	0.26	2.59	0.87	0.14	2.39
Educated (ref: uneducated)	0.14	0.04	1.15	0.28	0.29	1.32	0.57	0.24	1.77	0.2	0.47	1.22	0.69	0.14	1.99
1 morbidity (ref: none)	-0.16	0.05	0.85	-0.96	0.26	0.38	-0.92	0.16	0.40	-0.88	0.17	0.41	-0.88	0.1	0.41
Density of schools (ref: D ≥ 150 schools per 100,000 inhabitants)															
86 < D < 150	-0.01	0.07	0.99	-0.73	0.37	0.48	-0.46	0.28	0.63	-0.49	0.25	0.61	-0.46	0.21	0.63
D ≤ 86	-0.07	0.07	0.93	-0.8	0.38	0.45	-0.86	0.29	0.42	-0.62	0.29	0.55	-0.62	0.22	0.54
Development index low (ref: high)	-0.14	0.12	0.87	-0.15	0.36	0.86	-0.36	0.22	0.70	-0.44	0.22	0.72	-0.44	0.18	0.64
Variance															
Level 2	0.16	0.01		0.46	0.19		0.61	0.15		0.47	0.13		0.47	0.09	
Intra-class correlation															
ICC communes[a]	0.05	[]		0.12	0.16		0.16	[0.17]		0.13	[0.14]		0.13	[0.15]	

Note: [a] The intra-class correlation coefficient in square brackets is the coefficient associated with the empty model (without explanatory variables).
Source: Author's calculations.

Education, meanwhile, is associated with the perception of health for the wealthiest segment.

The results with respect to the effects of communal resources are particularly interesting. Although there is no perfectly linear progression in the odds ratios, the less wealthy segments and the wealthier one still present a contrast. The greater the women's individual wealth, the weaker the association between the setting in which the women live and their health status. For the wealthiest segment, no collective resource is associated with health; the odds ratios approach unity for each of the communal variables. The more limited the wealth of the individual, the more sensitive the health status becomes to setting and the stronger the relationship between the different collective resources and health.[9] The ratios fall into a range of 0.4 to 0.6 for primary schools.

The presence of public resources, particularly primary schools, would therefore seem to be relatively more strongly associated with the health of poor women than wealthy ones. We should note, though, that this association does not necessarily seem to extend to the poorest segment, evidencing an accessibility problem for those who are most deprived. The level of development of the commune, as presented here, is a composite of several factors, each of which differs in its relative importance in the perception of health depending on the standard of living of the women. For the poorest, electricity and water-purification systems seem to be the most discriminating factors.

Our analyses suggest, moreover, that the results obtained regarding the respective contributions of individual and communal factors to health status by standard-of-living segment are similar to those that can be obtained when the sample is stratified on the basis of education. Since education is instrumental in being healthy, I redid the previous analyses and obtained similar results. It is interesting to note that the income effect seems stronger for educated women, although the progression up to the four income levels is not constant or significant. This result tends to support my hypotheses that, the more educated women are, the more effectively income is used, allowing for better health production. Education thus interacts with resources and the vulnerability factors in the production function. Nonetheless, the association with standard of living is not negligible for uneducated women; to some extent, income seems to be a substitute for education for them.

No communal characteristics are apparently associated with the perception of health by educated women. For uneducated women, there is an association with both school density and level of development. It would seem that, in health production, the type of collective resources available might make up for these women's lack of formal education.

7 Discussion

With the specifications and form of the model I have adopted, empirical calculation does not allow me to explicitly determine the extent of the direct and indirect contributions of collective resources to the improvement of health. However, it does allow me to calculate the total 'effects' and their relative importance in explaining variations in state of health. My results suggest that the presence and number of primary schools enhance their accessibility and use by reducing the relative cost they entail (proximity). The results suggest too that primary schools may respond appropriately to women's educational needs, help increase their general and specific level of education, and consequently increase their effectiveness with regard to health production, or that the schools' proximity may allow women to allocate more time to other income-generating pursuits. The presence of such resources may also have a leverage effect, attracting other investments to the commune and increasing the potential for and diversity of jobs and sources of individual income. School density thus also seems to have an indirect effect on the perception of health by Moroccan women.

As for interactions between individual and collective resources, the results of the stratified analyses suggest that the quantity and diversity of available collective resources (particularly primary schools, but to some degree the level of development of the commune as well) affect the capacity to produce health, most especially for the most deprived or least educated women. The 'production technology' differs according to the characteristics of the women. For the poorest, availability and accessibility are critical and have to make up for the lack of individual resources; for the wealthiest, more specialized services and resources, which demand a minimum income or education level, will allow them to improve their state of health at the margin. One may thus suggest that the profile of the target population will determine whether the nature and quality of services are associated with population health.

This observation also contributes to explaining at least partially why I found no association between health infrastructure and health status, as reported previously. It is an indication of a lack of access to or a lack of quality of the services provided and it is central to the capability approach where, no matter what the level of resources, the capacity and the freedom to use them are non-existent. We should note though that this result could also be explained by the type of infrastructures considered and by using self-rated health rather than an indicator of ill-health.

Although interactions between collective and individual resources do not seem to be significantly associated with health in the model with the total sample, my results do at least support the hypothesis of the additive effects of individual characteristics and certain contextual ones. The results suggest that the characteristics of each different segment of the population must be considered before one may conclude that there are no contextual effects associated with the presence of collective resources. Even in a relatively homogeneous population (such as that of rural women), public investments may well affect the most deprived and the best off differentially. One can only imagine what may be overlooked with aggregate national- and international-level data.

The results also suggest that when we take into account the diversity among women and control for vulnerability factors (age and number of children) and initial state of health (presence of morbidity), standard of living remains an important determinant of health. Indeed, the results confirm the presence of a gradient, even within a population that is, by and large, as relatively homogeneous as that of rural women.

The results also show that income is more closely associated with the health status of the most educated women, suggesting that being educated may increase the effectiveness of individual health production. All things being equal, at equivalent income levels, one dirham would thus 'produce' more health for an educated woman than for an uneducated one.

It seems then that there are interactions between individual resources and vulnerability factors similar to the interactions between primary schools and individual resources. The results suggest, in fact, that experienced morbidity, age and number of children do not seem to affect the most and least affluent women in the same way. Income level and education apparently provide protection against individual risk factors.

8   Conclusion

The chapter extends the series by focusing on issues of individual and collective resource modelling, with the results suggesting that any intervention that jointly tackles individual, family, communal or regional mediators of women's socioeconomic status is likely to help improve their health. The results validate the proposition that individual resources contribute to improve health status and that individuals' freedoms to convert these resources into health depend on their vulnerability factors. Accessing collective resources, particularly the number of primary schools in my example, may also reinforce these capabilities. Any type of intervention that gives rise to greater individual and collective 'wealth' and capabilities may potentially make the environment more conducive to the production of health for individuals and the population. The results show, however, that, in choosing types of investments, consideration must be given not only to the health objectives but also to the initial conditions, that is, socioeconomic status and population vulnerability factors. The expected social benefits of public investments and collective resources will be that much greater if the capacity of individuals to access them – especially their capacity to internalize the return – is taken into account.

In addition, the results also suggest that public resources from different spheres of activity may create positive externalities with respect to health since they can increase the capacity of individuals and populations to be healthy. It therefore seems important to consider and include health benefits in calculating the expected returns of public investments in areas of activity other than health, most notably education. Nor must we ignore the possibility that investments that seem to yield individual returns may also create positive externalities benefiting the whole community. For example, Alderman et al. (2003) have shown that educating women affects the health not only of their own children but of the children in their 'neighbourhood' as well. There are important implications here for national and international policies designed to achieve, for example, the Millennium Development Goals. The argument thus exists to treat these goals as interconnected rather than as 'silos', each left to the relevant sectoral specialists and tackled with 'targeted' policies.

Throughout his writings, Amartya Sen has emphasized at length the fact that a healthy population is not necessarily a wealthy one and that the level of economic development is a necessary but not sufficient condition for improving the community's health. There is a whole series of intervening factors. Of these, the way in which a society creates and distributes its resources, freedoms and social opportunities would seem to help explain its health status and inform us about the health disparities and inequalities in the society (Sen 2002). My results suggest that better access to individual as well as to certain types of collective resources contributes to the maintenance and creation of individual and social capabilities to produce and maintain a decent health status.

Acknowledgements

This chapter is a revised version of a paper presented at the UNU–WIDER conference on Advancing Health Equity, Helsinki, 29–30 September 2006. I am indebted to Slim Haddad (University of Montreal) for his comments, advice and support. I have benefited from the comments of Bernard Decaluwe (Université Laval), Rohinton Medhora (IDRC) and the participants in the HDCA and UNU–WIDER conferences in Groningen in August and in Helsinki in September 2006.

Notes

1. The term collective resources refers to the public access dimension, not the source of finance which could well be private. This distinction is important because it assumes that all the resources are available to all the women within a region at the same 'cost'.
2. The findings by Esrey (1996) for Morocco also suggest that access to a better source of potable water would improve health when combined with better health infrastructures.
3. In a pure production model, age is a variable that affects the depreciation rate of the stock of health (Grossman 1972).
4. These initial conditions are the equivalent of the initial stock of health in production models. Several studies deal especially with estimation problems associated with heterogeneity in initial health (individual fragility) (Rosenzweig and Schultz 1983; Lee et al. 1997).
5. However, introducing a morbidity variable into the model allows one to at least partially control for endogeneity.
6. Despite the potential presence of multicollinearity between education and standard of living, the correlation structure of the model is not affected when one of the variables is added or deleted.
7. OR = odds ratio; and CI = confidence interval.
8. The cross-level interactions between standard of living and communal resources are not statistically significant for the sample as a whole, perhaps because of a number of factors, particularly the number of categories, the quality of the standard-of-living indicators, and statistical power (Zhao and Bishai 2003; Kreft 1996).
9. One of the referees of this article suggests that this result might also be driven by the possibility that in some developing countries public services are sometimes considered inferior goods. This is a valid point and could be part of the explanation of why the health status of richer groups of women seems not to be associated with public services. However, to be able to prove it definitively, we would require information on the existence of alternatives to public/collective resources as well as on the perceived quality of services offered.

References

Alderman, H., J. Hentschel and R. Sabates (2003) 'With the Help of One's Neighbours: Externalities in the Production of Nutrition in Peru', *Social Science and Medicine*, 56: 2019–31.

Caldwell, J. C. (1979) 'Education as a Factor in Mortality Decline: An Examination of Nigerian Data', *Population Studies*, 33 (3): 395–413.

Case, A. (2002) 'Health, Income, and Economic Development', *Annual World Bank Conference on Development Economics, 2001/2002* (Washington DC: World Bank), 221–41.

Deaton, A. (1999) 'Inequalities in Income and Inequalities in Health', National Bureau of Economic Research, Working Paper 7141 (Cambridge MA: National Bureau for Economic Research).

Deaton, A. (2001a) *Relative Deprivation, Inequality, and Mortality* (Princeton University: Research Program in Development Studies and Center for Health & Wellbeing).

Deaton, A. (2001b) 'Health Inequality, and Economic Development', CMH Working Paper Series WG1:3. Commission on Macroeconomics and Health (Geneva: WHO).

Direction de la Statistique, Royaume du Maroc (2000a) *Enquête nationale sur le niveau de vie des ménages 1998/1999: Premiers résultats* (ENNVM) [National Survey of Household Standard of Living], Rabat, Morocco.

Direction de la Statistique, Royaume du Maroc (2000b) 'La Base de données communales 2000' [Commune Database], *Annuaire Statistique du Maroc 2000* (Rabat, Morocco).

Drèze, J. and A. K. Sen (1989) *Hunger and Public Action*, UNU–WIDER Studies in Development Economics (Oxford: Clarendon Press).

Esrey, S. A. (1996) 'Water, Waste, and Well-Being: A Multicountry Study', *American Journal of Epidemiology*, 143 (6): 608–23.

Fielding, A. (2002) 'Ordered Category Responses and Random Effects in Multilevel and Other Complex Structures: Scored and Generalized Linear Models', in S. P. Reise and N. Duan (eds), *Multilevel Modeling: Methodological Advances, Issues, and Applications* (Mahwah: Lawrence Erlbaum).

Fielding, A., M. Yang and H. Goldstein (2003) 'Multilevel Ordinal Models for Examination Grades', *Statistical Modelling*, 3 (2): 127–53.

Filmer, D. and L. Pritchett (1998). 'Estimating Wealth Effects without Expenditure Data – or Tears: An Application to Educational Enrollments in States of India'. World Bank Policy Research Working Paper 1994 (Washington DC: Development Economics Research Group [DECRG], World Bank).

Frenk J., J. L. Bobadilla, C. Stern, T. Frejka and R. Lozano (1994) 'Elements for a Theory of the Health Transition', in L. C. Chen, A. Kleinman and N. C. Ware (eds), *Health and Social Change in International Perspective*, Harvard Series on Population and International Health (Cambridge MA: Harvard University Press).

Goldstein, H. (1995) *Multilevel Statistical Models* (London: Edward Arnold).

Grossman, M. (1972) 'The Demand for Health: A Theoretical and Empirical Investigation', NBER, Occasional Paper 11 (Cambridge MA: National Bureau of Economic Research).

Grossman, M. (2000) 'The Human Capital Model', in A. J. Culyer and J. P. Newhouse (eds), *Handbook of Health Economics*, Vol. 1A (Amsterdam: Elsevier), 347–408.

Gwatkin, D. R., S. Rustein, K. Johnson, R. P. Pande and A. Wagstaff (2000) *Socio-Economic Differences in Health, Nutrition, and Population in Morocco* (Washington DC: HNP/Poverty Thematic Group of the World Bank)

Kawachi, I., R G. Wilkinson and B. P. Kennedy (1999) 'Introduction', in I. Kawachi, B. P. Kennedy and R. G. Wilkinson (eds), *The Society and Population Health Reader: Income Inequality and Health* (New York: The New Press).

Kennedy, B. P., I. Kawachi and D. Prothrow-Stith (1996) 'Income Distribution and Mortality: Cross-Sectional Ecological Study of the Robin Hood Index in the United States'. *British Medical Journal*, 312: 1004–7; and erratum: *British Medical Journal*, 312: 1253.

Klees, R., J. Godinho and M. Lawson-Doe (1999) *Health, Sanitation and Hygiene in Rural Water Supply and Sanitation Projects and Other World Bank-Financed Projects* (Washington DC: World Bank, ECA Regional Studies Program).

Kreft, I. G. G. (1996) 'Are Multilevel Techniques Necessary? An Overview, Including Simulation Studies', Working Paper, California State University.

Lavy, V., J. Strauss, D. Thomas and P. de Vreyer (1996) 'Quality of Health Care, Survival and Health Outcomes in Ghana', *Journal of Health Economics*, 15: 333–57.

Lee, L.-F., M. R. Rosenzweig and M. M. Pitt (1997) 'The Effects of Improved Nutrition, Sanitation, and Water Quality on Child Health in High-Mortality Populations', *Journal of Econometrics*, 77: 209–35.

Leibowitz, A. A. (2004) 'The Demand for Health and Health Concerns after 30 Years', *Journal of Health Economics*, 23: 663–71.

Lindelow, M. (2004) 'Sometimes More Equal than Others. How Health Inequalities Depend on the Choice of Welfare Indicator', World Bank Policy Research Working Paper 3329 (Washington DC: World Bank).

Lynch, J. W. (2000) 'Income Inequality and Health: Expanding the Debate', *Social Science and Medicine*, 21: 1001–5.

Macintyre, S., A. Ellaway and S. Cummins (2002), 'Place Effects on Health: How Can We Conceptualise, Operationalise and Measure Them?', *Social Science and Medicine*, 55: 125–39.

Macintyre, S., S. McIver and A. Sooman (1993), 'Area, Class and Health: Should We Be Focusing on People or Places?', *Journal of Social Policy*, 22: 213–34.

Marmot, M. G., G. Davey-Smith, S. Stansfield, C. Patel, F. North and J. Head (1991) 'Health Inequalities among British Civil Servants: The Whitehall II Study', *The Lancet*, 337: 1387–93.

Ministère de la Santé Publique, Royaume du Maroc (1999) *Enquête nationale sur la santé de la mère et de l'enfant (ENSME) 1997* [National Survey of Mother and Child Health], Direction de la planification et des ressources financières, Ministère de la Santé, 333.

Pickett, K. E. and M. Pearl (2001) 'Multilevel Analyses of Neighbourhood Socioeconomic Context and Health Outcomes: A Critical Review', *Journal of Epidemiology and Community Health*, 55: 111–22.

Ranis, G. and F. Stewart (2000) 'Strategies for Success in Human Development', QEH Working Paper Series, 32 (Oxford: Queen Elizabeth House).

Rice, N. and A. Jones (1997) 'Multilevel Models and Health Economics', *Health Economics*, 6: 561–75.

Rosenzweig, M. R. and T. P. Schultz (1983) 'Estimating a Household Production Function: Heterogeneity, the Demand for Health Inputs, and Their Effects on Birth Weight', *Journal of Political Economy*, 91 (51): 723–46.

Rosenzweig, M. R. and K. I. Wolpin (1982) 'Governmental Interventions and Household Behavior in a Developing Country', *Journal of Development Economics*, 10: 209–25.

Sastry, N. (1996) 'Community Characteristics, Individual and Household Attributes, and Child Survival in Brazil', *Demography*, 33 (2): 211–29.

Sen, A. (1987) *Commodities and Capabilities* (New Delhi: Oxford University Press).

Sen, A. (2002) 'Why Health Equity?', *Health Economics*, 11: 659–66.

Shi, A. (2000) 'How Access to Urban Potable Water and Sewerage Connections Affects Child Mortality', Policy Research Working Paper, Development Research Group (Washington DC: World Bank), at: www.worldbank.org, date accessed 15 February 2008.

Snijders, T. A. B. and R. J. Bosker (1999) *Multilevel Analysis: An Introduction to Basic and Advanced Multilevel Modeling* (London: Sage).

Strauss, J. and D. Thomas (1995) 'Human Resources: Empirical Modeling of Household and Family Decisions', in J. Behrman and T. N. Srinivasan (eds), *Handbook of Development Economics*, Vol. 3A (Amsterdam: Elsevier).

Thomas, D., V. Lavy and J. Strauss (1996) 'Public Policy and Anthropometric Outcomes in the Côte d'Ivoire', *Journal of Public Economics*, 61: 155–92.

Townsend, P., N. Davidson and M. Whitehead (1988) *Inequalities in Health* (London: Penguin).

UNDP [United Nations Development Programme] (1990) *Human Development Report 1990: Concept and Measurement of Human Development* (New York: Oxford University Press).

Van der Klaauw, B. and L. Wang (2004) 'Child Mortality in Rural India', World Bank Policy Research Working Paper 3281 (Washington DC: World Bank).

Wagstaff, A., P. Paci and H. Joshi (2001) 'Causes of Inequality in Health: Who You Are? Where You Live? Or Who Your Parents Were?', World Bank Working Paper 2713 (Washington DC: World Bank).

Wang, L. (2003) 'Determinants of Child Mortality in LDCs: Empirical Findings from Demographic and Health Surveys', *Health Policy*, 65: 277–99.

Wilkinson, R. G., I. Kawachi and B. Kennedy (1998) 'Mortality, the Social Environment, Crime and Violence', in I. Kawachi, B. P. Kennedy and R. G. Wilkinson (eds), *The Society and Population Health Reader: Income Inequality and Health* (New York: The New Press).

Zhao, F. and D. Bishai (2003) *The Interaction of Community Factors and Individual Characteristics on Child Height in China*. Research report, World Bank and Johns Hopkins University, at: http://paa2004.princeton.edu/abstractViewer. asp?submissionId=42185

9
Health and Female Labour Market Participation: The Case of Uganda

Sarah Bridges and David Lawson

1 Introduction

There is growing evidence that reducing gender inequality in access to the job market and control of key productive resources necessary for growth are concrete means of accelerating and diversifying growth, making it more sustainable, and ensuring that the poor both contribute to, and benefit from, that growth (see, for example, World Bank 2001, Blackden et al. 2007). This has resulted in a common finding in many developing countries during the past decade that there has been a substantial growth in female employment (Standing 1999). Despite this, countries in sub-Saharan Africa (SSA) are still characterized by an under-utilization of their female labour, of which human capital, and health in particular, plays a major role. In many sub-Saharan African countries, as in many other developing countries, women who participate in the labour market are more likely to be in self-employment or, more generally, informal sector employment (Glick and Sahn 1997).

Although there is some prior evidence on labour supply issues for SSA,[1] these studies tend to provide only a partial analysis of the labour market, despite supporting the intuition that a high level of sickness results in low labour participation. For example, given the often huge gender differences associated with human capital, they lack a gendered focus. In addition, the lack of detailed labour force data for the region means that the findings of many of these studies are based on data for the mid-1990s or earlier. However, perhaps more than in most regions, labour markets in SSA have undoubtedly changed considerably since then, especially with respect to the role of females. But, more importantly, the growing HIV/AIDS epidemic has meant that much of SSA has experienced large increases in ill-health, especially among its working population.

For this analysis we focus on Uganda, a country that provides a particularly interesting focus owing to the decrease in HIV/AIDS prevalence over the past decade (from 15 per cent in the early 1990s to approximately 6.7 per cent in 2005). Although economic growth and poverty reduction performance have excelled, labour market participation is still limited. For Uganda, there is a wealth of household-level data, which enables us to focus on the impact health, relative to other human capital issues, has on participation decisions.

The theoretical basis of the analysis originates from a household production framework similar to that developed by Becker (1965), with health and labour market outcomes having a long tradition of theoretical focus, primarily through the efficiency wage models developed by Leibenstein (1957). Most of this literature focuses upon the association between better nutrition and higher productivity.[2] However, in this case we focus on how health and human capital affect the labour supply of an individual.

Ultimately an individual's stock of human capital may be influenced by his/her health status and other factors such as education. In the case of health, extended periods of illness are clearly likely to erode work capacity and the ability to participate in the labour market. Prior empirical evidence supports this view; for example, poor health has been found to have a negative effect on hours of labour supply (Pitt and Rosenweig 1986; Schultz and Tansel 1997) and participation (Lavy et al. 1995; Handa and Neitzert 1999).[3] However, the fact that a person ultimately starts life with a health endowment, therefore, means that an individual's stock of health depends upon prior decisions. This contrasts with other human capital components, such as education, which is often treated as predetermined, with most investment occurring in the early part of the life cycle (Currie and Madrian 1999: 3312).

Given this, it is therefore necessary to recognize the endogeneity problem of health and labour supplies. For instance, increased health status might result in higher employment potential/productivity and an increased ability to raise income, which, in turn, could result in increased health investment (Currie and Madrian 1999).

Such health/human capital and labour market foundations provide an appropriate analytical basis for SSA countries, particularly for Uganda where, despite impressive reductions in the prevalence of HIV/AIDS, there has been an increase in the proportion of adults reporting ill-health over the past decade and a half (from 17 per cent in 1992 to just under 30 per cent in 2002). However, there are now large gender differences in the incidence of morbidity, with females having a higher incidence than males.[4] Combined with facts such as the rates of paid employment participation for females being nearly half those for males, then we can see that the results and implications from earlier studies are far from understood in the context of a labour participation framework. Our analysis considers this gender dimension.

As noted, there is a lot of support concerning the negative influence that ill-health has on labour participation. However, it is also worth noting that the literature has expanded on this, as well as the broader human capital literature. For example, as noted in Currie and Madrian (1999), the empirical evidence on this issue shows that there is commonly a wide range in the estimated impact, an effect that is likely to be highly socially determined. Currie and Madrian also note the potentially unknown effect of mental illness, owing to relatively few data sets that collect such data with confidence.

From a broader human capital focus, specifically education, the general consensus of the literature supports intuition and human capital models that suggest that greater levels of education would imply greater participation, *ceteris paribus*. For example, this was found to be the case for a recent Kenya-based study. Evidence from Atieno and Teal (2006) notes that labour force participation rises more for women than for men as education increases. In general, there is notably limited evidence that is contrary to this.

In one of the few econometric studies that look at labour market issues for Uganda, Canagarajah et al. (2001) examine gender differences in employment and find that non-agricultural opportunities for female-headed households are often constrained. Again this provides further support for the view that the apparent underutilization of women in formal sector employment has negative implications for growth. Mugume and Canagarajah (2005), although focusing largely on issues concerning labour productivity and wages, find human capital to have a positive effect (through education) on participation.

2 Insights into labour market participation: data and descriptive statistics

This chapter uses the Ugandan national household survey (UNHS) for 2002–03, which is a multi-purpose study designed to elicit information on individual and household-level characteristics, health status and the economic position of a representative sample of households. Data were collected at the individual, household and community levels, therefore allowing for community-level identification of certain health information (in particular, the local health infrastructure). Given the labour market participation focus of this chapter, we restrict our sample to working-age adults, namely, those aged between 16 and 65 at the date of interview, which gives 21,083 individuals (9,915 men and 11,168 women).

The 2002–03 UNHS is a rich data set for examining labour participation decisions. In particular, respondents are asked detailed questions concerning their usual economic activity including, 'What is your employment status?' Here we define self-employment (informal employment) as comprising those who classify their usual economic status as an employer or own account worker, while our definition of paid employment (formal employment) includes permanent and temporary government or private sector workers.

In the case of the UNHS, this provides a self-reported measure of the respondent's health status. In the health section, interviewees are asked:

- 'Did you fall sick or get injured during the last 30 days?'

This is followed up with:

- 'What sort of sickness/injury did you suffer?' and
- 'How many days were lost (suffered) by you due to the illness/injury?'[5]

Focusing on the descriptive statistics, Uganda is characterized by particularly large gender differences in labour market participation.[6] Only 49 per cent of women participate in the labour market, compared with approximately 70 per cent of men (with an overall participation rate of 60 per cent). In addition, females who participate in the labour market are predominately engaged in some form of self-employment (83.6 per cent), compared with 69.5 per cent for males.[7] For both sexes, this self-employment usually takes the form of agricultural work. Of the labour market employees, only 16.4 per cent (30.5 per cent) of the women (men) are in paid employment, and of these the government employs a similar proportion of males and females (approximately 30 per cent).

Ill-health appears to be widespread throughout our sample; approximately 27 per cent of respondents report having been sick in the past 30 days (an increase from 17 per cent in 1992), and of these almost

60 per cent are women. Looking more closely at the effects of health status across occupation categories (Table 9.1), we see that a higher proportion of healthy individuals are concentrated in paid employment, relative to those who report being sick; 7.0 per cent (21.4 per cent) of sick females (males) participate in paid employment, compared with 8.5 per cent (22.5 per cent) for those who report being healthy. In contrast, for both men and women a higher proportion of those who report being sick participate in self-employment, relative to those who report being healthy; 46.9 per cent (56.3 per cent) of sick females (males) participate in self-employment, compared with 38.9 per cent (49.0 per cent) for those who report being healthy. In line with these findings, the average number of days lost owing to illness is also lowest for those in paid employment.

For the other main human capital variable, education, we find the highest education levels among those who participate in the formal sector (Tables 9.1 and 9.2). Important gender differences also emerge in this context. Although on average men and women have similar levels of education (see the summary statistics in Table 9.5 in the conclusion to this chapter), we find that females in paid employment have, on average, higher levels of education than males. In this setting it is impossible to separate the demand and supply effects. This finding may arise from discrimination on the part of the employer, with employers requiring that females have a higher level of qualifications than their male counterparts in order to participate in comparable jobs. However, it could also reflect cultural norms (either their own or their families') against female participation in market work, supporting the view that education is needed to help improve economic opportunities for women.

Interestingly, those who are not in the labour market have similar levels of education (on average) to those in self-employment. This result is more pronounced for females than for males, which again helps to reinforce the view that, for Uganda at least, it is not necessarily the lack of education that prevents individuals (especially women) from entering the labour market.

Disaggregating participation in paid employment further by education (Table 9.2), we see that, as education levels increase for both males and females, both the incidence of sickness and the number of days lost owing to sickness decrease. Again for both genders, not surprisingly, the trend in non-participation in paid employment also decreases as further education levels are completed.

Table 9.1. Percentage of individuals in each activity disaggregated by gender, health status, education and household demographics

	Female			Male			All		
	Paid employment	Self-employment	None[a]	Paid employment	Self-employment	None[a]	Paid employment	Self-employment	None[a]
Health status									
(By row, %)									
Healthy	8.54	38.86	52.60	22.49	49.01	28.49	15.42	43.87	40.71
Sick	6.98	46.91	46.10	21.39	56.26	22.35	12.84	50.71	36.45
All	8.08	41.26	50.67	22.24	50.68	27.08	14.74	45.69	39.57
(By column, %)									
Healthy	74.23	66.11	72.88	77.87	74.46	81.01	76.81	70.47	75.50
Sick	25.77	33.89	27.12	22.13	25.54	18.99	23.19	29.53	24.50
Av. no. of days sick	1.87	2.68	2.25	1.50	1.81	1.80	1.61	2.23	2.10
Education									
Av. no. of primary years completed	4.33	3.41	3.54	3.87	3.32	3.59	4.01	3.36	3.56
Av. no. of secondary years completed	0.95	0.47	0.52	0.77	0.43	0.60	0.82	0.45	0.55
Has university education (%)	2.43	0.41	0.26	1.45	0.28	0.45	1.73	0.34	0.32
Household demographics									
Household size	5.66	5.81	7.04	5.60	5.84	8.03	5.62	5.83	7.36
No. of children in household (%)									
0	23.13	15.07	11.27	26.83	17.57	10.74	25.75	16.37	11.10
1	16.59	15.01	13.07	13.89	12.94	8.18	14.68	13.93	11.49
2	17.04	16.61	14.37	13.85	15.21	10.11	14.77	15.88	13.00
3	14.49	14.70	13.88	14.52	13.44	11.22	14.52	14.04	13.02
4	10.84	13.36	13.07	10.72	13.48	12.89	10.76	13.42	13.01
5	8.85	9.72	10.72	6.65	9.35	12.86	7.29	9.53	11.41
≥6	9.06	15.53	23.63	13.54	18.01	34.00	12.23	16.82	26.97

Note: [a] Unpaid family worker plus individuals who are not usually economically active.
Source: Author's calculations.

Table 9.2: Proportion of men and women participating in the labour force (% sick, number of days lost) disaggregated by education

	Participating in labour market (%)	% sick	No. of days lost	Not participating in formal labour market (%)	% sick	No. of days lost
Females						
No education	18.7	26.0	7.8	27.0	29.7	8.3
Some primary	31.3	27.9	6.9	37.9	31.6	8.4
Completed primary	22.3	21.8	7.2	18.3	29.3	7.8
Some secondary	11.6	27.8	8.5	9.8	29	7.3
Completed secondary	16.0	25.5	6.3	6.9	26.4	7.0
Overall average	8.1	25.8	7.3	91.9	30.1	8.1
Males						
No education	22.7	23.1	6.6	27.0	23.3	7.8
Some primary	33.9	23.1	7.0	37.8	23.2	7.9
Completed primary	19.6	21.5	7.2	18.1	24.1	8.0
Some secondary	11.8	20.6	6.2	10.0	23.3	7.5
Completed secondary	12.0	18.1	5.2	6.9	20.5	6.3
Overall average	22.37	22.1	6.8	77.7	20.5	7.8

Source: Author's calculations.

3   Modelling and estimation

Modelling

We now examine the effect our key variables of interest (notably health status and the number of dependants) have on participation in a multivariate setting, before going on to look in more detail at the 'choice' individuals make between formal and informal employment.

As outlined in Bridges and Lawson (2009), we estimate here the probability that an individual i participates in the labour market ($y_{i0} = 1$) using a latent variable model of the form:

$$y_{i0}^* = \alpha H_{i0} + \beta_0' X_{i0} + u_{i0}, \qquad (9.1)$$

where y_{i0}^* is the latent (unobserved) propensity of participation, H_{i0} is a measure of current health status, X_{i0} are the set of exogenous regressors thought to affect participation, and u_{i0} is a random error that is distributed standard normally.

In line with Schultz and Tansel (1997), we argue that the number of days lost owing to illness/injury provides more information about current health status than the initial binary question asking whether the respondent had been sick/injured, and hence we capture current health status using our self-assessed measure of the duration of illness. There is also a well-documented endogeneity issue between ill-health and participation decisions. In light of these issues, we use the self-reported measures of health status to construct a more objective measure of an individual's health stock using a two-step procedure similar to that of two-stage least squares. [8]

Estimation results: health equation

We first look at some of the parameter estimates associated with self-reported health. Although we recognize that several earlier empirical papers have already looked at the determinants of sickness, we nevertheless feel the results are worthy of further note, especially in view of the focus of this chapter and in light of the modelling framework that we adopt.

To summarize health, ordinary least squares (OLS) estimates of the number of days lost owing to illness/injury are outlined in Table 9.3.[9] In line with expectations, the number of children has a negative effect on the number of days lost owing to illness/injury, which is less pronounced for men than for women. This may highlight the difference between males and females in the allocation of time and household

Table 9.3: OLS estimates of the number of days lost owing to illness/injury

Variable	Females	Males
Constant	2.033***	2.342***
Personal/household demographics		
Age	0.015	−0.018
Age-squared	0.000	0.001***
No. of individuals aged ≤5 in household	0.025	−0.016
No. of individuals aged 6–14 in household	0.026	−0.004
No. of individuals aged 60+ in household	0.047	0.011
1 child in household	−0.515***	−0.356*
2 children in household	−1.136***	−0.428**
3 children in household	−1.057***	−0.393**
4 children in household	−0.913***	−0.710***
5+ children in household	−1.082***	−0.588***
No education	−0.250	−0.290*
No. of primary years	−0.036	−0.041
No. of secondary years	−0.006	0.004
Educated to university	−0.501	−0.933
= 1 if married	0.419**	−0.255
= 1 if divorced	0.182	1.337***
= 1 if widowed	1.236***	1.595***
No. of working age individuals in household	−0.074**	−0.032
Sex of head of household	0.046	−1.079
Age of head of household	0.010*	0.001
Regional dummies		
Rural north	−0.214	0.152
Urban north	0.022	−0.223
Rural west	0.433**	0.585***
Urban west	0.324	0.214
Rural east	0.233	0.372*
Urban east	0.793***	0.199
Rural central	−0.047	0.030
Toilet facilities (base case: bush)		
= 1 if flush toilet	−0.811**	−0.936***
= 1 if covered latrine	−0.217	−0.581***
= 1 if uncovered latrine	0.283	−0.304
= 1 if borehole	0.062	0.102
Water source (base case: piped)		
= 1 if protected well/spring	0.074	−0.041
= 1 if rainwater	−1.092	−0.652
= 1 if water truck/water vendor	−0.617	−0.399
= 1 if unprotected	0.355*	0.166
= 1 if other water source	1.299	−0.025
Uses a mosquito net	−0.091	−0.190
Distance to local health unit (metres)	0.0001	0.0003**
Antibiotics available at health unit	0.423**	0.381*

(continued)

Table 9.3: Continued

Variable	Females	Males
Oral rehydration available at health unit	–0.600***	–0.337*
No. of doctors at health unit	–0.013	–0.002
No. of beds at health unit	0.00004	0.0004
Fee for malaria drugs	–0.0001	0.0001
Fee for malaria drugs (private)	–0.0001	–0.0001*
No. of observations	11,168	9,915

Note: * significant at 10%; ** significant at 5%; *** significant at 1%.
Source: Author's calculations.

responsibilities within the home. Women with children may, for example, be more reluctant to take time off from work while ill owing to their potentially greater family responsibilities.

On the part of both genders, being widowed has a positive effect on the number of days lost, although the effect is stronger for men than for women. This is likely to be health- or HIV/AIDS-related; widowed individuals are highly likely to have also contracted the disease.

The remaining parameter variables to affect self-reported sickness are associated with the local infrastructure, particularly interesting from a policy perspective. We find that the number of days lost owing to illness/injury is strongly associated with the household's living standards, or more specifically the household's public goods. The findings are in line with prior expectations – better sanitation leads to fewer diseases and therefore reduces the time lost owing to illness (Hoddinott 1997). Here, having a flush toilet (compared with using 'the bush') lowers the number of days lost owing to illness by about one day, while for men a covered latrine also has a negative, albeit smaller, effect on the number of days lost. In addition, there are associations with other living standard indicators; for females an unprotected water source (relative to piped water) increases the amount of time lost owing to illness.

Local health infrastructure also has an important role to play in explaining health status; for example, the distance to a health centre affects both the availability and use of healthcare services.[10] We find that, for men, distance to the nearest clinic/hospital has a positive effect on the number of days lost. It follows from this that, the greater the distance to the nearest health unit, the more difficult it is for an individual to seek medical treatment, potentially increasing their recovery time and hence days lost from illness. Similarly, Hutchinson (2001) finds that, the greater the distance to the nearest health facility, the more reliant individuals become on self-treatment and the use of traditional healers. For women, distance is insignificant, which may be reflective of the difficulties of developing-country females in receiving adequate medical care. Prior evidence for Uganda would support this. Lawson (2003), for example, found the lack of control over resources often means that women are less able to seek medical treatment when ill. Thus, making more health-care facilities available locally will not necessarily ensure greater uptake and use, especially among females. Changes in social attitudes, resulting in empowerment, are needed to enable women to invest more in their health (Mackinnon 1995).

The availability of certain drugs/treatments at the local clinic/hospital also appears to impact strongly on health status. For both sexes the availability of oral rehydration treatment at the local health unit has a negative effect on the number of days lost, while interestingly the availability of antibiotics has a positive impact.

Estimation results: participation

We now examine the effect ill-health has on labour participation decisions, disaggregated by gender. Maximum likelihood estimates of the probability of participation are illustrated in Table 9.4 for females and males, respectively. For each regression the table reports the marginal effects (evaluated at the means of the regressor variables) and levels of significance.

We begin our analysis by calculating the probability of participation for both men and women, and find that, in line with the summary statistics illustrated above large differences emerge between males and females in their likelihood of participation. A man with the average value (or mean probability) of male characteristics has a probability of participation of approximately 80 per cent, compared with just below 40 per cent for the 'average' female. It should be noted that here participation includes both paid employment and self-employment and, as we saw, a large proportion of those who participate are in some form of agricultural self-employment (45 per cent), which may help to account for the high participation probabilities that we observe here.

In line with the health/gender disparities that appear to exist in Uganda, we find that ill-health (for the 'average' worker) has a negative and significant effect on the probability of participating, which is stronger for females than for males. Such a finding is in line with other studies, which find that ill-health has a negative effect on labour market outcomes (see Strauss and Thomas 1998 for a review). Thus, one of the reasons for such a low participation rate amongst women is clearly their health status; individuals in poor health are likely to be less productive, making them less likely to participate in the labour market.

Table 9.4: Maximum likelihood estimates of the determinants of participation

Variable	Female (marginal effect)	Male (marginal effect)
Personal/household demographics		
Health stock (ill-health)	–0.059***	–0.038**
Age	0.056***	0.056***
Age-squared	–0.001***	–0.001***
No. of individuals aged ≤5 in household	0.003	–0.001
No. of individuals aged 6–14 in household	0.002	–0.005
No. of individuals aged 60+ in household	0.004	0.005
1 child in household	–0.017	–0.130***
2 children in household	–0.005***	–0.162***
3 children in household	–0.094***	–0.151***
4 children in household	–0.090***	–0.196***
5+ children in household	–0.133***	–0.208***
No education	–0.016	–0.019
No. of primary years	–0.002	–0.0005
No. of secondary years	0.006	–0.007**
Educated to university	0.216**	0.021
= 1 if married	0.157***	0.329***
= 1 if divorced	0.173***	0.091***
= 1 if widowed	0.148***	0.128***
No. of working age individuals in household	–0.016***	–0.012***
Sex of household head	0.489***	–0.039
Age of household head	–0.001*	–0.004***
Regional dummies		
Rural north	–0.125***	–0.171***
Urban north	–0.017	–0.173***
Rural west	0.090***	–0.016
Urban west	0.142***	0.024
Rural east	–0.030	–0.060**
Urban east	0.027	–0.082***
Rural central	–0.051**	0.013
No. of observations	11,168	9,915

Note: * significant at 10%; ** significant at 5%; *** significant at 1%.
See Bridges and Lawson (2009) for indicative results for the endogeneity tests.
Source: Author's calculations.

To obtain some understanding of the impact ill-health has on female participation we examine how the probability of participation varies for different values of predicted ill-health. As outlined above, the 'average' woman has about a 40 per cent chance of participation. If our 'average' female had the *highest* value of ill-health from her respective 'health' distribution, her probability of participation would fall to only 14 per cent. However, with the *lowest* value of predicted ill-health (in other words, the healthiest woman), her probability of participation would rise to 57 per cent.

Turning now to look at the effects of education, we see that a university education has a large positive effect for females on the probability of participation, raising her likelihood by approximately 22 per cent. Interestingly, but in line with growing empirical evidence for Uganda (Mugume and Canagarajah 2005), lower educational levels appear to have no significant effect (either individually or jointly) on the participation decision. Thus current education policies, for Uganda at least, that focus on providing a universal education for every child are likely to produce minimal returns in terms of their impact on labour participation. Only when families have the ability to ensure that their children can progress to higher educational levels do the labour market benefits start to accrue.

In contrast, for women, being a member in a female-headed household has an overwhelmingly large positive effect on her propensity to participate (Kabeer 1995 finds similar results for Bangladesh), raising her participation probability by nearly 50 per cent. Such a finding implies that women in households where there is an absence of a 'male breadwinner' are more willing/able to abandon their traditional role in the home and participate. This could at least in part arise out of economic necessity, and earlier empirical evidence for Uganda would support this. Lawson (2003), for example, finds that female-headed households have a larger number of dependent children – particularly orphans – and are thus more likely to face high levels of poverty, which may 'push' women into the labour market.

Of the other results, fertility (approximated here by the number of children) also has a role to play in this setting. Lundberg (1988), for example, observes a very different pattern to participation among couples with and without children, and between young and older children. Further, we find that the higher the number of children in the household, the lower is the participation probability, with a sharp fall in participation in households with five or more children. Interestingly, this effect is stronger for males than for females. In addition, perhaps rather curiously, the age of the children appears to have little effect on the participation decision. It should be noted, however, that, although the effects of children appear to be more pronounced for men than for women, this arises partly because here we are looking at overall participation. A different pattern merges when we look in more detail at the probability of an individual participating in paid employment (relative to self-employment).

In a similar vain, the composition of the household also affects the participation decision. For both genders, the number of working-age adults in the household has a negative effect on the likelihood of participation, which is stronger for females than for males. This may arise from the fact that, as the number of working-age adults in the household increases, there is potentially less need for a given individual to participate. An increase in the number of working-age adults in the household may also lead to an increase in the number of dependants, therefore increasing the need for greater hours and hence for individuals (and especially women) to dedicate time to domestic work.[11]

Of the remaining demographic variables, age and age-squared have the desired effect on participation; participation increases with age, after which it begins to fall. This is intuitively sensible, because we would expect old age to have a negative effect on the ability to work. Important regional differences also emerge. For both genders, living in the north (whether urban or rural) has a negative effect on participation, which is reflective of the lack of income-earning opportunities in this area relative to other regions.

4   Conclusions and policy implications

This chapter follows on from the previous one in this volume, which considered issues of intrahousehold allocation for rural women. Here we focus on one area of development analysis that has so far been deeply lacking, namely, furthering our understanding of how labour markets function in SSA, and the interaction of health with this. Labour market research and understanding the factors associated with the determinants of participation and the choice of employment are increasingly being recognized as being essential if we are to further our knowledge of how to combat poverty in developing countries.

Although many studies for Uganda have looked at the simple determinants of sickness, no research has advanced the analysis econometrically beyond this to examine labour market outcomes and the role of women in this. Given the high prevalence of ill-health in both Uganda and many other SSA countries, understanding the influence of these issues, especially relative to other major human capital issues such as education, is extremely important in guiding policy.

In line with prior empirical evidence, we find that health is highly significant and has a strong effect on labour market participation. Not

Table 9.5: Summary statistics

	Females		Males		All	
	Mean	SD	Mean	SD	Mean	SD
Personal/household demographics						
Age	30.36	11.71	31.21	12.18	30.76	11.94
Age-squared	1059.08	853.76	1122.80	896.85	1089.04	874.85
Sick	0.30	0.46	0.23	0.42	0.27	0.44
Single	0.22	0.42	0.35	0.48	0.28	0.45
Married	0.61	0.49	0.61	0.49	0.61	0.49
Divorced	0.09	0.28	0.03	0.16	0.06	0.23
Widowed	0.08	0.27	0.01	0.09	0.05	0.21
No education	0.26	0.44	0.26	0.21	0.26	0.44
Primary education	3.55	2.81	3.52	2.82	3.53	2.82
Secondary education	0.53	1.33	0.55	1.37	0.54	1.35
Sex of household head	1.32	0.47	1.12	0.32	1.22	0.42
Age of household head	40.45	13.33	39.86	13.18	40.17	13.26
Household size	6.42	3.40	6.38	3.51	6.40	3.46
Dependency ratio	1.27	1.03	1.07	0.88	1.17	0.97
No. of individuals aged 60+ in household	0.18	0.46	0.16	0.44	0.17	0.45
No. of individuals aged ≤5 in household	1.28	1.18	1.17	1.17	1.23	1.18
No. of individuals aged 6–14 in household	1.85	1.73	1.78	1.75	1.81	1.74
No children in household	0.14	0.35	0.17	0.38	0.16	0.46
1 child in household	0.14	0.35	0.12	0.32	0.13	0.34
2 children in household	0.16	0.36	0.14	0.34	0.15	0.35
3 children in household	0.14	0.35	0.13	0.34	0.13	0.34
4 children in household	0.13	0.34	0.13	0.33	0.13	0.33
5+ children in household	0.29	0.46	0.31	0.46	0.30	0.46
Urban west	0.11	0.31	0.11	0.31	0.11	0.31

Urban east	0.11	0.31	0.11	0.31	0.11	0.31
Rural east	0.17	0.37	0.17	0.38	0.17	0.38
Rural central	0.15	0.36	0.16	0.36	0.15	0.36
Urban central	0.13	0.33	0.12	0.32	0.12	0.33
Urban north	0.07	0.26	0.07	0.25	0.07	0.26
Rural north	0.11	0.31	0.10	0.30	0.11	0.31
Flush toilet	0.04	0.20	0.04	0.18	0.04	0.19
Covered latrine	0.77	0.42	0.78	0.42	0.77	0.42
Uncovered latrine	0.08	0.28	0.09	0.28	0.09	0.28
No. of doctors at local health unit	2.82	5.23	2.70	5.04	2.76	5.14
Distance to local health unit (metres)	348.51	398.21	347.75	350.99	348.15	376.73
Malaria drugs available at health unit	0.98	0.14	0.98	0.14	0.98	0.14
Oral rehydration available at health unit	0.91	0.28	0.92	0.28	0.92	0.28

Source: Author's calculations.

only are those in the poorest health less likely to participate but, perhaps more worryingly, these negative effects are stronger for women than for men. Ill-health clearly represents a substantial gender disadvantage to women. Extending the human capital perspective to consider education, and in contrast to the findings for other countries in SSA, the role of education interestingly appears to be limited, although high levels of education increase the probability of labour participation

In conclusion, the results of this chapter clearly continue to highlight the need to focus on health as a priority for achieving further formalization and labour market participation decisions. This is increasingly becoming recognized as a key to promoting economic growth in SSA countries. However, there is also clearly a need for policy to tackle gender-specific issues, such as the provision of suitable childcare arrangements, which would make it easier for females (and not only those in developing countries) to enter the labour market.

Acknowledgements

This chapter is a revised version of a paper presented at the UNU–WIDER conference on Advancing Health Equity, Helsinki, 29–30 September 2006.

Notes

1. See, for example, Schultz and Tansel (1997) for Côte d'Ivoire and Ghana; Lokshin et al. (2004) and Atieno and Teal (2006) for Kenya.
2. In addition, those with poor health might be rationed out of the employment market as they become too expensive to hire (see, for example, Rosenweig 1988).
3. Theoretically, we should, however, also note that health may reduce wages and effective time endowment and therefore the marginal rate of substitution between goods and leisure, thus potentially contradicting the axiom of ill-health reducing labour participation.
4. However, the proportion of sick individuals seeking health care is lower for females than for males (Lawson 2003).
5. In selecting the measure of ill-health, we recognize the extensive debate around the use of a self-reported health measure. For example, despite certain limitations, a large amount of empirical work validates the usage of self-reported health measures and has found it to be a favourable method of analysing sickness. For instance, Idler and Kasl (1991), Idler and Benyamini (1997) and Ferraro and Farmer (1999) all find the self-reported health status to be a reliable indicator of future mortality. However, contrary to this, Pitt and Rosenweig (1986) and Schultz and Tansel (1997) suggest that one interpretation could be that increased educational levels might increase illness

recognition because of heightened awareness of symptoms. If this is the case, then the self-reported illness data are subject to systematic reporting bias.

6. As is normal for this 'type' of paper, self-employed (agriculture and non-agriculture) and employment (agriculture and non-agriculture) is used – reflective of the interest of being able to access work outside the home.
7. Authors' calculations.
8. See Bridges and Lawson (2009) for indicative and extensive endogeneity testing.
9. The duration of illness may also be censored at zero. Our results are also robust to estimating our predicted measures of ill-health using a tobit specification. The results based on these different measures/specifications are not reported, for brevity's sake, but are available upon request.
10. And may also act as a proxy for the opportunity cost incurred in receiving medical treatment.
11. We acknowledge that household size could be endogenous in this setting due to unemployed people deliberately being in households inhabited by income earners. However we argue that this potential endogeneity does not detract from the main results.

References

Atieno, R. and F. Teal (2006) 'Gender, Education and Occupational Outcomes: Kenya's Informal Sector in the 1990s', GPRG Working Paper 050, Global Poverty Research Group, University of Manchester.

Becker, G. (1965) 'A Theory of Allocation and Time', *Economic Journal*, 75 (299): 493–517.

Blackden, M., S. Canagarajah, S. Klasen and D. Lawson (2007) 'Gender and Growth in Africa: Evidence and Issues', in George Mavrotas and Anthony Shorrocks (eds), *Advancing Development: Core Themes in Global Development* (Helsinki: WIDER).

Bridges, S. and D. Lawson (2009) 'A Gender-based Investigation into the Determinants of Labour Market Outcomes: Evidence from Uganda', *Journal of African Economies*, 18 (3): 461–95.

Canagarajah, S., C. Newman and R. Bhattamishra (2001) 'Non-Farm Income, Gender and Inequality: Evidence from Rural Ghana and Uganda', *Food Policy*, 26 (4): 405–20.

Currie, J. and B. Madrian (1999) 'Health, Health Insurance and the Labour Market', in O. Ashenfelter and D. Card (eds), *Handbook of Labour Economics*, Vol. 3 (Amsterdam: Elsevier), 3309–416.

Ferraro, K. and M. Farmer (1999) 'Utility of Health Data from Social Surveys: Is There a Gold Standard for Measuring Morbidity?', *American Sociological Review*, 64 (2): 303–15.

Glick, P. and D. Sahn (1997) 'Gender and Education Impacts on the Employment and Earnings in West Africa: Evidence from Guinea', *Economic Development and Cultural Change*, 45: 793–824.

Handa, S. and M. Neitzert (1999) 'Gender and Life Cycle Differentials in the Impact of Health on Labour Force Participation in Jamaica', Department of Public Policy, University of North Carolina, Chapel Hill.

Hoddinott, J. (1997) 'Health, Water and Sanitation: A Review', Food Consumption and Nutrition Working Paper Discussion Paper 25 (Washington DC: IFPRI).

Hutchinson, P. (2001) 'Combating Illness', in R. Reinikka and P. Collier (eds), *Uganda's Recovery – The Role of Farms, Firms and Government* (Washington DC: World Bank).

Idler, E. and Y. Benyamini (1997) 'Self-Rated Health and Mortality: A Review of Twenty Seven Community Studies', *Journal of Health and Social Behaviour*, 38 (1): 21–37.

Idler, E. and S. Kasl (1991) 'Health Perceptions and Survival: Do Global Evaluations of Health Status Really Predict Mortality?', *Journal of Gerontology: Social Sciences*, 46 (2): S55–S65.

Kabeer, N. (1995) 'Targeting Women or Transforming Institutions?', Policy Lessons from NGO Anti-poverty Efforts', *Development in Practice*, 5 (2): 108–16.

Lawson, D. (2003) 'Gender Analysis of the Ugandan National Household Surveys (1992–2003)', Background Paper for the Revision of Uganda's Poverty Eradication Action Plan (PEAP), CPRC, University of Manchester.

Leibenstein, H. (1957) *Economic Backwardness and Economic Growth: Studies in the Theory of Economic Development* (New York: Wiley).

Lokshin, M., E. Glinskaya and M. Garcia (2004) 'The Effect of Early Childhood Development Programming on Women's Labour Force Participation and Older Children's Schooling in Kenya', *Journal of African Economies*, 13: 240–76.

Lavy, V., M. Palumbo and S. Stern (1995) 'Health Care in Jamaica: Quality, Outcomes and Labour Supply', Living Standards Measurement Study Working Paper 116 (Washington DC: World Bank).

Lundberg, S. (1988) 'Labour Supply of Husbands and Wives: A Simultaneous Equations Approach', *Review of Economics and Statistics*, 70 (2): 224–35.

Mackinnon, J. (1995) 'Health as an Informational Good: The Determinants of Child Nutrition and Mortality during Political and Economic Recovery in Uganda', Working Paper Series 95-9, Centre for the Study of African Economies, University of Oxford.

Mugume, A. and S. Canagarajah (2005) 'Employment, Labour Markets, and Uganda's Structural Change', mimeo, World Bank, Washington DC.

Pitt, M. and M. Rosenweig (1986) 'Agricultural Prices, Food Consumption, and the Health of Indonesian Farmers', in I. Singh, L. Squire and J. Strauss (eds), *Agricultural Household Models: Extensions, Applications and Policy* (Baltimore: Johns Hopkins University Press).

Rosenweig, M. R. (1988) 'Labour Markets in Low Income Countries', in H. B. Chenery and T. N. Srinivasan (eds), *Handbook of Development Economics*, Vol. 1 (Amsterdam: North-Holland).

Schultz, P. and A. Tansel (1997) 'Wage and Labour Supply Effects of Illness in Côte d'Ivoire and Ghana', *Journal of Development Economics*, 53 (2): 251–86.

Standing, G. (1999) 'Global Feminization through Flexible Labor: A Theme Revisited', *World Development*, 27 (3): 583–602.

Strauss, J. and D. Thomas (1998) 'Health, Nutrition and Economic Development', *Journal of Economic Literature*, 36 (2): 766–817.

World Bank (2001) 'Engendering Development: Through Gender Equality in Rights, Resources, and Voice', World Bank Policy Research Report, Washington DC.

Index

Page references in **bold** refer to figures, page references in *italic* refer to tables.